501

Answers

to Frequently Asked Questions

D1445406

501
Answers
to Frequently Asked Questions

WALTER REEVES

COOL SPRINGS PRESS

Franklin, Tennessee

Published by Cool Springs Press
101 Forrest Crossing Boulevard
Suite 100
Franklin, Tennessee 37064

Cataloging in Publication Data is available.
ISBN-10: 1-59186-377-5

First Printing 2008
Printed in the United States of America
10 9 8 7 6 5 4 3 2 1

Managing Editor: Ramona Wilkes
Designer: Bruce Gore, Gore Studio, Inc.
Production: S.E. Anderson

Visit the Cool Springs Press Web site at **www.coolspringspress.net**.

DEDICATION

This book is dedicated to all the gardeners who have posed questions to me over the past twenty years. I hope I've been helpful to you, but you perhaps don't realize how helpful your questions have been to me.

Some questions have been asked dozens of times . . . but each of my answers after the first was a better answer than the one I gave previously.

Your questions have forced me to become a better gardener, and for that I am grateful to each of you.

CONTENTS

Introduction, 8

INTRODUCTION

The process of gardening inevitably raises questions. They may be asked of someone else: *"Which grass are you growing over there, neighbor?"* Or they may be part of an internal monologue: *"Wonder why the boxwoods near the downspout look so puny?"* The hundreds of questions I've chosen for this book represent the thousands I've been asked over the past twenty years.

I'm sometimes asked if I get tired of being asked garden questions. My answer? *"Never!"* In fact, questions always stimulate me. They can be of two kinds: a question I've been asked before, or a question I have never been asked. Either type delights me. If I have heard the situation before, my challenge is to match my answer to the knowledge base of the questioner. If the person is a beginning gardener, my answer will be much different than if he or she is a Master Gardener.

On the other hand, if I have never been asked the question, I get the pleasure of doing a bit of research and discovering something new, knowing that in all likelihood, the question will come up again.

Most *frustrating*, though, are folks who don't ask anything. They blithely water their lawn every day for thirty minutes, never considering that their unquestioned habit might be the cause of diseases and bare spots. They plant whatever they see on sale at a "big box" store, never wondering if there might be better plant choices available for almost the same price.

I take no pleasure in pointing out their mistakes. I just wish they had *asked* before leaping into action. I *do*, however, take pleasure in counseling beginning gardeners.

In this way, my wife and I are alike. She is a reading specialist, a teacher who diagnoses children's reading problems and coaches them to better reading skills. She loves seeing the light suddenly dawn in children's eyes as they make the connection between a series of letters and a word they hear used every day.

It's the same light I see in the eyes of someone I've reassured that leaf galls are harmless or that his crapemyrtle will eventually bloom.

I love good-naturedly preaching about the joy of gardening. Here's an answer I gave a beginning gardener several years ago:

Q: *I am a little intimidated by gardening. I have a couple of holly bushes that I've had in pots near my entryway for months and they look like they need planting. How do I know where to plant them? Do I need a plan before I plant them? Where should I start? I always seem to kill plants.*

A: Gardening intimidating??!! If you are unnerved by the prospect of gardening then I, and all gardeners, bear the blame. Let me drag out my soapbox here and preach for a moment.

Gardening is simple. Gardening is fun. Gardening is neighborly. Gardening is educational. Gardening is meditative. Gardening should never be scary or dismaying. If there is any part of gardening that seems unachievable, then we gardeners who enjoy it so much have not communicated our joy to you successfully.

My young son plays in a soccer league where, for the first few seasons, they don't even keep score at games. The coaches have agreed that soccer is more fun when the emphasis is on learning skills rather than scoring points.

I think you would profit by thinking the same way about gardening. If you haven't grown anything before, give yourself at least a year of killing everything you plant. Don't compare your yard to others; compare it to how it looked last month. As for the hollies, find a sunny spot, dig a hole, put the roots of the holly in the hole, cover with dirt, and add some water. If the holly lives, it is the equivalent of scoring a goal in your first game. If it dies, you will have gained some knowledge to apply next time you plant something.

Do you need a plan? Not particularly; although I can imagine the howls of landscape and garden designers reading this. My point is that you don't need a plan now because you're just beginning to garden. Later, when you are reasonably sure you can keep plants alive, you'll need a plan. And plans are everywhere!

9

Drive around on a Saturday afternoon and look at other folk's landscapes in your neighborhood. Surely you will find an arrangement of plants that appeals to you. If you have a camera, take a couple of pictures of plants you like but can't identify. Take the pictures to any garden center and ask an employee to put those plants on your cart. Go home, dig holes, and plant them.

Hey! Now you're a gardener! And you'll continue to score goals in your garden for the rest of your life!

I think the fear of seeming uneducated is what keeps most folks from asking questions about gardening. But gardening is no longer a part of growing up, as it was in my childhood on the farm. Fewer and fewer people have family members who gardened habitually. As a result, when they buy that first home and landscape, many folks have a steep learning curve.

I've tried to include a wide mix of questions in this book. I give the simple information on fertilizing a lawn but also cover how to make "ballfield stripes" in your grass. I cover the basics of using lumpy fertilizer but also the complexity of why frost forms.

Each of these questions was asked by someone who wanted to be a better gardener; someone building on his or her own experience; someone who, in Garrison Keillor's words, ". . . is looking for answers to life's persistent questions."

I am hopeful you'll find these questions, and their answers, useful in your quest to have a more successful landscape!

EDIBLES
Q&A

1 Fire Blight – In Pear

Q: *I have an old pear tree that suddenly has shown signs of distress. After blooming, the top 12 inches of some branches turn black. The leaves hang on the tree. The problem has spread to other branches in the lower part of the tree. What's going on?*

A: You have an infestation of *fire blight*, a bacterial disease of apples and pears. Copper-containing sprays are bactericidal, but they might cause *russeting* (freckling) of the fruit. At this point in the disease cycle, your best bet is to prune out all diseased branches, cutting at least 12 inches below the first visible symptom on each stem. Disinfect your pruner with a 1:10 mixture of bleach and water after each cut. Destroy the cuttings after removal. Another avenue is to spray at leaf emergence each year with **harpin**.[1] This chemical causes a tree to think it's being attacked, making it more resistant to disease and insects.

2 Cherry – Sweet

Q: *I recently purchased a 'Tartarian' sweet cherry tree. I can't find much information on growing it.*

A: Sweet cherry trees do not thrive in Georgia; our heat and disease pressure is too great. You might get a 'Stella' or 'North Star' sour cherry to survive, but they rarely produce fruit because the flowers are hurt by late frosts. Why not grow something easy like raspberry, blackberry, blueberry, or fig?

---

1. **harpin:** www.gardenword.com/harpin

3 | Citron – Growing

Q: *We used to grow a thing called a* citron, *a watermelon-type fruit. It looked exactly like a watermelon, but the darn thing was harder than a rock. My younger buddies think I'm crazy when I tell them how hard it was.*

A: In the watermelon fields of south Georgia, the citron is a noxious weed, good only for pranks. I have a friend from Reidsville who relates breaking open citrons and putting them under the tires of cars. The wheels would spin helplessly while the kids laughed their heads off! Citron flesh is used in fruitcakes and to make preserves. I'll leave it to you to demonstrate its hardness.

4 | Vegetable Garden – Till in Rye

Q: *I have raised beds for vegetables in which I planted annual ryegrass as a green manure crop. When should I till it under in order to provide nitrogen to the soil?*

A: Mow green manure crops like ryegrass, clover, or peas two weeks before you plant. This chops up the foliage and starts the process of decomposition. Till it into the soil one week before you plant.

5 Broccoli – Gone to Seed Early

Q: *I planted my broccoli plants on February 22. Now in mid-March they are only a foot high but have already gone to seed. I feel cheated!*

A: Broccoli plants flower and make seed (*bolt*) when the young plants are exposed to warm, then cold, then warm temperatures. It's common in February to have temperatures in the low 70s. March brings in chilly weather, followed by a few hot days. Faced with that roller coaster ride of highs and lows, broccoli senses that spring is coming fast and that they'd better get busy and reproduce, thus the flowers. Try again in fall by starting broccoli seed indoors in early August and planting seedlings outdoors in mid-September. If it is still hot then, shade the plants with a white sheet until days cool off. For a spring crop next time, try planting broccoli in a spot that gets morning sun but afternoon shade.

6 Tomato – When to Pick

Q: *I want "vine-ripened" tomatoes, but mine are too ripe and mushy when I eat them. When should you pick a tomato?*

A: As you've probably noticed, tomatoes ripen in stages. Commercial growers pick them when there is no color showing and artificially ripen the fruit with ethylene gas. But once a tomato has turned 10 percent orange, usually around the blossom end, it's in the "breaker" stage and can ripen all by itself, without being outdoors. My advice? Pick your tomatoes when they are at least 80 percent colored and ripen them in your kitchen window. Keep some mayonnaise and white bread ready to receive slices of perfectly ripened fruit.

14

7   Asparagus – Found in Wild, Edible?

Q: *My husband and I noticed asparagus ferns growing along a fence row on our property. Is it safe to eat? Is there such a thing as wild asparagus?*

A: My parents made a hobby of transplanting wild asparagus seedlings, which they found under farm fences, into their vegetable garden. The spears were never very big, but we did enjoy a mess or two of asparagus each spring. As you might suspect, birds deposited the asparagus seed under the fence. Someone in your neighborhood is growing asparagus and is not removing the berries from female ferns as they ought. You can collect the chance seedlings you find, but if you really like asparagus, buy crowns of a good variety like 'Jersey Giant' or 'Jersey Male'.

8   Bell Pepper – Growing from Seed

Q: *I just bought a red bell pepper last night from the grocery and saved some of the seeds that fell out while I was slicing it. Will these seeds actually produce peppers?*

A: The seeds probably won't produce anything. Most bell peppers are picked before they are fully ripe, before the seeds inside are mature. It would be better to buy seeds or young plants each spring at a garden center.

9   Asparagus – Weed Control by Harvesting

Q: *My husband has a very large asparagus patch. The weeds get in there and are difficult to eradicate. Is there a weed killer that would not hurt the asparagus?*

A: According to the Ohio Extension Service, harvesting and weed control go hand in hand. Harvest asparagus by snapping 7 to 9 inch spears with tight tips. You can do this regularly for two or three weeks in spring. Stop the harvest when the diameter of most of the spears becomes less than 3/8 inch. At this point, snap all the spears off at ground level. Apply 1/2 pound of 34-0-0 fertilizer per 50 feet of row. Since no asparagus greenery is aboveground, spray the patch with **non-selective herbicide**.[2] This will kill any existing weeds. New spears will emerge, fern out, and provide a large canopy to cover the space between the rows. Once a dense fern canopy is formed, weed growth will be shaded out.

10   Cipollini Onions – Planting Seeds

Q: *I am interested in growing cipollini onions. They're the little flattened ones from Italy. When should I try to plant seeds?*

A: I've never grown them, but according to one source, cipollinis are "medium-sized flat onions that come in white, yellow, and red varieties. They start out sweet and at maturity combine a sublime creamy texture with the perfect balance of sweetness and pungency." Sounds tasty! Plant seed in September, 1/2 inch deep and 3 inches apart. Onion seedlings easily overwinter and begin rapid growth in spring. Fertilize regularly. When the leaves turn yellow next summer, bend them completely over, wait a few days, and then dig your fresh ingredients for shish kebab.

---

2. **non-selecxtive herbicide:** www.gardenword.com/nonselective

11 Banana – Growing from Seed

Q: *While contemplating a banana split at an ice cream shop, I noticed the seeds in the banana slices. Can bananas be grown from seed?*

A: The black spots in banana slices are remnants of immature seeds. Banana fruit, at least the commercial varieties, develops *parthenocarpically*, meaning pollination does not have to occur for fruit to grow. Commercially grown bananas are propagated by offsets that grow at the base of a mature plant, not from seed. Before your curiosity is engaged once again while regarding a dish of fried plantain, I'll remind you that banana and plantain differ botanically only in the amount of sugar and starch they contain. One is raised and eaten for its sweet taste, the other for its starch and nutrition.

12 Peach – Liming

Q: *How much lime does a peach tree need?*

A: One of the best ways to increase the health of peach or plum trees is to regularly add lime to the soil. They prefer a soil pH of 6.5. If you have never limed before, measure the trunk thickness 3 feet from the ground. Sprinkle 1 pound of garden lime per inch of trunk diameter under and beyond the tree limbs. Repeat every year for three years and then have the soil pH tested by your local Extension office (1-800-ASKUGA-1).

13   Blackberries and Raspberries – Fruit Growth

Q: *Do blackberries and raspberries produce fruit off old growth or off new growth?*

A: It depends on which varieties you have. *Brambles* (the common name for both blackberries and raspberries) typically send up green, leafy stems (*primocanes*) initially. The following year the primocanes turn into *floricanes*. They flower, bear fruit, and die by autumn. Most brambles behave this way, so you are generally safe to prune out all brown, formerly fruiting canes in late summer each year. Observe carefully as you prune and let the green primocanes in the thorny tangle continue to grow. They will fruit next summer. In contrast, there are a couple of "fall-bearing" or "ever-bearing" brambles which produce fruit on cane tips in late summer and then flowers (and fruit) on the lower parts of the same cane early the next summer. 'Heritage' raspberry is the only bramble of this nature you're likely to run into. It can be pruned to the ground in winter and allowed to fruit on the cane tips the following fall.

14   Basil – Preserving

Q: *How do I preserve basil leaves?*

A: Pull your plants before frost and hang in a cool place until the leaves are completely dry. They can be crumbled and stored in a jar for winter use. You can also place the leaves between two paper towels in a microwave oven. Heat for one-minute intervals, checking to see when the leaves are crisp. Store herbs in a dark place to preserve their flavor.

15   Blueberries – Pruning

Q: *When do you prune blueberries? I had fruit from June through July! I need to know how to keep it this good for next year.*

A: Immediately after harvest is the best time to prune blueberries, but only if they need it. Your biggest task is to keep the bush at the right size for picking. If there are any sprouts taller than 6 feet, cut them back to 4 to 5 feet high. This will encourage horizontal branches, where fruit is formed. Every couple of years, cut the oldest central stem down to 2 feet, promoting new growth low in the plant.

16   Blueberry – Recommended Varieties

Q: *I have recently moved to a new place and want to plant blueberries. Are highbush or rabbiteye blueberries best for my spot south of Gainesville?*

A: Cultivated blueberry production in the South consists predominantly of the northern highbush blueberry and the native rabbiteye blueberry. The southern highbush blueberry is a relatively new type of blueberry and is a hybrid of the northern highbush and one or more native southern blueberry species. Which blueberry type or variety to plant is a fundamental question. For Georgia, I recommend southern highbush or rabbiteye blueberries. Good southern highbush blueberries include 'Cape Fear', 'Georgia Gem', and 'Ozarkblue'. Try 'Climax', 'Briteblue', and 'Delight' rabbiteye blueberries.

17 Blueberry – Transplanting

Q: *Last summer I had several small sprouts near my blueberry plants. I cut the root connection between them and the mother plant then. When can I transplant them?*

A: The best time is when the weather warms up in late winter. Your blueberry sprouts should be well-rooted by then. Dig them carefully and put them in a well-tilled new bed. Water and fertilize moderately the first year. Don't expect berries for a couple of years. Your sprouts will spend most of their energy growing strong roots and stems rather than making fruit.

18 Blueberry – Yellow Leaves

Q: *I have four blueberry bushes. This year the leaves on two of the bushes are turning yellow but not falling off. Are they missing a mineral?*

A: When blueberry leaves are yellow with green veins, the condition is called *chlorosis*. It is usually caused by a lack of iron in the leaves. There is plenty of iron in Georgia soil . . . so why is your blueberry not getting enough? My guess is that the pH of your soil is too high. Blueberries, like azaleas, thrive in acid soil but become chlorotic when the soil pH is above 6.0. To know your exact soil pH, have a soil test done by your local Extension service (1-800-ASKUGA-1). If you don't want to wait for the test results, try sprinkling .5 pounds of sulfur per 100 square feet of area around your blueberries. For a temporary solution, spray the foliage with soluble **iron**.[3]

3. **iron:** www.gardenword.com/iron

19 Carrots – Growing

Q: *We are trying to grow carrots in our garden. The carrots are very short and many have two or three short roots. What am I doing wrong?*

A: You may be preparing the soil well enough for most vegetables, but your carrots are proving that more work is needed. Twisted, short, or split roots are a sign that the carrots encountered stones or clods of clay. Next time dig a trench in your garden 12 inches wide and as long as you care to excavate. Mix native soil, soil conditioner, and gritty sand at a 1:1:1 ratio and fill the trench with it before planting the seed. You can plant carrot seed in mid-August and harvest a fall crop.

To keep the soil moist at all times during germination, soak the soil and cover the row with a board after planting. Lift the board each day to see if seedlings have emerged and remove it when you first notice them. Thin the seedlings to one plant every 2 inches. A few should be eating size by mid-October, but you can leave the plants in the garden, eating a few each week, until severe cold arrives. Try a second planting in mid-February each year.

20 Collards – Aphids

Q: *I have a beautiful crop of collards, but cannot control the lice on them.*

A: *Turnip aphids* and *green peach aphids* (collard lice) are common pests of collards. Try insecticidal soap or **spinosad**[4] insecticide. Spinosad is an insect nerve toxin derived from a naturally occurring bacterium (*Saccropolyspora spinosa*). It is generally considered safe to use on vegetable crops.

4. **spinosad:** www.gardenword.com/spinosad

21 Corn – Falling Over

Q: *How do you keep corn stalks from falling over? I have a small vegetable garden with three rows of 'Silver Queen' corn. After every heavy rain, just about all the stalks are on the ground! I don't remember my grandfather, who had large fields of corn, having this kind of trouble.*

A: One thing your grandfather probably did was to plant with a mule. He could cut a deep furrow and plant the corn at the bottom. After the corn sprouted, a trip down the rows behind "Jack" would push nearby soil into the row to strongly anchor the plants *and keep them from lodging* (falling over). If you have well-drained garden soil, try planting your corn in furrows 8 inches deep and anchoring the plants with soil as I've described, minus the mule. A few years ago I had the same problem in my piddly backyard corn patch. I finally resorted to running a wire between posts at both ends of my corn rows. I laboriously tied the stalks to the wire with string. The corn plants stayed upright and bore a good crop of corn. Then the raccoons harvested *every ear of it* the day before I planned to pick it!

22 Collards – Treated Seed

Q: *My pack of collards seeds says they are not for consumption. Does this mean the seeds or the plants?*

A: The seeds have been treated with a fungicide powder, usually pink, to protect the young seedlings when they emerge. You can't eat the seed, but you can safely eat all of your collard leaves.

23 Corn – Pollination

Q: *I am an organic gardener and would like to know if I plant popcorn next to regular corn, will it cross-pollinate and ruin my corn crop?*

A: Unlike other vegetables, the taste of corn *is* affected by the pollen an ear receives. For squash, beans, tomatoes, and others, the taste of *future* crops is affected but not the current one. In your case, it depends on what you want. If you want good sweet corn, popcorn planted nearby will cause the sweet corn to be a little less sweet. On the other hand, if you want good popcorn, cross-pollination won't affect the popping ability of the corn, but it may taste a bit more "corny." However, there is a way around your problem. Plant your two corn crops a couple of weeks apart. In this way they won't be shedding pollen at the same time, and you'll likely get a good harvest of both kinds of corn.

24 Muscadine Grape – Recommended Varieties

Q: *What muscadine grape varieties do you recommend growing in the Atlanta area for eating, jellies, and jams?*

A: Muscadines are native grapes and rarely have pest problems in Georgia. Their sweet juice and pulp is a September treat for many Southern gardeners. Unfortunately, their thick skin precludes grabbing a bunch and munching away. You have to take a moment to spit out the skin before swallowing the juice. 'Carlos', 'Fry', 'Noble', and 'Triumph' are among the best muscadines.

25 Crabapples – Pollinating Regular Apple Trees

Q: *I have read that planting crabapples with regular apple trees will insure better pollination. How close should you plant them?*

A: Your information is correct. Apples are considered "self infertile." They require pollen from another apple variety in order to set fruit. The problem is that apple trees don't produce a huge amount of pollen. Crabapple trees, however, *do* produce lots of pollen and can be used to increase fruit set. Plant a couple of crabapple varieties such as 'Donald Wyman', 'Dolgo', or 'Profusion' nearby.

26 Cucumber – Bitter Taste

Q: *What makes my cucumbers so bitter?*

A: Cucumber stems, leaves, and roots are naturally bitter to stave off the attack of insects. In fact, the bitter chemical has a name: *cucurbitacin*. When a cucumber plant is stressed, the chemical can spread to the green skin of the fruit. One way to avoid having bitter cucumber in your salad is to peel them in a certain way: slice the peel *away from* the blossom end *toward* the stem end of the cuke. Quickly rinse the knife or peeler between cuts. This technique prevents cucurbitacin, which concentrates in the stem end, from being spread over the rest of the cucumber. Anything that reduces stress on your garden cucumber plants will help reduce bitterness. Mulch your plants, do not allow the soil to dry between waterings, and don't overfertilize in hot weather.

27 Walnut – Poisoning Apples?

Q: *I have ordered an English walnut tree for my backyard. The only available spot will place it within 30 feet of young apple trees. Very recently I learned that English walnut cultivars are grafted to black walnut rootstock. Will such a tree produce soil toxins and harm my apples?*

A: This situation could eventually be a problem, but I am not sure you should worry about it now. Black walnut roots do exude a chemical that is toxic to apples, tomatoes, hydrangeas, azaleas, and many others.

However, dozens of other plant species are perfectly happy growing near a walnut. The question boils down to how much of the walnut root zone will intermingle with the roots of the apples. In the years while your trees are small in stature, I don't think there will be any contact. Ten years from now, the roots may be in contact and cause problems. Here's an idea: install a root barrier midway between the trees. Simply dig a narrow trench 18 inches deep and 20 feet long, and insert aluminum flashing into it edgewise. By keeping the roots away from each other, your apples can prosper. You'll have the ingredients for a Waldorf salad in a few years!

28 Okra – Priming Seed

Q: *How can I get my okra seed to sprout faster?*

A: Experienced gardeners soak them overnight in a pint of water to which a tablespoon of bleach has been added. This makes the seed coat softer.

Q: *I have heard several descriptions of how to prune a fig, but some seem to conflict. What is the timing and severity of pruning the trees?*

A: The best way to prune a fig is to decide how big you can allow it to grow and prune it to half that size in January. Prune monthly in the summer by removing the tips of vertical sprouts when they are 2 feet long. Do any further corrective pruning right after your fig fruits in fall. (Be sure to water regularly after pruning in fall.) Try to remove the more vertical limbs and leave most horizontal limbs alone, since these will bear most of the fruit. Don't prune in winter again; let summer and fall pruning be your main chore. With this schedule you may get a pretty good early crop (if it doesn't freeze), and you'll surely get a good fall crop each year.

To explain further: Southern figs try to bear two crops per year. After a mild winter, a small breba fig crop will be produced in midsummer on old wood (twigs that grew the previous autumn). The main crop occurs on new wood (twigs that grew and matured in the current spring and summer). If you *severely* prune a fig in the winter, you remove all of the old wood. Thus, no breba figs will be produced the following year since the old wood has been removed. Much new juvenile wood is produced after a severe winter pruning. It takes at least six to eight months of growth after a winter pruning before new fig twigs begin to produce flowers and make fruit. Thus, your harvest will be small if you rely only on winter pruning.

30　Fruit Trees – For Schoolyard

Q: *I'm in charge of planning a fruit tree garden for elementary school students. Can you give me some ideas on fruits that will ripen before the end of May or after August?*

A: Not many fruits ripen in late spring. Try serviceberry (*Amelanchier × grandiflora* 'Autumn Brilliance'), which may have a few sweet fruit before school lets out. In fall, apples are first to come to mind. Elisa Ford at Johnson Nursery in Ellijay recommends 'Freedom', 'Liberty', and 'Arkansas Black' for their disease resistance and late ripening. You might also try a 'Jiro' Asian persimmon. The fruit is as large as a fist and does not have the astringency of American persimmons.

31　Fruit – Definition Of

Q: *My sister's nine-year-old has a book that states a banana is a berry. Can you please tell me if this is a fact?*

A: Oddly enough, bananas *are* berries. A berry is botanically defined as a fruit with a skin that has a pulp covering its seeds. That describes how a banana grows—as well as other berries such as grapes, tomatoes, and apples!

You might think that fruits and vegetables would be easy to distinguish, but one dictionary definition of a fruit is: "Any product of a plant that is useful to humans or animals." Accordingly, pears, pecans, squash, corn, and cotton could be fruits.

Most people have a narrower meaning that only includes "the edible, juicy part of a plant that contains seeds." Melons, peaches, and blueberries could be included in this list. Unfortunately, a strawberry could not be a fruit under this definition because its seeds are *outside* the juicy part! Scientists might define a vegetable as any edible part of a plant, which would make wheat and pineapple vegetables. Most of us, though, would define a vegetable as "a plant or any of its parts, other than fruits and seeds, which is used for food." Sweet potatoes, spinach, and rhubarb would be vegetables in that case, but squash, beans, and peas, the quintessential vegetables, would be left out. Don't inform the nine-year-old of these confusing definitions unless you want a dinnertime debate about what is meant by "Eat your fruits and vegetables before dessert!"

32 Garden – Amending Soil

Q: *My husband and I are novice gardeners. Last year we planted a vegetable and herb garden. Our soil was mostly red clay so I added store-bought dirt and manure: about twenty bags of each in an 8 feet × 10 feet area. The only thing that grew well was the cucumbers. Everything else died. Is there anything that you can suggest?*

A: I am not a fan of "store-bought dirt," particularly the $.99-a-bag topsoil. The product seems too silty and poorly drained for my liking. There *are* good bagged soils to buy. They are usually labeled "Planting Soil" and cost several dollars per bag. I think your soil had poor drainage. It didn't dry out quickly after being irrigated, and your plant roots suffered. I'd add a 2-inch layer of mini-size pine bark chips over the garden area plus a pint of 10-10-10, plus 4 pints of lime, and mix it to a depth of 10 inches. That should increase drainage and fertility enough to show improvement next growing season.

33 Planting – Soil Temperature

Q: *Is there a general rule for when soil temperatures reach plantable levels for gardens?*

A: Cool season vegetables, like lettuce, parsley, radish, and turnip greens, need soil at least 45 degrees F. Warm season vegetables, like tomato, corn, squash, and beans, like the soil to be at least 65 degrees F. To determine soil temperature in your area, go to **www.georgiaweather.net**.

34   Garlic – Growing

Q: *I was wondering if you could give me some advice on growing garlic.*

A: Plant garlic in the fall; it requires a long growing season to develop large bulbs. Garlic prefers a location in full sun with loose, well-drained soil. Planting in compacted soil will result in small, misshapen bulbs. Start garlic from the cloves (sometimes called *toes*), which you've separated from a bulb. Plant individual cloves 2 inches deep and 4 inches apart in rows 1 foot apart. To have straight necks on the bulbs, keep the pointed clove ends up. Make sure garlic has plenty of water if the weather turns dry. Garlic begins to bulb when the days get longer in May and June. The larger the plants at that time, the larger the bulbs will be, so it is important to keep the plants growing healthily. If a flower head begins to develop, snip the stalk off to force energy back down into the bulb. Harvest garlic as soon as most of the leaves have turned yellow, usually in early summer. Save some of the very best bulbs for planting the next season.

35   Malabar Spinach – Spot Fungus

Q: *My Malabar spinach is very vigorous and beautiful, except I've gotten a spot fungus on the leaves. Can we eat those leaves?*

A: Malabar spinach, *Basella rubra*, is an excellent summer substitute for regular spinach. It is not kin to the cool season crop but tastes remarkably similar. Malabar spinach grows as a vigorous vine and does very well in a large container. It's very ornamental, with deep green leaves and red stems. As you've found, the leaves get fungal spots occasionally. Simply cut them out and prepare the leaves as you normally would.

36 Gourd – Drying

Q: *How do I dry and utilize gourds?*

A: Allow your gourds to ripen on the vine. The best way to determine if they are ripe is to wait for the stem to wither in cool fall weather. Clean the gourds with mild soapy water and a soft brush. In humid weather, mold can grow on the gourd rind before it dries. To prevent this, try a recommendation from the American Gourd Society: mix 1 cup of 20 Mule Team Borax into 3 cups of hot water. Stir until dissolved. Let the mixture cool to lukewarm. Bring another pot of water to a boil. Dip the gourd into the boiling water briefly, then soak it in the borax solution for fifteen minutes. Do not rinse, but hang gourds in a cool place to dry for several weeks. You can leave the gourds whole or cut a small hole and remove the seeds. Vigorously shake a handful of gravel inside a gourd to loosen the fibrous interior and then pour everything out. When the gourds are completely dry, make them shine with a good quality liquid floor wax.

37 Grapevines – Bleeding

Q: *I pruned my grapevines in mid-March, and they bled a lot! Was I too late, or was it just the mild winter?*

A: Bleeding is a common phenomenon but no problem for the plant. Grapes can bleed quarts of sap without suffering any harm at all. To avoid worries, try to finish pruning by February each year.

38 Bunch Grape – Pruning and Variety Selection

Q: *I have two 'Concord' grapevines growing along the lattice around our patio. When do I cut them back, and how much do I remove? The vines are two years old, and I had plenty of grapes this year.*

A: Bunch grapes need to be pruned severely each year to avoid disease buildup on the plant. Properly done, you should remove nearly 90 percent of the vine each February. This is easy to do when the grape is growing on a wire arbor but very difficult on lattice. Your best bet is to simply shorten as many canes as you can reach to make an attractive vining cover for the lattice. Grapes will be produced on the new growth next spring.

The 'Concord' you've planted is not really the best variety for Georgia. 'Fredonia' is much better; the fruit ripens more evenly. Other good choices include 'Delaware', 'Mars', and 'Niagra'. American bunch grapes are characterized by their hardiness and pest resistance and are generally well adapted to Southeast growing conditions. American-French hybrid grapes have good disease resistance but don't have the sharp "foxy" taste of American grapes. European grapes like 'Chardonnay' and 'Pinot Noir' are difficult to grow in the Southeast and are generally not recommended.

EDIBLES

39 Growing Days – How Many?

Q: *I want to have a vegetable garden. What is the length of our growing season?*

A: It depends on where you live. Here are some representative city statistics, with average last frost, first frost, and length of season:

Athens	Mar. 24	Nov. 8	224 days
Atlanta	Mar. 27	Nov. 12	228 days
Macon	Mar. 27	Nov. 11	220 days
Savannah	Mar. 10	Nov. 15	250 days
Waycross	Mar. 19	Nov. 15	229 days

40 Horseradish – Growing in Georgia

Q: *We are establishing a new garden in Rabun County. Can we grow horseradish in this part of Georgia?*

A: This hardy member of the cabbage family is unforgettable to people who have tasted more than a small bit of wasabi with their sushi! The hot, biting, pungent taste makes it valuable as a condiment on prime rib or corned beef. Horseradish requires a long, cool growing season, so your garden in north Georgia should be perfect. The easiest way to start is to buy a horseradish root at the grocery. Lay the long root at an angle, with the thick top higher but slightly belowground. Cover the entire root with soil. Big leaves will soon emerge. Be careful to control it; the plant is somewhat invasive. Harvest fresh horseradish all season by cutting pieces of root from the outside of the root clump as you need them.

41 Vegetables – Growing Indoors

Q: *My family is trying to eat as many homegrown fruits and vegetables as we can. I am arranging my complete basement to be able to garden year-round. Do you see any problems with this?*

A: My guess is that your basement setup will include fluorescent lighting. You must always remember that *light* equals *food*, both for the plant and for you. Even if you have windows and sliding-glass doors, you'll need lots of light fixtures to provide the energy that food-producing plants require. Plants like tomatoes, squash, and dwarf citrus require approximately 1,000-foot candles of light per square foot of growing surface. A two-tube, 80-watt shop light provides close to this amount when the tubes are hung a few inches above the foliage of your plants. If they are any higher, light intensity drops tremendously. When the tubes are 12 inches above the leaves, your plants will get less than 500-foot candles. This means you'll need to cover most of your floor space with fluorescent fixtures.

"Cool white" tubes provide vital blue light but not much red light. They must be supplemented with incandescent bulbs. Add together the watts of the fluorescent tubes you'll use; divide in half and add that wattage amount in incandescent bulbs. This, of course, brings problems with heat control and energy cost. My advice? Try growing leafy vegetables like lettuce, radishes, and spinach in your basement. You'll have enough success to be proud, but you won't waste lots of money trying to garden in your basement year-round.

Q: *Until four years ago my tomatoes covered the side of my garage and bore fruit until frost. Then the hornworms got my address. The first year they defoliated an entire plant overnight. Soon I couldn't pick them off fast enough. Is there anything I can do before planting?*

A: *Hornworm caterpillars* have a voracious appetite. When they grow large, usually by July, one can devour a foot-long tomato leaf in one day. Small ones are almost impossible to spot. Their green coloration is excellent camouflage against human and animal predators. Fortunately, there are two insect enemies that have no problem finding tomato hornworms: both are wasps. The tiny braconid wasp lays her eggs on an unlucky hornworm. The immature wasps consume the caterpillar from the inside and then make numerous white cocoons on the creature's skin. Additionally, the common paper wasp loves to eat small hornworm caterpillars.

To avoid hurting your insect friends, spray or dust an organic garden insecticide containing ***Bacillus thuringiensis* (B.t.)**[5] on your plants in early May and every week thereafter. The B.t. is harmless to animals and insects but is fatal to caterpillars. In this way you'll have safe control of the worms but won't endanger your friends, human or otherwise.

---

5. ***Bacillus thuringiensis* (B.t.):** www.gardenword.com/bt

43 Irish Potato – Planting in Tires

Q: *I have heard of planting Irish potatoes in a stack of tires. You fill it with straw or dirt of some sort. Can you give me a better description?*

A: Sure I can! First gather four old automobile tires. Deeply dig a 2 feet × 2 feet area, mixing in ¼ cup of 6-12-12 or 5-10-15 fertilizer. Place a tire on its side over the area. Cut a certified disease-free Irish potato into four pieces and press them shallowly into the rich soil. Fill the tire with damp, rotted hay or rotten leaves mixed with planting soil. When potato foliage emerges a few inches above the upper tire rim, add another tire and fill it with more rotted material. Continue thus until late June, when you can knock over the tire pile and count your harvest. Be sure to water regularly—the tires really heat up in bright sunshine. Conditions can be somewhat improved by painting the tires white . . . and when you get tired of planting potatoes in them, you can half-bury the white tires on edge and line your driveway!

44 Manure – Using in Garden

Q: *YAY!!! I have been given a garbage can full of composted horse manure. Should I wait until we get some rain to spread it?*

A: If the manure is aged, it won't burn plants, if applied immediately, as long as the layer is less than an inch deep. Keep it 3 inches away from the stems so moisture isn't held there, and your plants will be as excited as you!

45 Lettuce – When to Plant

Q: *I was at a local home improvement store in late February when I noticed they had lettuce transplants for sale. Isn't that too late to plant lettuce in north Georgia?*

A: Lettuce can withstand a freeze. The recommended planting date for transplants is three to four weeks before the spring frost-free date. The average date of last frost is March 13 to 28, so planting lettuce in early March is not as big a gamble as you imagine. Spring-planted lettuce will be harvested and out of the garden by early summer, but you can begin planting again in August and September. If you plant some seed every two or three weeks, you can harvest fresh lettuce well into the New Year.

46 Luffa Gourd – Harvesting

Q: *How do you harvest luffa gourds?*

A: In autumn, mature gourds will begin to turn brown and brittle. Check vines frequently and remove any dried gourds. These will feel light and dry and will rattle with loose seeds when shaken. After the first killing frost, remaining gourds can be brought inside to dry. Cut off the ends of the gourds and beat them together to shake out the seeds. Save the seeds from the most vigorous vine for planting next year. Soak the dry, brown gourds in warm water until the skin is easy to peel off. Soak the fibrous interior in a 1:10 solution of bleach and water, respectively, for a few minutes to lighten the color. Cut the sponge along its length or across its width and allow it to dry completely. *Rub-a-dub-dub!*

47 Asparagus – Male vs. Female

Q: *We have a nice asparagus bed, but I think I remember you saying that you should pull out the female plants. Are they the ones with the berries?*

A: Females have the berries and produce a few less spears than male plants each year because they give energy to seed production rather than root growth. Cut off the berries as they are seen in order to make the plant concentrate on making sturdy roots. There is no need to remove the plant if you remove the berries each year.

48 Mexican Bean Beetle – Identification

Q: *I have bright yellow, many-legged bugs eating the leaves on my half runner beans. What can be done?*

A: The yellow critters are *Mexican bean beetle larvae*. Both larvae and adults feed on bean and pea foliage, leaving large holes in tattered leaves. The adults are one of the few harmful members of the lady beetle family, which they closely resemble. Keep an eye out for them in early summer. If you see them, spray with **spinosad**[6] or an insecticide labeled for **gardens**.[7]

6. **spinosad:** www.gardenword.com/spinosad
7. **gardens:** www.gardenword.com/gardeninsecticide

Q: *Four years ago I planted a 'Cowart' muscadine vine. To this day I have had no grapes. Little grapes show up, but they never get large.*

A: I am considering seeking licensure as a registered plant sexologist. Public knowledge about the sexual habits of humans and animals seems adequate, but I sense a deep need for more information about plants. Each summer I am asked why squash (cucumber, melon, gourd, etc.) flowers fall off the vine without making fruit. The answer is simple: male flowers appear first. They wither and fall off after being open for only a few hours. Female squash flowers begin appearing several days later. Pretty soon both are opening at the same time and squash *amour* is the natural result.

Muscadine grapes are a bit different, but I still believe your problem stems from a lack of sex amongst the vines. You see, some muscadine varieties have perfect flowers, which contain both male and female organs. These varieties do not require another variety nearby to achieve pollination. However, some varieties have flowers with only female organs. These varieties require a perfect-flowered variety nearby to contribute pollen.

My bet is that your grapevine was mislabeled and you have a female-flowered variety, not a perfect-flowered 'Cowart'. The lack of pollen would explain why the little grapes never develop to maturity.

Plant a perfect-flowered grape like 'Cowart', 'Triumph', or 'Carlos' nearby. If you harvest grapes next year, I will use you as a reference in my new profession.

50 Ornamental Pepper – Edible

Q: *We have ornamental peppers in a planter. I know they aren't hardy outdoors in winter, but can we eat them before they freeze?*

A: If you have not sprayed them with pesticides, they are eminently edible! Be sure to taste them first, though; some are quite hot. 'Chilly Chili' was named an All-America Selections Ornamental a few years ago. If you decide not to eat them, you can bring the peppers indoors in a pot for the holidays. The red fruit are quite eye-catching. Keep in mind that not all holiday plants are edible: Jerusalem cherry has round, bright orange fruit, but they are poisonous in the extreme.

51 Peach – Scab Disease

Q: *Every year my peaches are covered by little black spots. I have golf-ball-sized fruit now, and it is beginning again. What should I do?*

A: The better question might be "What should I have done?" *Peach scab* is a fungal disease that infects when the fruit first appears. Some varieties of peach are slightly resistant to the disease, but yours does not seem to be one of them. In May, thin your fruit to leave 6 inches between each fruit. This will make them larger and better able to resist the fungus. Pick up all fruit you thin out and all fruit that falls from the tree, and dispose of them away from the tree. Next year, when buds begin to swell, begin spraying with any **fungicide**[8] labeled for disease control on fruit trees.

---

8. **fungicide:** www.gardenword.com/gardenfungicide

Q: *We are trying to find 'White Acre' peas for our garden. We cannot locate them anywhere. We had some of these at a diner for lunch, and they were really tasty.*

A: Let me educate you a bit about this favorite Southern food. According to M. J. Stephens at the University of Florida, there is great confusion among consumers about Southern peas. The first mix-up is whether "cowpeas" and "Southern peas" are peas at all. In fact, they are beans, members of the *Vigna* genus, not the *Pisum* genus of true peas. There are many different named varieties of Southern pea as well as many unnamed strains. Part of the confusion comes from folks who save their seed. One gardener might name his peas "Carolina Blackeye," and another might name the identical plant "Florida Straightpod."

Varieties with seeds that are so closely spaced that the seed ends are pressed against each other are called *crowders*. Each seed has slightly blunted ends from this compression. Seed color varies but is either concentrated around the seed-eye or is general all over the seed coat. Those varieties that have no color are called *creams*. Most of the cream peas are loosely spaced; they are also called "conch" peas. Your 'White Acre' is a cream pea. Colored hull peas like 'Pinkeye Purple Hull' and 'Purple Tip Crowder' are also common Southern pea varieties.

There are many online vendors of heirloom vegetable seed. Start your search there.

53 Peach – Curculio

Q: *The peaches on my tree are oozing a clear sap. This is becoming a yearly problem. Any suggestions?*

A: *Plum curculio* is a small "snout beetle" that attacks peaches and plums. Adults overwinter in debris near a fruit tree and emerge in spring. The female lays her eggs in small wounds she carves in the fruit, leading to a clear ooze afterward. These insects are active at night, which explains why you don't see them. Once the eggs hatch, they feed inside the fruit, leading folks to say they find "worms." Organic control of plum curculio is nigh impossible. Now and in years to come, use a **home orchard spray**[9] according to label directions. Note that most of these sprays should not be used during bloom, or they will kill pollinating insects. Destroy all blemished fruit. When you pick them off, do not leave them on the ground.

54 Sweet Corn – Harvesting

Q: *When should I pick sweet corn? In the past I have left the corn on the stalks and picked it as we needed it. When the corn first gets ripe, it is delicious, but it seems that within a week or two it turns very bland and sticky.*

A: For a blueberry, it's easy to tell when it's ripe: deep blue means it is time to harvest. But for corn or Irish potatoes or watermelons, it's not that easy. The answer to your corn conundrum is to use your thumbnail to pierce the grains. When they all appear full-sized and contain lots of milky liquid, the corn is at peak ripeness.

If you really like "sweet" corn, try varieties like 'Peaches & Cream', 'Kandy Korn', or 'Jubilee Super Sweet'.

9. **Home orchard spray:** www.gardenword.com/homeorchardspray

41

55 Pear – When to Pick

Q: *I have a pear tree that is full of fruit this year. Is there a way to tell if they are ready to pick?*

A: Unlike most fruits, pears continue to ripen after picking. Rather than letting them fully ripen on the tree, pick them when the fruit surface changes from hard to firm, about the firmness of a softball. There is often a slight color change from bright green to yellow-green. The small dots on the pear skin are white on immature fruit but brown when the fruit is ready to pick. Place harvested fruit in a bowl or paper bag and let stand at room temperature until soft and ripe.

56 Pecan – Fertilizing

Q: *I would like to know how to fertilize my pecan trees. I have two large trees, and I want them to do their best.*

A: Pecan trees produce nuts based on how many leaves were present the previous year. The best way to have lots of leaves is to fertilize regularly. Go to each of your trees and measure how thick it is at chest height. For every inch of thickness, broadcast a pound of 10-10-10 under and slightly beyond the canopy. Do this three times a year, in February, June, and September. In addition, apply 1 pound of zinc sulfate to four- to ten-year-old trees and 3 to 5 pounds for older trees each year. This prevents pecan rosette, which causes limbs to have thick knots of leaves at the ends.

57 Pecan – Scab Disease and Recommended Varieties

Q: *I have two eight-year-old pecan trees. The nuts turn black, sort of like mildew, on the hulls. Is there anything special I can do to correct this?*

A: I'll bet your trees have *scab*, a common disease of pecans. The fungus moves into the tree from infected leaves and fallen nuts stirred up by spring storms. In south Georgia, pecan farmers use huge blowers to direct a mist of fungicide into the tops of their trees. They also plant scab-resistant varieties like 'Stuart', 'Elliott', 'Curtis', and 'Gloria Grande'. It's almost impossible for a homeowner to control scab. Rake and destroy every fallen leaf, nut, and twig each autumn; spread mulch over the area in winter, and pray for a dry spring.

58 Squash Bug – Control

Q: *Do you have any suggestions for controlling squash bugs, not squash vine borers, on yellow squash?*

A: Adult *squash bugs* are a bit more than a $1/2$-inch long and a $1/4$-inch wide. They are dark brown, sometimes mottled with gray or light brown, flat-backed, and they stink when crushed. Both nymph and adult squash bugs suck sap from leaves and stems, simultaneously injecting a toxic substance that causes stem wilt. **Garden insecticides**[10] work very well on young insects. Spray as needed.

10. **garden insecticides:** www.gardenword.com/gardeninsecticide

43

EDIBLES

Q: *I recently purchased an attractive plant from a hardware store. The clerk knew nothing more than that it was a pepper. It has dark green leaves, purple flowers, and purple fruit. What do you know about purple peppers?*

A: As a child, I was scarred for life when I took a bite of dried jalapeno pepper. I distinctly remember running to a nearby metal cabinet and licking it frantically to get the fiery taste out of my mouth. Your question, though, caused me to venture into my garden to do a taste test. I'd planted a purple-leaved ornamental pepper this spring because it caught my eye in a garden center. Believing it to be similar to yours, I took a small bite of the fruit. It was hot . . . but not so hot that my dentures melted. Since your plant has green leaves, not purple, I think it is the 'NuMex Centennial' variety. This was one of the first ornamental/edible chili peppers released by New Mexico State University. If purple, red, and yellow fruit are on the plant at the same time, it could be the 'NuMex Twilight' variety. My purple-leaved pepper, on the other hand, is probably the 'Pretty Purple' variety. The fruit originates purple but changes to red when it is mature. 'Tepin' pepper is very hot, but the plant is so sprawling, it's unlikely to be found at a nursery.

Q: *Growing wild near my dad's garden plot were small plums. The fruit were about twice the size of a cherry and seemed to be growing on a small bush. They were light yellow when ripe. Are you familiar with the plum I am referring to?*

A: My guess is that you are remembering either the hog plum (*Prunus americana*) or the Chickasaw plum *(Prunus angustifolia)*. It is difficult to describe the slight difference between the two, but both have fruit like you remember. When I was a child, plums were a staple of my early summer diet. The yellow and red fruit, when consumed to excess, guaranteed a technicolor stomachache. I notice them growing along country roadsides when their fragrant white blooms appear in spring, but I don't know of a specific retail source for the plants. Perhaps the best way to find a plant for yourself is to cruise the backroads next April and ask permission from the landowner to dig one.

EDIBLES

Q: *I am keeping a pomegranate plant in a large pot. During winter I move it indoors. I love this plant and want to see it grow in my garden. Please advise if the plant would be tolerant of the winter here.*

A: Pomegranates are dense, bushy shrubs, 6 to 12 feet tall with thorny, slender branches. Orange-red, bell-shaped flowers appear on new growth in the spring and summer. The leathery fruit contains numerous seeds surrounded by sweet, pink, juicy pulp. Commercially, the juice was once used to make grenadine syrup, the red coloring in the Tequila Sunrise mixed drink.

One way to enjoy the fruit is to roll it firmly on a hard surface, then cut a hole in the end to suck out the juice. This is best done in your birthday suit because pomegranate juice stains are very difficult to remove from clothing. Pomegranate fruits also make nice ornaments for fruit bowls or Christmas wreaths. The plant may be damaged by unexpectedly low temperatures in the spring or in midwinter by temperatures below 10 degrees F. That said, I still think you should try planting it outdoors. If unseasonably cold weather threatens, simply cover it with a large cardboard box.

62 Potato – Varieties for Georgia

Q: *My mother was born and raised a farmer in Galicia, Spain, but I have not inherited her farming skills. I bought 12 pounds of 'Shepody' seed potatoes online for her. I tilled, fertilized, and planted the potatoes in a good spot. The vines grew like crazy, but I only harvested four marble-sized potatoes out of a 100-square-foot area. What did I do wrong?*

A: Your mother probably adjusted to living in the States better than the 'Shepody' potatoes adjusted to growing in Georgia. 'Shepody' potatoes were specifically developed for Canada. 'Shepody' is best grown in places that have sunny, cool summers. In Georgia's heat I can understand why your plants made all vines but few potatoes. Next year try 'Yukon Gold', 'Kennebec', or 'Sebago' for spring planting. You can plant some 'Red LaSoda' for a fall crop if you get them in the ground before mid-August.

63 Pomegranate – Pollenation

Q: *My coworker tells me that every year his pomegranates look healthy but always drop their blooms before they can set fruit. Do you have any ideas why?*

A: Very likely the problem is caused by failure of the flowers to be pollinated. Small insects, moths, and hummingbirds normally do the job. But if he's spraying insecticides nearby, that could be the problem. A solution is to plant flowers close by that attract pollinators. Catnip, mint, parsley, marigold, phlox, zinnia, cosmos, salvia, bee balm, Shasta daisy, iris, and coneflower are full of the nectar that pollinators crave.

64 Potatoes – When to Plant

Q: *I ordered some potatoes from a catalog in Maine. They won't ship until April. Isn't March the best time to plant potatoes in Roswell? Will April be too late?*

A: The key indicator for when to plant potatoes is soil temperature. You *can* plant at 45 degrees F, but you'd be better off planting when the soil is 50 to 55 degrees F, in Atlanta, the soil warms up to the right temperature for potato planting between March 15 and April 15. If your potatoes arrive around the first of April, you'll be harvesting new potatoes in mid-June and fist-sized spuds a couple of weeks later. You could also make an earlier planting of locally available seed potatoes in March while you wait for the Maine arrivals.

65 Apple – Recommended Varieties

Q: *Which apple varieties do you recommend?*

A: 'Red Delicious', 'Mollie's Delicious', 'Fuji', 'Gala', and 'Yates' all do well in most parts of Georgia. Remember to plant at least two varities to get good pollination. You can also plant a flowering crabapple nearby to contribute pollen. If you don't have much room, look for these varieties grafted onto a dwarfing rootstock. It's best to buy fruit trees from a vendor you trust. I know of examples where the labels on young trees at a "big box" store were not accurate.

66 Raspberry – Virus

Q: *What is wrong with my 'Heritage' raspberries? About 25 percent have healthy green leaves, but the rest have mottled leaves with a mosaic of yellow in the green.*

A: It's *raspberry virus*. Raspberries and blackberries are susceptible to several virus diseases, including raspberry mosaic, raspberry leaf curl, and tobacco ringspot virus. Symptoms include odd-looking, stunted canes or yellow, mottled, curled, or puckered leaves. Viruses are tricky to diagnose and may easily be confused with herbicide damage. There is no spray to cure a virus. The disease is spread by insects that suck sap from one plant and transmit it to other plants. If you think a virus is the problem, remove all raspberry plants exhibiting symptoms, roots and all.

67 Tomato – Low Acid

Q: *I have read that sprinkling baking soda around a tomato plant will make the fruit sweeter. How much baking soda should I use?*

A: I don't know where your tip came from, but it is false. Tomato taste is determined more by genetics and sunshine rather than the pH of the soil. "Low-acid" tomatoes just have more sugar, which masks the acidity. Almost all tomatoes have a fruit acidity pH of approximately 4.6. Tomatoes like a soil pH between 6.0 and 6.5. Baking soda would raise the soil pH, but it wouldn't affect the tomato taste.

EDIBLES

Q: *I recently moved here from Canada, and I really miss growing and harvesting rhubarb for pies and jams. Can it be grown here?*

A: Transplants to Atlanta from northern climes long for two things: lilacs and rhubarb pie. Both are difficult to grow here. Our summer heat and lack of deep winter cold keeps these plants from doing their best. Rhubarb *can* be grown here with a little preparation. The roots should be planted in the coolest yet sunniest site in your garden. Rhubarb prefers full sun but will grow better and survive longer in Atlanta in partial shade (lightly filtered sun all day or protection from hot afternoon sun). Try planting on the eastern side of your garage where the sun will hit the plants during the morning, but the earth will stay cool.

Dig the soil thoroughly and add one bag of soil conditioner for every 10 square feet of rhubarb bed. Plant several roots: when the stems are harvested in spring, they will not be as large as they grow in the North. In one of the wonderful coincidences of nature, strawberries become available at the same time as rhubarb, leading to delicious strawberry-rhubarb pie!

69 Rosemary – Recommended Varieties

Q: *I have a lovely 18-inch-wide decorative pot I want to center in the middle of my herb bed. It gets full sun all day. What would you recommend?*

A: I have a single recommendation: rosemary! There are several varieties of rosemary available: 'Athens Blue Spires', 'Tuscan Blue', 'Arp', etc. You could use either an erect or trailing type. Better yet, why not buy a rosemary topiary and plant it in your pot? If you need something to trail over the edge of the pot, try thyme. It is usually winter-hardy and does well under the same conditions as rosemary. Both love fast-draining soil and prefer to be watered once each week.

70 Seed – Saving and Drying

Q: *I am saving seed for next year in baby food jars. I know that moisture is a big enemy to these seeds, and I've seen desiccant packs for sale in seed catalogs. I'm wondering if I can simply use those little desiccant packs that come with new shoes.*

A: The shoe desiccant packs will work fine as long as they are "dry" to begin with. Silica gel is the usual chemical contained in the packs. A pack can be dried by heating in a 200-degree oven for fifteen minutes. Another way to dry the air in a seed storage jar is to wrap 2 tablespoons of dry milk powder in tissue paper and drop the package into the jar before you seal it.

71 Seedless Fruit

Q: *Why do limes not have seeds? I assume they're propagated the same way lemons are, but I've had a fresh lime every day for the last two years and have yet to see a seed.*

A: It's because the common lime (*Citrus aurantifolia*) aka Persian lime, is *parthenocarpic*, meaning the flowers do not require pollen to produce fruit. There are many common examples of parthenocarpic fruit: seedless grapes, seedless watermelons, banana, 'Brown Turkey' fig, etc. 'Burfordi' holly sets its bright red berries without pollination. One can even induce parthenocarpy in tomatoes by spraying the flowers with a hormone. You'll get a juicy tomato but no seed. Although lime and holly parthenocarpy occurs without human intervention, seedless watermelons and seedless grapes are a bit different. Seedless watermelons are produced when diploid and triploid plants are planted near each other. Pollination, but not fertilization, is the result.

Melon fields are planted annually. Seedless grapes, in contrast, come from a grapevine that lives for many years. The original 'Thompson Seedless' grape was the result of careful breeding. Growers developed a grape that would abort its seeds before forming much seed tissue. Look closely and you can see the aborted embryos in a seedless grape. Rooting cuttings, not planting seed, propagates a seedless grapevine, as well as your lime tree.

72 Seedless Tomatoes – Hormone?

Q: *What kind of hormone do you use to get a seedless tomato?*

A: It's intriguing, isn't it? Certain plants can be sprayed with hormones during flowering to induce the flower to set fruit without being naturally pollinated. Tomato gardeners in cooler parts of the country commonly perform this hormonal activation. **Tomato Blossom Set Spray**[11] contains cytokynin and will produce the effect you want.

73 Squash – Cross-pollination

Q: *I have a watermelon planted next to a cucumber vine. The watermelon flesh is white. Did the cucumber pollinate the watermelon? How did this happen?*

A: With apologies to Cole Porter, *Birds do it . . . Bees do it . . . Even melons and zucchinis do it . . . Pollination! Plants falling in love . . .* Cross-pollination among the melons, pumpkins, and squashes is a confusing subject. In general, summer squash and most pumpkins will cross-pollinate each other. Watermelons and cucumbers do not cross-pollinate. But remember: just because one plant pollinates another, it does not determine the shape or taste of the fruit. It is the *offspring* (seed and seedlings) from such plants that may produce fruit that looks or tastes odd. The watermelon might have white flesh because it was picked too early or because it did not receive enough sun. Or perhaps the watermelon vine rose from a seed saved from last year. Now if we could just get kudzu and watermelon to cross, we'd have a self-trellising fruit!

11. **Tomato Blossom Set Spray:** www.gardenword.com/blossomset

74   Strawberry – Fertilizing

Q: *What sort of fertilizer should I use on my strawberry bed?*

A: If your bed is more than a year old, you can get by with a single fertilization each spring. Do it in mid-March, using 2 pounds of 10-10-10 per 100 square feet. For a new bed, use 1 pound of 10-10-10 in March, 1 pound again in June, and 2 pounds in mid-September.

75   Summer Vegetable Gardening – Information

Q: *I'm new to gardening in Georgia so I'm curious. Many gardens are planted very early in the spring, compared to my New York State home. Is it just too hot down here to have fresh vegetables all summer long?*

A: Your enthusiasm is inspiring! You can plant summer vegetables two or three times each summer in Georgia. Add to that the cool-season crops of spinach, mustard, and other greens that you can plant each spring and fall, and there is hardly a month you can't be harvesting something. Your local Extension office (1-800-ASKUGA-1) can send you excellent publications on gardening in Georgia.

76 Sunflower – Harvesting Seed

Q: *Please tell me how to harvest sunflowers. I would like to have seeds for next year and let the birds have the rest.*

A: The back of a completely ripe sunflower head is brown and dry, with no green left in it. Birds are the best indicator of harvest time. Sparrows and wrens will work for hours removing individual seeds as they fly back and forth under the seedhead. Cover the flower with cheesecloth to protect the seeds from hungry wildlife. It is possible that your sunflower blooms might rot from heavy rain in summer. If that occurs, when the seedhead seems mature and dry, cut it off and let it dry completely in your attic or carport. The seeds can be rubbed off with a gloved hand.

77 Caterpillars – On Parsley

Q: *I found a bunch of yellow and black caterpillars happily munching on my parsley. Any idea what they are?*

A: They are the caterpillars of swallowtail butterflies. They are sometimes called *parsley worms*. The butterflies lay their eggs in July. They are too tiny to notice at first but soon grow large enough to do some damage to your leaves. Unless you desperately depend on the size of your parsley crop, I recommend you let the caterpillars do their thing. You can plant fresh parsley plants in fall, and the caterpillars will be long gone by then.

Q: *My wife and I are growing tomato plants in two locations. Mine are in the garden; hers are in containers on the back deck. Tomatoes on her plants are turning black on the bottom. All ten of mine are much healthier and have more tomatoes than hers, not that we're having a contest or anything. Any ideas as to what can be causing the blackened tomatoes?*

A: *"Not that we're having a contest or anything . . ."* Hmmm . . .

Blossom end rot is common on tomatoes growing in containers. The condition is caused by a lack of calcium in the fruit when it is young. A container usually doesn't have enough soil to moderate moisture swings and heat accumulation during the day. This leads to calcium uptake problems and onset of the disease. In case you *do* decide to have a contest in the future, I recommend your wife start with one tomato plant per half-barrel-sized container, no smaller. Use a planting soil mix specifically designed for outdoor containers. The results will be a lot more in her favor. In the meantime, get some **Blossom End Rot Spray**[12] containing calcium chloride, and spray the foliage of her plants until it is dripping wet.

---

12. **Blossom End Rot Spray:** www.gardenword.com/blossomendrotspray

79 Tomato – Cracking Fruit

Q: *I have tomatoes planted in whiskey barrels on my porch (full sun). Both barrels show signs of cracking fruit—but only on some of the fruit. Any help would be greatly appreciated.*

A: Your tomatoes have what is called *physiological cracking*. In simple terms, it is caused by the skin hardening during times of dry soil and then being unable to expand when the soil is wet. On some tomatoes the crack goes from stem to flower end (*longitudinal cracking*). On others the cracks are more circular around the stem. Although growing tomatoes in barrels is a good practice, somehow the soil got dry or hot. Be sure to have only one plant per barrel and to check soil dryness daily. If the cracks do not cause the inner fruit to rot, you can eat it safely.

80 Pecan – Pruning

Q: *I planted four pecan trees two years ago. Two are doing great, while the other two are not. The weaker two are sprouting new growth from the soil line, while the tops look dead. How should I prune these two?*

A: I think the weak ones are partially dead, but they may be salvageable. I'd let the stem suckers at the base grow to 3 feet tall this spring, and then select the straightest one on each tree, removing the others. The sprouts you keep will be the trunks of your new trees. Fertilize each of them with a few tablespoons of 10-10-10 in April, June, and September this year. If my hunch is correct, you'll have producing trees in five years.

81 Tomato – Curling Leaves

Q: *I planted a tomato six weeks ago, and just recently the leaves have started to curl from side to side. Any idea what causes this? It seems to be otherwise doing well in its bushel basket filled with potting soil.*

A: Many serious tomato diseases, including curly top, mosaic, fusarium wilt, and herbicide injury, begin with rolling leaves. But if your plants are green and no other symptoms appear, it's probably plain old *tomato leaf roll*. It's a temporary disorder resulting from excessively wet soil, especially after heavy rains, or bright sunshine on young plants. It doesn't affect the plant's growth. A normal crop of fruit is usually produced. The rolling typically disappears in a few days when the soil dries out. 'Big Boy', 'Floramerica', and 'Beefsteak' seem to be affected most often.

82 Loquat Trees

Q: *I know that loquat trees are hardy enough to fruit in southern and coastal Georgia, but do you know a loquat cultivar that will fruit in Atlanta?*

A: Loquat (*Eriobotrya japonica*) is cold hardy down to the lower teens, but the problem isn't the cold; it's the tree's habit of fruiting in winter. They bloom profusely in October to November and set multitudes of fruit, all of which are usually frozen in January. I think it would be possible to have a loquat produce fruit in Atlanta if it were in a very sheltered location, but I don't know of one that has consistently done so.

83   Tomato – Early Blight

Q: *What is the cause of the bottom limbs on my tomato plants turning yellow?*

A: Most tomato gardeners have seen the symptoms: lower leaves get dark spots, turn bright yellow, then drop off the plant. As the season progresses, most leaves drop off the tomato vine, leading to sun scald if any fruit forms. The disease is early blight, *Alternaria solani*. The fungus is present in most soils and cannot be eliminated. It attacks tomatoes when humidity and temperatures are high. The best practice to limit disease occurrence is to mulch under the plant *immediately* after planting. In this way infected soil cannot splash onto lower leaves. Water using a soaker hose, keeping the leaves as dry as possible at all times. **Fungicides**[13] labeled for garden use can also be used to keep the disease from spreading up the plant.

84   Plums – Frozen Blossoms

Q: *I have two five-year-old 'Santa Rosa' plums. Last year the trees bloomed in full glory in January, but most of the blossoms froze. Are there any tricks?*

A: I recognize the signs of a fellow stubborn gardener! I won't go into the trials I've had with my porch-side daphne, but suffice it to say that success has eluded me. 'Santa Rosa' plum gets stem cankers and leaf blights besides the frozen bloom problem you've encountered. Are you sure you want to continue playing with them? Why not cut down the unsuccessful trees you have and plant 'A.U. Amber', 'A.U. Rubrum', 'A.U. Roadside', or 'Methley' plums instead?

---

13. **fungicides:** www.gardenword.com/gardenfungicide

85 Tomato – Pollinating

Q: *How are tomatoes pollinated? Should I use a "blossom set" product? I just want the best tomatoes I can get.*

A: Blossom setting sprays contain a plant hormone that induces tomato flowers to develop fruit without pollination. This type of development is technically known as *parthenocarpy*. Tomato growers in cool climates use the spray to get fruit when nothing else works. Since the tomato develops without pollination, some might be misshapen, due to uneven development of the ovules. Temperature and humidity both affect tomato pollination, which occurs without a bee's involvement. Vibrations and air currents are usually sufficient to shake pollen loose and achieve pollination in Georgia gardens. Here's a trick to try: lightly tap each flower cluster a couple of times each day with a wooden pencil or chopstick. You may well get the best pollination and the biggest tomatoes with this simple method.

86 Tree Tomatoes

Q: *I saw a newspaper ad for "Tree Tomatoes." Have you ever heard of these?*

A: *Tree tomato* isn't a tomato at all. The fruit is more tart and jelly-like, and it has more seeds. It's botanically known as *Cyphomandra betacea*, a very different species from garden tomatoes. Actually, the tree tomato is a tropical, semi-woody shrub. It grows as much as 10 feet high and starts bearing fruit in the second or third year. However, the least amount of frost will kill the plant. Don't waste your money.

87   Vegetable Seed – How Long to Save

Q: *Are last year's seeds for our vegetable garden still viable or should they be thrown out?*

A: If the seeds have been kept cool and in darkness, they may well be viable this spring. Here's a test that will tell the tale: Put five seeds from a questionable packet in the center of a damp paper towel. Roll the towel around the seeds and put it in a resealable plastic bag. Place the bag in a warm place (on top of your refrigerator, in an upper kitchen cabinet, on the water heater, etc.). In five to ten days, unroll the towel and check on the seeds. If they are still viable, the seed will have sprouted in the towel. If you handle them carefully, they can be planted outdoors along with the rest of your untested seed.

88   Vegetable Seeds – Time Frame for Starting Seeds Indoors

Q: *What is the time frame for starting vegetable seeds for spring planting? Is there any rule of thumb as to when seeds are started indoors for Southern gardeners?*

A: Starting seeds indoors is a great way to save money when you need lots of plants for your garden. With a sunny window, a sunroom, or an artificial light setup, you can raise hundreds of dollars worth of plants with just a few dollars investment. Judging when to start the seeds indoors is a bit tricky. Seeds take various lengths of time to germinate and to grow to planting size, which should coincide with the first warm weeks of spring. Call your local Extension office (1-800-ASKUGA-1) to get a pamphlet on home gardening.

89　Watermelon – Judging a Ripe One

Q: *This is the first year I have grown watermelons. They are taking over my garden! When is the right time to harvest them? The largest melon is the size of a basketball.*

A: I have a gourd vine right now that seems headed in the direction of I-85. If you hear traffic reports of a green, slimy mess on the Interstate, you'll know it arrived and tried to cross. Watermelons are no less rampant—the typical spacing in a garden is at least 6 feet between plants. Let the vines spread as best you can. The leaves absorb the sunshine that is turned into the sugar that makes a watermelon sweet. The easiest way to tell when one is ripe is to find the little "pigtail" sprout that occurs on the vine just opposite of where a melon is attached. While the melon is unripe, the pigtail is green. When the melon is dead ripe, the pigtail turns brown. Being the impatient sort personally, I'd wait until the pigtail turns yellow, then use a knife to take a deep, narrow plug out of the fruit. If it seems to be ripe enough to eat, dig in!

90　Tomatoes – Producing More Fruit

Q: *My tomatoes grew to 7 feet tall in three weeks in June but have only had five tomatoes between them. What do I do to get more fruit?*

A: Stop fertilizing. A tomato will put all of its energy into vine growth and none into fruit production when it is overfed. I recommend fertilizing tomatoes once at planting, once when it has doubled in size, and once again when a few fruit appear on the plant. If you have a big crop, fertilize again when you notice less vigorous growth in August.

91 Spiders – In Garden

Q: *I have a small vegetable garden. I see a lot of little spiders running around. I'm wondering if the spiders will be beneficial or if I need to spray the entire yard.*

A: Spiders are overwhelmingly beneficial to a garden. They eat aphids, small caterpillars, and many other soft-bodied insects. I use wheat straw to mulch around my garden plants and between rows because it provides a good habitat for my spider allies.

92 Vegetables – Shade Tolerance

Q: *Are there any shade-tolerant vegetables?*

A: The "leafy" vegetables like spinach, collards, turnip greens, etc., are more shade tolerant than tomatoes, corn, or beans. Most leafy vegetables are also grown in the cool season, when leaves are more likely off the trees surrounding them. It's simply a fact of science that sunshine is the energy source that powers fruit formation. If you have little sun, your plants will produce few fruits. If you have more shade than sun, try gardening in large containers. These can be placed in the sunniest spots of your yard and moved around to gather as much light as possible.

93 Yellow-Neck Caterpillars – On Blueberry

Q: *Some very large, fuzzy, black caterpillars with yellow stripes are devouring the leaves of my blueberries. Should steps be taken to eliminate them?*

A: You are seeing *yellow-neck caterpillars*. Notice how they lift their front and hind quarters to form the letter *C* when disturbed. They can be voracious on blueberries in August, but plants are rarely killed. Spray the critters with **spinosad**[14] or any caterpillar control product containing *Bacillus thuringiensis* (**B.t.**).[15]

94 Fire Ants – Controlling in Garden

Q: *I have a vegetable garden, and there are fire ant mounds in it. What can I do to kill them without hurting my vegetables?*

A: Managing fire ants in a garden is a challenge. One option would be to pour boiling water on the mounds on a warm morning when the pests are working in the top of the mound. Scalding water will kill an ant mound 60 percent of the time, but take care not to cook your vegetable plants in the process. If you work quickly, you could simply shovel the mound out of the garden. **Fire ant baits**[16] are effective, but the label on bait products does not allow them to be used in gardens. There is no prohibition on scattering the bait around the perimeter of a garden and allowing foraging ants to take the bait granules back to their mound. Inside the garden, spinosad organic insecticide can be used as a mound treatment.

14. **spinosad:** www.gardenword.com/spinosad

15. *Bacillus thuringiensis* (**B.t.**): www.gardenword.com/bt

16. **fire ant baits:** www.gardenword.com/fireant

FLOWERS

Q&A

95 Pokeweed (Poke Sallet) – Defined

Q: *The Yankees in our Sunday school class are not familiar with the Southern plant known as poke salad. Do you know about it?*

A: Yankees?! In Georgia?! My heavens, next we'll have Republicans!! *Poke salad* (also called *poke sallet*, *pokeberry*, and *pokeweed*) is an absolutely and truly Southern plant. The scientific name is *Phytolacca americana*. The broad green leaves and violet stem are vaguely tropical looking. The purple berries make excellent food for every bird in the neighborhood. The bird droppings keep car wash emporiums humming each autumn. The dark purple berries and mature stems and leaves are poisonous. Some Southerners harvest and eat the young poke salad leaves, but that's not a chance I'm willing to take. Most gardeners consider it a weed. It can be controlled either by digging out the root or by spraying with **non-selective herbicide**.[17]

96 Squirrels – Plant Protection

Q: *Squirrels are uprooting my recently planted pansies. Is there anything I can do?*

A: Try removing mulch around the plants and laying 4-inch wide, 2-feet long strips of chicken wire between your plants. Anchor the wire with "hairpins" made from wire clothes hangers. Re-cover the chicken wire with mulch. The animals will have a hard time digging anything up thereafter.

17. **non-selective herbicide:** www.gardenword.com/nonselective

97 Spreading Monkey Grass – Eradication

Q: *I was given some "spicato" border grass several years ago. It has taken over my more desirable grasses and is rampant in my beds. How can I eradicate it?*

A: I think the invasive plant you have is *Liriope spicata*, spreading monkey grass. I have it in my backyard as well, mixed with clumping monkey grass (*Liriope muscari*). My weapon of choice is **non-selective herbicide**.[18] I make a slow tour of my landscape every four weeks during the growing season. Every sprig of an invasive plant gets a squirt of herbicide.

98 Plants – For Damp Areas

Q: *How do I get rid of mold and mildew from the area where my air conditioner drains into my yard?*

A: Why not make lemonade out of the "lemony" wet spot and install plants that like wet feet? There are many plants from which to choose. Virginia sweetspire, sweet shrub, canna, iris, curly sedge, cardinal flower, and 'Gateway' Joe-Pye weed would be happy to make their home in the area near your air conditioner.

Mix a 2 cubic foot bag of soil conditioner into a 10-square-foot area to prepare the spot for the plants you select. Then sit back and enjoy some *real* lemonade to reward your effort.

FLOWERS

18. **non-selective herbicide:** www.gardenword.com/nonselective

67

99 Plants of the Bible – Growing in the South

Q: *We are landscaping an area and would like to feature biblical plants. Do you know how I could find a list?*

A: It turns out that Professor L. J. Musselman at Old Dominion University has done extensive research on plants mentioned in the Bible and the Koran. Here are some biblically mentioned plants that are easy to find and grow in the South:

Aloe (*Aloe vera*); apple (*Pyrus malus*); bean (*Vicia fava*); cane (*Arundo donax*); cattail (*Typha domingensis*); coriander (*Coriandrum sativum*); cotton (*Gossypium* sp.); dill (*Anethum graveolens*); garlic (*Allium sativum*); gourd (*Citrullus colycinthus*); grape (*Vitis vinifera*); lily-of-the-valley (*Convallaria majalis*); mustard (*Brassica nigra* or *B. alba*); onion (*Allium cepa*); papyrus (*Cyperus papyrus*); pomegranate (*Punica granatum*); walnut (*Juglans regia*); willow (*Salix alba*).

100 Lady's Slipper Orchid – Transplanting

Q: *Can I transplant the lady's slipper orchids I found on my daughter's property?*

A: You can try, but you have to be very careful in the transplanting process. Pink lady's slippers are generally found in acid soils near pine trees. They require certain soil fungi to be present in order for their root tips to absorb sufficient moisture and nutrients. If you want to attempt the transplant, scoop a big shovelful of soil around each plant. Nestle the root ball while transporting so soil doesn't fall away from the roots. You should also observe the conditions in which the lady's slippers thrive on your daughter's property. Try to mimic those conditions as best you can in their new home. Frankly, it might be best for you and your daughter to enjoy them where they are.

101 Broom Sedge – Identification

Q: *We are building a rural homestead display at Rock Eagle 4-H Center and using broom sedge for thatch and for brooms. Can you give me the scientific name of broom sedge?*

A: It's a grass, not a sedge, but broom sedge's technical name is *Andropogon virginicus*. Most Southerners consider it a weed, but I suppose it has its practical uses. I found it for sale on the Internet for $4.00 per plant. Many pasture owners in rural Georgia would be millionaires if they could find willing buyers at that price.

   Broom sedge stems are too fragile to be used for an outdoor broom, but they work tolerably well in old log cabins where you could simply sweep tracked-in dirt through the floorboards. My grandmother "Bubber" used a "bresh broom" made from dogwood twigs to sweep the sand by our back door when I was a kid. My mother remembers that that area was 2 inches lower than the nearby soil under our house, due to the daily sweepings Bubber performed.

102 Perennials – Liming

Q: *How do I apply lime to an established perennial garden?*

A: Just scatter it over the top of the plants, then rinse it off the leaves. A ballpark amount to apply is 4 pounds per 100 square feet. Since lime is so slow to dissolve into the soil, you can lime at any time.

103 Spider Mite – On Foglove

Q: *My foxgloves looked wonderful in May, then became increasingly "fried" looking. I haven't seen any webs from spider mites.*

A: Despite the lack of webs, your foxgloves are likely infested with *spider mites*. In my experience, webs are seen on houseplants infested with spider mites but rarely on outdoor plants. These creatures live under leaves, where they suck sap and chlorophyll from individual cells.

Spider mites make foxglove leaves dry up and turn brown. Sound familiar? To avoid insecticides and protect bees, try modifying the mites' environment. Spider mites hate moisture, so use a water hose to direct a strong spray of water under the leaves every two days for two weeks. If you choose to go the chemical route, look for products labeled for **mite control**[19]. Not all insecticides kill spider mites.

104 Spanish Moss – Control

Q: *Is there a chemical for controlling Spanish moss in crapemyrtles?*

A: Why do you want to control it in the first place? Spanish moss doesn't hurt the crapemyrtles. It simply uses the branches as support. Spanish moss is actually kin to pineapples; it survives on the nutrients dissolved in rainwater. If it is objectionable to you, pull it out of the trees with a fishing pole and hang it in neighboring landscapes. It's a misconception that chiggers live in Spanish moss. Chiggers live in grass and shrubbery close to the ground where they can crawl onto passing deer, dogs, and humans.

19. **mite control:** www.gardenword.com/miticide

Q: *I am having bad luck growing peonies. I have purchased several in the past, but they die within two years. I love peonies because my grandmother had them. I always think of her when I see them, and I want some of my own.*

A: Three things strike me as essential for success with peonies in Georgia: loose, well-draining soil, protection from afternoon sun in summer, and chilly winters. To increase your success with the plant, choose a planting spot that gets six hours of morning sunshine but dappled shade in the afternoon. Amend the soil with plenty of soil conditioner before planting.

Since peonies need to be cold in winter, plant your roots shallowly, barely an inch deep in the soil. You can fertilize in fall with an organic all-purpose fertilizer or in spring with bulb fertilizer.

These peony varieties seem to do best in the South:
- 'America': large fiery-red flowers with golden center tuft
- 'Blaze': early single-petaled red with a sunny yellow center
- 'Bride's Dream': creamy white with soft yellow center
- 'Coral Charm': deep coral buds that soften to coral-peach when open
- 'Festiva Maxima': large, early, white double flowers with crimson flecks
- 'Kansas': large, early double flowers of watermelon red
- 'Miss America': snow-white petals that open to a full flower
- 'Paula Fay': glowing pink, early semi-double with waxy, textured petals
- 'Shirley Temple': blush daughter of Festiva Maxima; fragrant

106 Wildflowers – Planting

Q: *How should I plant a wildflower meadow?*

A: The name wildflower implies that these plants will grow and flourish just about anywhere. Gardeners found out long ago, however, that a blend of wildflowers that prospered in California would languish in Georgia. The reason is that wildflower blends contain seeds of plants that come back from their roots year after year (*perennials*) and plants that must reseed themselves each year (*annuals*) in order to survive. Weather conditions in different parts of the country determine which blend of particular flowers can coexist, without one plant dominating the others. Most garden centers carry a blend of wildflower seed appropriate for our region. Fall is the best time to prepare and seed the spot where you want wildflowers next spring.

107 English Ivy – Killing

Q: *I have a large mass of ivy, and it is in terrain that keeps me from mowing it. Would you please recommend an available spray and how to most effectively use it to kill the ivy?*

A: I've spent many enjoyable afternoons with my wife pulling it out! Mark your calendar on successive Saturdays six weeks apart during the growing season. Spray **non-selective herbicide**[20] on the ivy that offends you when each marked day arrives. By next spring, it will be almost all gone. You just have to be persistent and patient.

20. **non-selective herbicide:** www.gardenword.com/nonselective

FLOWERS

Q: *I have a 7-foot-tall angel trumpet plant. It has numerous large white trumpet flowers. I would like to keep it alive for next year, but someone told me it would freeze. Can I cut it down and cover the stump with pine straw?*

A: These coarse shrubs are covered with stunning flowers each autumn. But the plant, which is in the same botanical family as tomatoes, can sometimes be killed by north Georgia winters. Your idea of covering the stump with mulch after the first frost is good. Wait until Thanksgiving to cut the main stem down to 6 inches in height. Put a gallon pot over it and cover it with a mound of straw. For insurance, though, you should collect some green stems in October to root indoors. Use your pruning loppers to cut off a couple of large branches, then strip off the biggest leaves.

Cut a dozen 12-inch lengths of the branches, noting which end of each section pointed toward the branch tip and which end pointed toward the plant's trunk. Place the "trunk" ends of the sections in a small plastic bucket and cover the ends with 6 inches of water. Put the bucket and branch sections in a sunny window in an unused bedroom.

You'll be surprised to find how fast the ends of the lengths will sprout roots. The other ends will soon sprout leaves. You can plant the rooted pieces in individual pots by late December and then plant them outdoors in April.

109 Garden Plants – Poison Worries

Q: *I have been told that angel trumpet plants are poisonous. Since we have a lot of small children living near us, I don't want to grow a possibly hazardous plant.*

A: If you're worried about poisonous landscape plants, you'll have to remove every azalea, rhododendron, Carolina jessamine, boxwood, daffodil, clematis, and Virginia creeper. Also take out any privet, burning bush, elephant ear, lantana, oleander, arborvitae, caladium, or Easter lily you have in your garden. In my opinion, a case could be made that most plants are poisonous, depending on how much and how often you make contact.

Eat enough beans, and you'll have a violent stomachache. Does that make it "poisonous"? Rub against an angel trumpet, and you'll usually have no reaction at all. That doesn't keep it from being classified "non-poisonous."

It is true that angel trumpet leaves and seed cause tremors and blurring of vision if you eat them. But so will the foliage of a tomato. Unless your neighborhood children are likely to chew the leaves of your angel trumpet, enjoy the flowers and keep in mind that while the plant *can* be poisonous in certain situations, it is not likely that it *will* be poisonous in yours.

110 Bulbs – Depth to Plant

Q: *Various bulbs require being planted at a certain depth. When you plant at a specific depth, does the addition of mulch add to the depth?*

A: Excellent question! Since the soil holds moisture and nutrients around the bulb and protects it from predators and weather, recommended depth always refers to the depth to which you plant beneath the soil surface. A thin layer of mulch (1 to 2 inches) simply keeps the soil from drying or eroding. The rule of thumb for bulb-planting depth is two to three times the diameter of large bulbs and three to four times the diameter of small bulbs. Remarkably, some bulbs can move themselves to the correct depth if you make a mistake. Their extensible roots slowly move the bulb into correct position. Even if you plant a bulb *upside down*, it will grow normal shoots, roots, and flowers.

111 Confederate Rose – Rooting

Q: *I have a 6-foot-high Confederate rose. What is the best way to propagate this plant? Can it be rooted?*

A: Propagating a Confederate rose is easy. You can do it by seeds or cuttings. After the flowers fade, they leave behind a brittle seed capsule. You can collect seeds from them in fall and plant them in spring. Rooting is even easier. Just collect several 12-inch-long cuttings from the limb tips in fall, before the first frost, and stick them into a bucket or deep vase with 6 inches of water. Keep in a sunny, warm spot indoors. Roots will form by December. You can transplant the cuttings to gallon pots in January and plant them outdoors in spring.

112 Resurrection Fern – On Trees

Q: *I've seen resurrection fern on trees and would like to know if it is a good sign or not, realizing mushrooms on trees are not a good thing.*

A: Resurrection fern (*Polypodium polypodioides*) is completely harmless. The fern confines its growth to the bark of the trunk and major limbs and is not parasitic, nor does it prevent the tree from performing photosynthesis.

It is an interesting weather gauge. During dry weather it turns brown, but the first bit of rain "resurrects" the fern into greenery.

113 Flattened Stem – Fasciation

Q: *I have a 'Sterling Star' lily. Its stem is about 1-inch wide and flat, not round. It has loads of flowers/buds. What causes this mutation? Will it continue to grow like this in years to come?*

A: The phenomenon of abnormally flattened stems is called *fasciation*. Many plants are known to occasionally produce fasciated limbs. The fasciation results from bacteria in some cases and genetic abnormalities in others. It is difficult to predict whether the lily will fasciate again. Grow it and see what happens!

114 Rabbit Tobacco

Q: *I grew up knowing about the wild rabbit tobacco, but I have just now discovered how to use it in decorations. Its fragrance is amazing!*

A: I, too, grew up familiar with rabbit tobacco. I smoked it occasionally as a kid, but the resulting headache dissuaded me from regular use. There are several species of rabbit tobacco, which is also called *cudweed*. *Gnaphalium spicatum*, shiny cudweed, develops from a distinct round silver-white rosette of leaves that grows flat on the ground. *Gnaphalium purpureum*, purple cudweed, has the gray-white narrow leaves along the stem that you probably think of as rabbit tobacco. All cudweeds grow as annual or biennial plants. The best way to propagate more is to collect seeds from mature flower heads in fall and plant them in spring.

115 Equisetum

Q: *I have been given a plant that I think is called* **equiseedem**. *It is only a bunch of tall green straws in a pot. Can you tell me something about this plant and how to care for it and what to expect in the future?*

A: The real name of your plant is *equisetum*, commonly called *scouring rush*, and yours is likely the dwarf form. It is an ancient plant, representing a single living genus, a single family, a single order, and a single class of plants. There is no other organism like it in the world. Dinosaurs likely munched on an ancestor of your small equisetum.

A pot is an appropriate container since scouring rush can become a weed if planted in a damp spot outdoors. Equisetum is one of the few native plants that is invasive. It has invaded many lake- and stream-sides across the country. That said, it does make a nice addition to the landscape when confined. It is said to be eaten by wildlife, but in my neighborhood the rabbits and squirrels leave it alone. I can't imagine a deer being hungry enough to chew through all of the abrasive silica in the stems.

116 Dodder – Identification and Control

Q: *I have a yellow-orange vine covering my impatiens. It's coming directly out of the stem and almost looks parasitic.*

A: As you should know if you watch horror movies, there is no such thing as "almost parasitic." This plant IS parasitic, and its name is dodder. The seeds of dodder germinate in the spring and send up a short sprout that attaches to any nearby plant. The vine tendrils wrap around the plant stem and invade it with parasitic roots. The dodder extracts water and nutrients from the host plant and can severely weaken it or kill it outright. There is no chemical that will kill the dodder and not harm your flowers. Pull and destroy any plants the dodder has touched, since the parasite can still grow from infected plants. Consider removing the top 1 inch of soil from your impatiens bed to eliminate dodder seed.

Red Hot Poker – Care

Q: *A few years ago my dad gave me some plants he called* **red hot poker.** *I planted them around my mailbox, and they have done well. I think it is time to dig, split, and spread them to other places in the yard. Since the leaves stay green all year, what is the best time to do this?*

A: There are several species and varieties of red hot poker, or *Kniphofia*, which is also commonly called *torch lily*. Although it is a member of the lily family, it doesn't grow from a bulb. Rather, the thickened roots (*rhizomes*) spread slowly from a single plant as the years pass. Given good growing conditions, they will sometimes become crowded and flower output will decline.

The best way to divide a clump is to remove young plants from the edge without disturbing the middle. You can certainly lift and split an entire mass of roots, but you won't get many flowers this year as they all recover from being moved. Cut away dead leaves with scissors.

When they bloom in summer, watch for hummingbirds attracted to the bright red-orange tubular flowers hanging from each flower spike. Cut off the spike immediately when most of the flowers on it are brown. Give the plant water and fertilizer, and it will bloom again in six weeks.

118 Flower Bed – Conditioning Soil after Planting

Q: *I have an existing flower bed that was tilled with soil amendments at the beginning, but maybe not enough. Will top-dressing the entire area with soil conditioner this fall help areas that are lacking in amendments? The bed is too big to till and replant—too many plants!*

A: It's a common occurrence to skimp on soil preparation and live to regret it. But you're astute to realize your situation and to think about how to rectify it. Hot weather literally cooks soil-softening organic matter out of the soil in a few years. Even gardeners who go the extra mile to amend their soil at the beginning need to prevent it from hardening over the long term.

My suggestion is that you mix 2 cubic feet of soil conditioner with a bag of composted cow manure or mushroom compost. Place a 1/2-inch layer of the resulting mixture under all of your plants in early fall, while the soil is warm. Note that you'll have to remove mulch under the plants before this topdressing is done.

Repeat the process next spring when the soil warms up in early April. Soil warmth is important. Earthworms have to be near the surface in order for them to take the organic matter belowground and keep the soil soft. Beginners and experts alike should do this each year.

119 Four-o'clock – Japanese Wonderflower

Q: *I purchased some Japanese wonderflower roots (**Mirabilis jalapa***) at a garden show. How do I plant them?*

A: A root of the common four-o'clock (*Mirabilis jalapa*) will grow just about anywhere you put it. Plant the thick end uppermost. Some gardeners find that the root exhausts itself after a couple of years. However, the multitudes of seed a four-o'clock scatters keep it happily reproducing from year to year. In fact, you may find yourself wondering how to eradicate the wonderflower a few years hence.

120 Hollyhock – Rust

Q: *Something is devouring my hollyhocks. There are yellow dots on the underside of affected leaves. Eventually the leaves look like lace.*

A: You have *hollyhock rust*. The disease causes lots of orange-yellow pustules underneath hollyhock leaves and corresponding yellow dots on top. Thousands of spores are in the rust pustules. They are carried by splashing water and breezes to nearby healthy plants and cause new infections. The fungus overwinters in infected plant debris.

   Spray with a **garden fungicide**[21] when you see the first yellow dots in spring. To break the disease cycle, cut all of your hollyhock stalks back to ground level in the fall. Afterward, collect all leaves and destroy them.

121 Fuchsia – Care

Q: *I have a 'Dark Eyes' fuchsia and would like to plant it in the yard. Is this a wise thing to do?*

A: You are welcome to plant it, but I can't guarantee success. In the first place, fuchsia does not like summer temperatures above 85 degrees F. When it gets hot, they quit producing new flower buds and become susceptible to disease. Winter temperatures below 25 degrees F will kill them. Southern gardeners get the most enjoyment from fuchsia by planting it in a pot in spring, and placing it in a spot that gets only a few hours of morning sun. When summer arrives, move the pot to a shady porch or under a small tree. Never let the soil dry or become waterlogged. Fuchsia will drop all of its leaves if the roots are unhappy.

---

21. **garden fungicide:** www.gardenword.com/gardenfungicide

122 Hosta – Propagating

Q: *I have a number of mature hosta plants with seed pods along the stems. I would like to plant these seeds. Is there a trick?*

A: You can collect seed from the crumbly brown pods and plant them in September in a sunny, well-drained spot. They will sprout in spring. Feed with houseplant fertilizer every six weeks to help them quickly grow to mature size. Don't expect the seedlings to be identical to the parent plant. The leaf color of the seedling will be derived from the color in the center of the leaf of the parent plant.

123 Native Plants – Neighborhood Covenants

Q: *This may seem like a ridiculous question, but the covenants for my subdivision require plant material "native to the southeastern U.S." What qualifies as "native"?*

A: In my opinion, they are ridiculous covenants. "Native to the southeastern U.S." means no one could plant fescue (Europe), zoysiagrass (Korea), bermudagrass (Asia), or centipedegrass (China). 'Bradford' pear (China) and Leyland cypress (Wales) would also be forbidden. While yaupon holly and American holly would be acceptable, 'Burford' holly (China) and 'Convexa' holly (Japan) would not. Many of the flowers we cherish, like daffodils and iris (Europe), butterfly bush and tulips (Asia), gladiolus (Africa), and zinnia (South America) are not "native" plants. I certainly recommend native plants, but someone wasn't thinking when he or she wrote the rules. I think the covenants need clarification.

124 Fragrant Plants

Q: *I know you like winter daphne, but can you list other fragrant plants that do well in our climate?*

A: I don't think I appreciated the value of landscape fragrance until the last few years in my garden. I was delighted in May when I discovered, by nose alone, a newly blooming gardenia. Here is a list of fragrant plants that do well locally, in approximate order of blooming:

Winter honeysuckle (*Lonicera fragrantissima*); daphne (*Daphne odora*); Koreanspice viburnum (*Viburnum carlesii*); Coastal flame azalea (*Rhododendron austrinum*); Piedmont azalea *(Rhododendron canescens*); Alabama azalea (*Rhododendron alabamense*); Lily-of-the-valley (*Convallaria majalis*); Confederate jasmine (*Trachelospermum jasminoides*); rose (*Rosa*); gardenia (*Gardenia jasminoides*); Southern magnolia (*Magnolia grandiflora*); moonflower vine (*Ipomoea alba*); Stargazer lily (*Lilium* × 'Stargazer'); Flowering tobacco (*Nicotiana alata*); summersweet azalea (*Rhododendron viscosum*); ginger lily (*Hedychium coronarium*); eleagnus (*Elaeagnus umbellata*); osmanthus (*Osmanthus fragrans*); sweet autumn clematis (*Clematis maximowicziana*).

125 Geranium – Hardy Type

Q: *On your radio show you mentioned hardy geraniums to use as a ground cover. I didn't catch all of the conversation. Could you fill me in?*

A: In my opinion, hardy geraniums are vastly underused in Georgia gardens. Unlike the gaudy red and orange flowers of annual geranium, which more accurately is a *Pelargonium* rather than a *Geranium*, perennial geranium has more muted purple-to-lavender blooms. Given good drainage, hardy geraniums form a weed-free mat of foliage that tolerates both drought and rainy weather. The flowers and attractive leaves are a bonus.

I like *Geranium sanguineum* 'John Elsley' and any of the cultivars of *Geranium macrorrhizum*. You may sometimes see hardy geraniums labeled "cranesbill geranium" due to their distinct seedpod, which resembles a bird's beak.

126 Daffodil vs. Jonquil – Identification

Q: *My office would like to know: what is the difference between daffodils and jonquils?*

A: Bringing light to the dark corners of garden knowledge is my specialty! Daffodils belong to the genus *Narcissus*, most of whose members have the familiar six flat flower petals surrounding a central cup. Daffodil is the common name for all members of the Narcissus family. You can use either *daffodil* or *narcissus* correctly when referring to any of this familiar family of bulbs. The American Daffodil Society divides members of the Narcissus family into thirteen divisions, based on the shape of the flower. There are Cyclamineus daffodils, Double daffodils, Miniature daffodils, etc. Narcissus is sometimes used as the common name for a few members, i.e., paper-white narcissus.

Older Southern gardeners would commonly refer to any early, yellow, fragrant narcissus as a jonquil. However, *jonquil* is properly used only as the common name for the Jonquilla group of daffodils.

127 Mums – Transplanting to Bed

Q: *Our church recently put out one hundred mums in pots for our dedication. Someone told me that these cannot be planted in a garden. Can they be successfully transplanted?*

A: They absolutely can be transplanted into gardens . . . and would be, in years to come, a nice remembrance of the church dedication. Truth be told, florist mums grow taller than garden mums. But with a bit of care, they can look spectacular next fall. If the flowers have faded, cut the foliage down to 3 inches tall now and plant each mum in a sunny garden spot. Mulch lightly around them with pine straw. New foliage will sprout up next spring. Shear it to 4 inches tall in late May, and shear again to 8 inches tall in mid-July. There will be plenty of regrowth by September, on which the chrysanthemums will make a mass of flowers.

128 Dahlias – Storing for Winter

Q: *I'm confused about whether or not to store dahlias for the winter. Will they make it through an Atlanta winter or should I dig them up?*

A: I've had them freeze in winter several times, so I recommend that you dig them up and store them. In contrast, I've observed a big clump of them in front of a house a mile away from me that have *never* been dug up and have done just fine for five years. Just to be safe, dig up your dahlias for storing, clip off the stems, dust the cuts on the tubers with garden sulfur, and store in a box in a cool spot until planting time next May.

129 Ginger Lily – Winter Care

Q: *I received a clump of ginger lily, which I planted like an iris. There isn't any foliage in winter. Is it dead or just dormant?*

A: Ginger lily (*Curcuma* and *Hedychium* species) is usually hardy in Atlanta, although a layer of pine straw over the clump is appreciated in frigid weather. As you guessed, the clump is dormant in winter. The green foliage will spring up in April, followed by the fragrant flowers in summer. The *rhizomes* (roots) can be divided in a few years and clumps passed along to your friends.

130 Salt-Tolerant Plants

Q: *We just bought a house on the beach. We need to put in grass and shrubs for landscaping. Can you recommend salt-tolerant plants?*

A: Depending on how far you are from the ocean, there are plenty of plants that will grow for you. Yaupon holly, cabbage palm, daylily, purpleheart, and bermudagrass all have good salt tolerance. This is a great opportunity for you to meet your new neighbors: just knock on their doors and inquire about the successful plants you see in their landscapes.

131 Verbena – Rejuvenating 'Homestead Purple'

Q: *For two consecutive years I have planted 'Homestead Purple' verbena, and it dies without fail. The site is on the side of my stone patio wall, sloped slightly, and is completely in the sun.*

A: You have the right planting spot for 'Homestead Purple'. Maybe you need to help it establish more thickly during the summer. This verbena produces blooms at the growing tips of branches. As it elongates during hot weather, most of the blooms occur in a doughnut around the original center of the plant. Old stems become hard and woody. Hot, dry soil keeps the young branches from rooting vigorously.

Try this method to rejuvenate the verbena. In mid-July, make several light vertical "chops" with a shovel in a circle 12 inches out from the center of the verbena clump. This will cause young branches that have already started rooting to root further and establish themselves before cold weather. The old branches in the center will be shocked into forming new growth and eventually flowers. Water regularly for a few weeks, until you see new leaves near the center of the plant, then leave your verbena to its own devices for the rest of the season.

132 Burial Plot – Recommended Plants

Q: *We have a family burial plot that needs some upkeep. Is there a low-growing grass I can plant in a semi-shade spot that won't require mowing?*

A: All of the turfgrasses used on lawns will require mowing. Centipedegrass will not require as much mowing as the rest, but you'll have to lug a mower over there a few times each year. Why not try mondo grass? This plant is not a true grass, but it stays low to the ground and never needs mowing. It doesn't like much traffic, but that won't be a problem in your situation. Mondo grass spreads by underground runners. If you have a friend with a big patch, ask if you can dig some of it and divide it to plant on your plot.

133 Asparagus Fern – Mysterious Bumps

Q: *I just purchased an asparagus fern, and the roots have big bumps on them. Are these root galls?*

A: The swollen parts are normal—just root nodules where water is stored. If you keep the plant in a plastic pot for very long, the strong root expansion will crack the plastic. Divide the plant when it begins to look crowded.

Although asparagus fern is kin to the plant that produces edible asparagus, parts of this houseplant are poisonous. On the Georgia coast it is an invasive perennial outdoors.

134 Aspidistra – Growing and Transplanting

Q: *Could you tell me where it's best to grow an aspidistra plant? Are there any instructions on how to transplant?*

A: Aspidistra is sometimes called *cast-iron plant* because it adapts to so many situations. However, until recently, I had never seen what I would call a good-looking clump of aspidistra. The bedding plants all seem to get leaf spot or have bleached leaves or floppy foliage or a generally messy character. Then I visited the Cloister, on Sea Island, and talked with their landscape director. She showed me several nice aspidistra beds on the property. In every instance they were in *deep shade*.

My jaundiced observations have been of beds that got more than a couple of hours of direct sun. Aspidistra is a plant that can grow happily in the shade under a magnolia or a tree-form 'Burford' holly, but more than a few hours of sunshine will cause it to complain loudly. The plant has creeping roots that grow shallowly under the soil, so transplanting it is no harder than digging up part of a clump and moving it to a new shady site.

135 Liriope – Crown Rot

Q: *A large section of liriope suddenly turned yellow. When you gently pull on it, it breaks away easily and has a black area at the base.*

A: Most gardeners consider monkey grass to be bulletproof, but you are not the first to complain about dying liriope. Yours has crown rot, caused by *Phytophthora palmivora*. The disease is exacerbated by wet soil, so cease any irrigation. Fungicide drenches can control the disease, but they are too expensive to consider. One source reports that compost tea or a topdressing of compost can help liriope recover. If you decide to replace the plants, add plenty of coarse paver underlayment sand to the spot to increase drainage.

136 Roses – Growing in Georgia

Q: *My husband and I are moving to St. Mary's from south Florida. Although roses will grow here, they don't thrive. How do roses do in coastal Georgia?*

A: Roses grow very well in south Georgia, as long as you pick the right ones. Sandy soil, heat, humidity, and soil nematodes sap the strength of roses that are not suited for the climate. Roses for the coast are usually grafted onto a 'Fortuniana' rose rootstock because this rose has a vigorous, nematode-resistant root system. Any rose that is so grafted will do fine.

137   Hosta – Variegated Turning Green

Q: *I have several hostas that once had a green center and white edge, but each year the variegation seems to fade more and more. In fact, some of them are solid green this year.*

A: This reversion to green is called *viridescence* and is a physiological response to our warm summer nights. In regions where the nights are cool, the leaf color of 'Albomarginata' hosta remains unchanged. Full sun tends to exacerbate the change in color and appearance of the leaves. You could force your hosta to return to its original color by cutting it down to ground level when the leaves begin to turn green. Afterward new white-margined foliage will emerge and remain unchanged into the fall. However, if you perform this drastic operation too often, expect to see smaller leaves in the clump in subsequent seasons.

138   Thyme – Between Stone Pavers

Q: *I have a stone walkway with sand and gravel between the rocks. I've heard that thyme makes a good green mat between the rocks and holds the sand and gravel. What do you recommend?*

A: I had a similar situation in front of my backyard water feature. The flat stepping stones were laid on clay. I used a shop vac to suck out loosened clay until I had a 6-inch deep slot between the stones. I filled the depression with planting soil and planted creeping thyme (*Thymus serpyllum*). The thyme thrived and now gracefully covers the stone edges.

139 Houttuynia – Chameleon Plant

Q: *I bought a plant labeled* Houttuynia *'Chameleon', labeled as a colorful perennial. It leaves a very unpleasant odor on your hands. What can you tell me?*

A: Your plant is *Houttuynia cordata*, but I'm not sure you should keep it. Chameleon plant is very invasive in most garden spots, particularly those that are shady and moist. I had some in a daylily bed a few years ago. I finally had to dig up every daylily, wash the soil from the roots, and replant them in another spot. I sprayed the remaining chameleon plants with **non-selective herbicide**[22] but had to likewise deal with new sprouts every three weeks for three months.

    I often see chameleon plant for sale in garden centers. I shudder when I pass the pots, warn customers of their aggressive ways, and consider surreptitiously spraying them with poison before another gardener suffers the fate I did.

140 Tansy – Deterring Japanese Beetles

Q: *I read in a book that tansy is good for deterring Japanese beetles. I have roses and other flowers that the beetles have a good lunch on for a few months. I don't like to use sprays due to my pets and grandkids. What do you think of tansy as a deterrent?*

A: For hundreds of years, gardeners have looked for plant combinations that would reduce pests. Despite numerous anecdotes from gardeners, little scientific research has been done to determine the specific situation in which companion plants really work. We *do* recognize that it's best to avoid planting a monoculture (one plant type) because a diverse environment confuses damaging insects. We *do* know that some plants attract beneficial insects. But we *don't* know scientifically if tansy repels Japanese beetles, or if chives repel aphids, or if mint deters cabbage moths.

    Honestly, I'm doubtful if any plant scent could keep Japanese beetles off roses.

---

22. **non-selective herbicide:** www.gardenword.com/nonselective

90

141 Lantana – Winter Pruning

Q: *I bought a lantana plant last spring, and it has grown into an unruly bush! Should I trim it back to the ground for the winter?*

A: Lantana was virtually unknown in Georgia horticulture until fifteen years ago. Then Goodness Grows Nursery in Lexington, Georgia, introduced a semi-hardy variety known as 'Miss Huff', and the plant exploded in popularity. There are several popular varieties, including 'New Gold', 'Athens Rose', and 'Confetti'. Only 'Miss Huff' survives winter in Atlanta. If your lantana has multicolored pink and yellow flowers, it is probably 'Miss Huff'.

There are two schools of thought on winter lantana care: some folks believe in cutting the plant to 12 inches tall in December and piling pine straw around the crown. Others passionately believe that the plant must be left untouched until it sprouts new growth in spring.

I fall into the first group because brown lantana stems are so ugly in winter. I'm careful to mound straw around the plant but not over it, so as to keep the stems dry. Nature, though, might bring unexpected cold temperatures in winter, meaning that even 'Miss Huff' will be compost by spring!

FLOWERS

Q: *I want to plant a small flower garden in my yard. I'm a beginner and have no idea of what type of gardening tools I need or what type of flowers to plant. How should I get started?*

A: One Atlanta expert says that in order to learn to garden, "You have to be willing to take a pile of cash and set it on fire!" You nor I have a pile of cash that we're willing to set afire, so let me suggest that you start with only a couple of tools: a round point shovel and a trowel. Begin with a small flower bed, perhaps 4 feet × 10 feet. The key to success in any garden is the soil. When you go to a garden center, buy 10 cubic feet of bagged soil conditioner. Mix it thoroughly into the bed before you plant. My feeling is that if you can first be successful with just a few plants, you'll be encouraged to build on that success in the future.

In winter, plant pansies as soon as you find them available. You'll need fifty plants for the bed. Plant them 10 inches apart and fertilize every month with liquid houseplant fertilizer. Next May pull out the pansies and replace them with daylily, black-eyed Susan, 'Homestead Purple' verbena, and bearded iris. Buy five of each, plant them a foot apart, and you'll have a very nice flower bed with blooms throughout the summer.

143 'Lavender Wave' Petunia – Growing

Q: *I twice planted some 'Lavender Wave' petunias, but they are not thriving. Could it be that there is not enough drainage?*

A: Although I've seen spectacular displays of 'Wave' petunias, they can sometimes be problematic. In my experience, these newer petunias are more sensitive to wet soil than older types. I also suspect that some are overwatered in the nursery and may bring the beginnings of root rot with them at planting. Check the prepurchase health of petunia roots by pulling a couple of plants from their pots. Plant in free-draining soil that has plenty of coarse sand mixed in. Water deeply once per week and feed often. These steps seem to be key to having good-looking 'Wave' petunias.

144 Poppy – Growing Legally

Q: *I'd like to grow breadseed poppy. Do you have instructions?*

A: Breadseed poppy is the common name of *Papaver somniferum*, also known as opium poppy. Poppies grow very well in Georgia, but possession of the seed is a bit tricky legally. As I understand it, if you *do not know* that opium poppy can be used to make opium, possession of the seedpod and/or flowers is legal. On the other hand, if you *know* the pod can be used illegally, you can be charged with possession of a controlled substance. Lest you worry about the poppies grown in highway medians, they are corn poppies (*Papaver rhoeas*).

145 Poppy – Planting

Q: *When can I plant poppy seeds?*

A: Poppies are most commonly planted in late October. Several kinds of poppy are grown in the South: Shirley poppy (*Papaver rhoeas*), Iceland poppy (*P. nudicaule*), Oriental poppy (*P. orientale*), and the infamous opium poppy (*P. somniferum*). All have gorgeous flowers when in bloom. Some gardeners simply scratch the soil and scatter the seed in areas where they grow large warm-season perennial plants like agastache, perovskia, and gaura. The poppy blooms are very noticeable before the other plants begin to flower. Afterward, the poppies disappear in the heat. Although some are touted as being perennial, I wouldn't count on it. If you don't want to take a chance on seed, poppy plants are common at area nurseries in spring. Plant them as soon as they are available.

146 Plumbago – Hardiness

Q: *My plumbago plants were covered with light blue flowers this summer. Will they make it through the winter?*

A: Plumbago is also known as *leadwort*. However, confusingly, there are two different leadworts commonly sold in nurseries. One, *Plumbago auriculata*, is a lanky half-hardy perennial, meaning it usually dies in winter here. The other, *Ceratostigma plumbaginoides*, is a fully hardy groundcover. The difference is that the first leadwort blooms all summer long while the second only makes blooms in fall. You have *Plumbago auriculata*, Cape leadwort. My advice is to cut dead stems back to 4 inches tall in November and lightly mulch with pine straw. If the winter cold doesn't kill them, you'll enjoy plumbago again next year. And if you see another plant that is also called leadwort, you'll now know the difference.

147 Pansy – Slow to Bloom

Q: *I put out four flats of pansies in October. They were small, healthy plants. They had blooms then but have not bloomed since. What's wrong?*

A: The plight of your poorly pansies is directly connected to the size of their root systems. If they were planted after the middle of October or if they were not fertilized every two weeks since then, the plants just aren't big enough to make many blooms. Fertilize now with liquid houseplant food and repeat every two to three weeks. The pansies will slowly get bigger and will be blooming by March. To assure winter blooms next year, plant only pansies growing in 3-inch pots.

148 Pansy – Nitrate Nitrogen

Q: *I have read your advice to use a fertilizer that contains "nitrate nitrogen" on pansies. How do I find it?*

A: Products containing a nitrate form of nitrogen are a bit better for cold weather plants like pansies, ornamental kale, and fall garden vegetables. Nitrate nitrogen is absorbed quickly by roots in cold soil. Other forms of nitrogen have to be broken down by soil bacteria first. There aren't many of these critters working when soil temperatures are below 40 degrees F. Read the labels of garden fertilizers, looking for those that contain at least 6 percent nitrate nitrogen.

149 Pansies – When to Plant

Q: *Even in October, my summer annuals look good. What is the latest date I can plant and still have thriving pansies?*

A: You can plant as late as December if you choose, but you'll have to spend more money on larger plants then. A pansy plant needs a root system as big as a softball in order to bloom in cold weather. Smaller plants, like those in nursery "six packs," need four weeks of strong growth in warm soil before they can bloom reliably in winter. To get good blooms, gardeners should plant the smaller pansies in early October, larger 3-inch pots in November, and even bigger 4-inch pots of pansies in December.

150 Money Plant – Growing

Q: *I was given a bag full of silver dollar money plant seeds but don't know anything about them.*

A: Money plant is lots of fun to grow. The silvery seed can be used by kids to purchase all manner of pretend goods from each other. The purple flowers are attractive in spring. Plant the seed in spring but do save a few and plant them in fall as well. The reason for the staggered planting is that money plant is a biennial. The seeds germinate, and the plant grows during one year, but the flowers and "money pods" don't come until the next year. Some of the seed you plant in spring may sprout and have enough time to flower this year. Once you have the pretty purple flowers in spring, you won't need to worry about having plants again. It reseeds readily, and you can give away your excess wealth each autumn.

151   Millet – Ornamental

Q: *I've recently purchased two 'Purple Majesty' millet plants. I was wondering if this plant comes back true from seed.*

A: 'Purple Majesty' millet was discovered at the University of Nebraska in their agricultural millet breeding program. The scientists in Lincoln recognized that although it didn't meet expectations for a grain plant, the millet was certainly ornamental. "Tall, dark and handsome" is the phrase some gardeners use to describe it. The purple foliage surrounds several tall, stiff seed spikes. Since 'Purple Majesty' is an F1 hybrid, the seed will not produce plants identical to the parents. Some of the offspring may not turn purple at all, although some probably will do so.

152   Mexican Heather – Is It Evergreen?

Q: *I thought Mexican heather would make it through the winter. Now in December my twenty mature plants are yellow. Do I need to cut them to the ground so they'll come back in the spring?*

A: The name *heather* fooled you, didn't it? Members of the true heather family are winter-hardy in Atlanta and, if planted where the soil drains well, will sometimes survive our summers for several years. Unfortunately, Mexican heather is a member of the "false heather" family. It vaguely resembles real heathers but is decidedly *not* winter-hardy here. It will survive outdoors only in far south Georgia and in Florida. Mexican heather is a great plant for our hot, dry summers, but it is best treated as an annual.

153 'Magilla' Perilla – Winter Care

Q: *Last spring I purchased a perennial and accidentally lost the tag. The plant leaf resembles a coleus and is magenta, cream, and green. I remember the name was something like "magilla."*

A: I remember watching *The Magilla Gorilla Show* back in the early sixties. Magilla had somehow come to live at Peebles Pet Store. Mr. Peebles, the owner, tried unsuccessfully to sell him in each episode. In contrast, 'Magilla' perilla has become more and more desired over the past few years. The bright purple and yellow splashed leaves make it look like a coleus, to which it is kin. It is a carefree plant, thriving in part shade to full sun. It will not survive winter cold. Remove a few 6-inch cuttings and put them in a cup of water on a windowsill. They will form roots in six weeks, after which you can plant in small pots before moving them outdoors in spring.

154 Plectranthus 'Mona Lavender'

Q: *Is 'Mona Lavender' plectranthus an annual or a perennial?*

A: If lived in tropical South Africa, where it was developed, "Miss Mona" would be perennial. If you live where it freezes in winter, it is used as an annual. Unlike other plectranthus, 'Mona Lavender' develops woody mature stems and forms a low shrub. The dark green leaves have wine-purple veins, making it very attractive in summer. When day length is fewer than twelve hours in fall, numerous lavender-colored, 6-inch-long flower spikes appear. Your plants will be covered with flowers from September up until the first frost. Remove old flower heads as the blooms fade. Plant in filtered sun, fertilize monthly, and irrigate if the plants begin to droop. Take 6-inch stem cuttings in early October and root in a glass of water so you'll have even more of these great plants next year.

155 Impatiens Seed – Planting

Q: *I am having great fun sharing with friends the popping of impatiens seedpods. Now what do I do with them?*

A: You can easily save impatiens and other flower seed over the winter. All you have to do is collect them and keep them cool and dry until spring. Pop some of the mature seedpods over a sheet of newspaper. Brush away the chaff and dry them on the paper for a week. Put the seeds in an envelope, label, and place the envelope into a pint jar. Also put in the jar two tablespoons of dry milk powder wrapped in tissue. The milk powder absorbs any moisture in the jar after sealing. Screw the jar lid on tight and put in the back of a refrigerator drawer. They will be safe and sound all winter.

In late April, sow the impatiens seeds on top of a flat of sterile seed-starting soil outdoors in a shady spot. Pat the seeds gently into the soil. Don't cover them—they need light in order to germinate. Water with a mister immediately, and daily thereafter, to keep the soil moist. Tiny seedlings will emerge in two weeks. Transplant the seedlings into your garden in late May. You'll notice that plenty of large, healthy impatiens are available at nurseries when yours are just beginning to sprout. Your impatiens may not bloom until late June, while those that your neighbors bought earlier will be blooming the day they are planted.

FLOWERS

Q: *I bought a hollyhock plant last spring. It did nothing but make lots of leaves. This spring it has grown enormously and has a weird-looking thing on the end of the stalk. What should I expect from this plant?*

A: I think you're seeing a flower pod waiting to open. My bet is that as the stalk grows taller, you'll have more side leaves and more flower buds to enjoy along the stem. Hollyhocks usually behave as a biennial. They sprout and grow several leaves in the fall of one year, overwinter, then grow tall and set their flowers the following spring and summer. That explains why yours did nothing last year but is preparing to flower this season.

Some hollyhock strains behave as annuals. They can sprout and bloom during the same growing season. You might try persuading your hollyhock to behave more as a perennial. After a couple of months of bloom, plants will look ratty and there will be only a few flowers at the top of the stalk. Cut the plant back to just above its lowest leaves. These leaves will feed new leaves, which sprout around the base of the stalk. Just before frost, cut off the stalk just above the basal leaves. If the winter is not too severe, the leaves will remain on the plant, and it will reflower the second year.

157 Geranium – Keeping over Winter

Q: *I have a prized geranium that I would like to carry over during the winter. What is the best way to do this?*

A: There are two ways. You could make several 3-inch long cuttings and root them individually in paper cups filled with a 1:1 mix of sand and peat moss. Alternatively, dig up your plant before night temperatures go below 40 degrees F and put it in a brown paper bag. Place it in your garage where it does not freeze but is kept cool. Check on it in late December. If the rootball is powder dry, take it out of the bag, soak it, let it dry until slightly moist, then put the plant back in the bag.

Don't worry if many leaves turn yellow and fall off. If the stems shrivel, the plant is being kept too dry. In mid-March, remove the plant from the bag, soak it in a bucket of water, and put it in a pot. It can be put outside when all frosts are past. It is surprising how fast those little sticks perk up and sprout leaves once again!

158 Curcuma – Winter Care

Q: *I love the flowers of a plant labeled "curcuma." What should I do with it this fall and winter?*

A: You have a Siam tulip (*Curcuma alismatifolia*). It is not hardy outdoors in winter and so must be brought indoors before first frost. Try placing it in a sunny window and taking it outdoors when night temperatures are above 55 degrees F next spring. It hates soggy soil, so I suggest you replant it in cactus potting mix when you take it inside this fall.

159 Sweet Peas – When to Plant

Q: *When is the best time to plant sweet peas? Would mid-February be too early?*

A: Mid-February would be just right for starting sweet pea seed indoors, but you should wait until early March to plant seed outdoors. Although the plants can endure frost without much problem, keep some black plastic on hand to cover the little arbor where you've planted them in the garden if temperatures below 28 degrees F appear. Another idea would be to plant in a container and leave it outdoors except on the coldest nights. Place the seeds an inch deep just inside the rim of the container and use several 3-foot-long slender branches to make a teepee on which the vines can climb.

160 Jonquil Bulbs – Storing

Q: *Someone gave me three bags of jonquil bulbs in April. Can these be stored during the summer so that they will keep until I can plant them in the fall?*

A: All things considered, I think you should plant them. If they send up flower stalks, cut them off so the plant can concentrate on growing new roots and leaves.

161 Cotton – Planting

Q: *Would you tell me how to plant cotton seeds?*

A: Before you plant the cotton seed, you must have permission to grow it. The Georgia Department of Agriculture only grants permission to educational or historical organizations. Their reasoning is that uncontrolled homeowner cotton gardening could lead to an outbreak of the cotton boll weevil.

The response may seem extreme, but you have to look at the situation through the eyes of Georgia cotton farmers. Their crop averages more than $500 million at the farm gate each year. They could not be so successful if the cotton boll weevil ever again became epidemic in Georgia like it once was. The Georgia cotton crop declined by *80 percent* only seven years after the boll weevil appeared in Thomasville in 1915. It spread to forty Georgia counties in four months.

From this you can grasp the fear that cotton producers have for this destructive insect. In 1980, researchers found that they could dramatically reduce the amount of poison used if they closely monitored the weevil population with pheromone traps placed alongside cotton fields. By 1996, the boll weevil was considered eradicated in Georgia, and a $720 million crop was harvested. Now you can see why homegrown cotton is viewed with such consternation by farmers. If a few weevils develop undetected, an entire crop and livelihood could be threatened.

162 Ornamental Sweet Potato – Propagating

Q: *I planted some ornamental sweet potatoes this year. Do you have suggestions on how to keep them for next year?*

A: You can certainly keep the potato tubers over the winter, but planting them next spring is not the process you might expect. Dig up the potatoes when the foliage dies in fall. Use a permanent marker to mark the end from which the roots grew (R) and the ends from which the vine grew (V). Keep the tubers in a dry, dark, and cool spot until early next March. At that time suspend each potato in its own glass of water so that the root end is half-submerged. Place the glasses in a sunny window, and wait for potato sprouts and leaves to appear.

When the sprouts are 6 inches long, clip them from the mother tater and submerge them halfway in another glass of water in the window. The sprouts will form roots in a few weeks and can then be planted in a sunny spot in your garden.

163 Celosia – Growing

Q: *Have you seen cockscomb celosia? The flower looks like a red fuzzy brain. I have some seeds from a bouquet, and I'd like to know how to cultivate them.*

A: Celosia is an annual flower that has three distinct flower forms: *plumosa*, *spicata*, and *cristata*. As the names imply, plumosa flowers are tall and feathery while spicata flowers are narrow and spiky. Cristata flowers remind many gardeners of convoluted brains. Save the seed from your bouquet flower and keep them cool and dry until spring. Plant in a sunny bed when nighttime temperatures are consistently above 55 degrees F.

164 Cleome – Planting

Q: *A friend of mine recently gave me some cleome seeds from her garden. What do I do with these seeds?*

A: Cleome self-seeds to a fault, but the flowers are beautiful. It is a tall plant, so choose a planting spot in the back of your flower bed. Scratch the ground there next April and scatter your seed. Cover with a bit of dirt, and they will sprout in three weeks.

The pink-lavender flowers are very attractive in midsummer, but most gardeners find the plants leggy and unattractive by August. You can prevent this by removing each flower stem, even if it has a flower on it, when it is 12 inches long on the end of a larger branch. Remove the faded plants next fall, but note that the trunk is lined with slender seedpods, many of which will have opened and scattered seed by that time. Regular cleome grows 3 to 5 feet tall; the variety 'Linde Armstrong' grows only 12 to 16 inches tall and doesn't self-seed so vigorously.

165   Butterflies – Plants to Attract

Q: *My neighbor showed me four monarch butterfly caterpillars on his fennel plant. I want to be the butterfly queen in my neighborhood. What should I plant this fall?*

A: Planting some fennel would be a good start. The green and yellow caterpillars will be all over your plants each August. You have to plant two kinds of plants to make butterflies happy. Some plants are in a butterfly garden to feed caterpillars. Others are there to attract the adult "flutterby's." Parsley, butterfly weed, passionflower, and elm trees also host caterpillars. Nothing beats a combination of butterfly bush, lantana, and annual zinnias for attracting the pretty adults. If you bury a plastic basin in the ground and fill it with wet sand or mud, you'll provide the other element that attracts the insects: a moist place on which to land, drink, and bask in the sun.

166   Butterfly Houses – Not Helpful

Q: *My daughter gave me a butterfly house that was treated to keep out wasps. It didn't work. Any ideas?*

A: Butterfly experts have concluded that a butterfly box rarely benefits butterflies. Few, if any, use it for hibernation, shelter, or forming their chrysalis. They are, however, excellent homes for paper wasps. My solution would be to put screen wire on the inside of the slots and keep *all* insects from going inside.

167 Butterflies – Attracting with Nectar

Q: *I have a very nice glass butterfly feeder. How do I make the nectar to attract them?*

A: Experienced butterfly fanciers are unconvinced that butterfly feeders attract or feed butterflies. One breeder warns against using a concentrated sugar solution like you'd use for hummingbirds. He recommends Gatorade™ spiked with a few splashes of soy sauce. Also, rotting fruit is very attractive to butterflies. Place a saucer on a flat-topped post near your flower garden and put sliced bananas, apples, and oranges in it. I think you'll see more butterflies dining on the fruit than at your nectar feeder.

168 Carpenter Bee – How to Repel

Q: *I had carpenter bees boring in my deck last year, and now they are back again. Is there any way to keep them away?*

A: The best you can do is to reduce the local population each year. Although carpenter bees are active pollinators, the damage they do to siding, decks, and garages sometimes outweighs their usefulness. The ones you see hovering around the wood are males, guarding the egg-laying tunnels made by female bees. Squirt a bit of insecticide into each hole you can locate and seal it with caulk. This will do more to reduce next year's family than swatting the males when they buzz you.

FLOWERS

Q: *I found a caterpillar in the backyard. I asked my mom if it was a boy or a girl caterpillar, and she didn't know. I asked my neighbor if it was a boy or girl, and he didn't know. Do you know?*

A: I don't know if your caterpillar is a boy or a girl, but I am sure *it* knows! You probably already know that a caterpillar is just one of the four stages of life through which a butterfly goes: adult, egg, caterpillar, and *pupa* (cocoon). The easiest time to determine if a butterfly is male or female is when it is an adult. A butterfly identification guidebook will show you the wing markings that distinguish the two. When a female butterfly lays her eggs, each one is either a boy or a girl. The eggs hatch in a few days into tiny caterpillars.

Even though the caterpillars are either male or female, this doesn't matter to them and the two sexes look identical. What *does* matter to a caterpillar is to *eat, eat, eat* in order to gain the size and energy to change into a butterfly. Once the caterpillar is mature, it will attach itself to a twig or leaf and harden into a pupa. Inside the pupa, the caterpillar body will change into a butterfly.

When the butterfly emerges from the pupa, he or she will go looking for a flower from which to feed. Later, he or she will look for a mate. They don't use their eyes to find each other; they use a special perfume (a *pheromone*) that each can detect. Even though this seems complicated, butterflies and moths have somehow managed to figure out who is male and who is female for millions of years. It must be simple to them—but even the smartest scientists would have a hard time figuring out whether your caterpillar is a boy or a girl.

170 Clover Mites – Identified

Q: *I have tiny red bugs on my house walls and windows. What are they?*

A: Just a few sunny days in April can cause clover mites to hatch in your lawn. These tiny, red mites feed on clover and tender grass. They do no harm to people, buildings, or pets, but they can be unsightly if found in or on your house. The easiest solution is to wash them off your house with a hose. There is no need to use an insecticide, but you could spray with any outdoor **garden insecticide**[23] if you *must* do something. Cold weather retards their hatching; they finish hatching in mid-spring. You usually won't see them any more after April.

171 Daisy Beetle – Control

Q: *I found little beetles eating the petals of my brown-eyed Susans and coneflowers. What are they?*

A: The beetle is a member of the leaf-feeding beetle family: *Chrysomelidae*. Other common leaf-feeding beetles include potato beetle and elm leaf beetle. There are hundreds of Chrysomelid species, and since I am not an entomologist, I can't specifically identify the one that afflicts your flowers. I've decided to call it "daisy beetle" since it consumes the flower buds of daisy family members. In any case, spraying with a garden insecticide will take care of the problem.

23. **garden insecticide:** www.gardenword.com/gardeninsecticide

172 Columbine – Leaf Miner

Q: *In a matter of days after planting, most of my columbine leaves had serpentine patterns on them. Is this a leaf miner?*

A: Anyone who grows columbine (*Aquilegia* spp. and hybrids) will have columbine leaf miner on the plant foliage. In fact, I often see the trails on columbines for sale in nurseries. The insect adult is a tiny fly. The female lays single eggs at different spots on leaves. When the egg hatches, the larva burrows into the leaf and begins tunneling between the upper and lower surface of the leaf. As the larva grows bigger, the serpentine trail becomes wider. In early June, the larvae will pupate and drop to the ground to wait for next year's victims.

Other than causing visual disfigurement, the columbine leaf miner doesn't seem to hurt the plant. Columbine itself is usually a short-lived resident of Atlanta-area gardens. I think the best control is to shear off the foliage immediately after blooms fade, when you can see tiny seedpods. Scatter the seeds nearby. The original plant may sprout new leaves by midsummer, but if it dies, the seed will sprout to give fresh plants for next spring.

173 Bearded Iris – Propagation

Q: *What are the pods on a bearded iris for? Do they have seeds?*

A: If you are both adventurous and patient, you'll get lots of enjoyment from propagating iris from seed. The swollen seedpod below the faded flower contains several seeds. When the pod dries and begins to split (which may take several weeks), you can collect the dark seed and plant them in a sunny, evenly moist spot. Like daylily seed, they seem to germinate best when sown in the current year, not kept for next spring. Some seed will sprout almost immediately, but some may wait until next spring. Next May transplant the little sprouts to a sun-filled "nurse bed," feed them regularly, and wait. Vigorous plants will have blooms within two years of germinating.

174 Easter Lily – Care

Q: *I received an Easter lily in April. How should I care for it? Can I make it bloom next year?*

A: Easter lilies are hardy outdoors in Atlanta. The best thing to do is to plant them in a spot with dappled shade in your garden. The foliage will disappear by midsummer. The next year it will bloom in early June. Your Easter lily was forced in a greenhouse to bloom earlier than it would normally do so. Be sure to plant in the shade. Otherwise the plants seem to last only a few years in full sun. The shade also keeps them from emerging too early.

175 Siberian Iris – Care

Q: *I have several Siberian iris in my garden. They are one of my favorite spring flowers, but I am not fond of the foliage that looks untidy all summer long. Can I remove this foliage?*

A: The iris will be damaged if you remove the foliage while it is green. Leaves store the energy needed for blooms next May. I have a suggestion to camouflage the untidy foliage. Why not plant coneflower, black-eyed Susan, or daylilies among your irises to hide the leaves as they fade? If you use these companion plants, you'll have more than two months of flowers in the same area rather than just the week of blossoms that the Siberian iris provides.

176 Elephant Ear – Blooms

Q: *My elephant ear bloomed this year and last. Can you tell me how often to expect this?*

A: I can't say how often flowering will occur. My guess is that older, crowded plants will bloom more often than newly planted elephant ears. Elephant ear is in the same family as peace lily and anthurium, the common houseplants. Their blooms are technically called *spathes*. Botanically, a spathe is a *bract* (modified leaf) enclosing a *spadix* (fleshy spike of tiny flowers). If the flowers are pollinated, tiny "berries" will form along the spadix. Save them from your elephant ear to plant outdoors in spring.

177 Iris, Daisies – Care in Fall

Q: *By August my iris and daisies have all bloomed, but they look dreadful. Would it be all right to cut them back now?*

A: Any time a leaf is green, it is providing food for the plant to which it is attached. Even though your plants are floppy and leggy, like mine are, it is better to leave green leaves in place. To hide the disheveled foliage, consider planting dwarf goldenrod, aster, or sedum 'Autumn Joy' around your untidy flowers. All of the plants I've listed are late bloomers and will make a nice transition away from the summertime blooms of iris and daisy.

178 Spring Bulbs – Winter Care

Q: *I planted bearded iris roots in early November, and now they have shoots about 6 inches tall. Will these survive the winter? Should I trim or replant?*

A: This is a common question each winter. Fall-planted bulbs (daffodil, tulip, iris, hyacinth, etc.) often send up greenery before winter sets in. The good news is that the leaves will not be harmed by cold. If you need something to do, lightly cover the bulb foliage with pine straw. All of those noted will bloom normally next spring.

113

179 Tulips – Planting in Pots

Q: *I have some tulip bulbs that I would like to plant in pots on the deck. Do I need to pre-chill the bulbs for eight weeks and then plant in December?*

A: You should plant the tulips in outdoor pots in October and let Mother Nature provide the refrigeration. Consider putting the tulips near the bottom of the pot and placing early-blooming daffodils above them. Fill the pot with potting soil and carefully plant pansies on top. You'll have in the pot a succession of blooms to delight your eyes for months. The tulips and daffodils will bloom next spring, but tulips generally decline and produce few blooms after the first year. For that reason, remove the bulbs in May and plant them in a sunny bed where they can naturalize if they care to. Use fresh bulbs in the pot next fall.

180 Daylilies – Fertilizing

Q: *Is April the time to fertilize daylilies?*

A: The general rule of thumb is to fertilize plants when they are most vigorously growing, which would be late March through early April for daylilies. Since most time-release fertilizers depend on warm soil to release nutrients, I recommend you use a tablespoon of 10-10-10 per plant in late March, followed by the label-recommended amount of time-release fertilizer. Water it in thoroughly so the 10-10-10 can get to work in the plant. Fertilize again with 10-10-10 or with a liquid fertilizer as the last blooms fade in summer. This will stimulate new growth, assuming you water regularly, and may induce new flowers a month later.

181 Tulip – Reblooming

Q: *Do tulips come back every year, or do I have to replant new bulbs every fall?*

A: My mother proudly informed me that her tulips bloomed regularly in the same spot for three (!) years. I make it a habit never to argue with success (particularly my mother's), but I will say that tulips are not ordinarily perennial in Atlanta. In order for tulips to flower strongly from year to year, they must grow in cool temperatures but bright sunshine for two months after flowering and then go bone dry. That isn't what we have in Georgia in May. In summer heat, the leaves fade away and fail to absorb the energy they need to produce flowers the next spring.

However, if you want to experiment, all is not lost. Next fall excavate a bulb planting area 12 inches deep. Discard half the soil you bring out; mix the other half 1:1:1 with soil conditioner and gritty sand. Refill your bed area halfway with this mixture. Position the tulips on the loose soil, scatter a tablespoon of bonemeal around each one, and finish filling the hole with your soil mixture. By doing this you will give the tulips good drainage below the bulbs and a cool place in which to grow. The best site for them would be bright shade—never full sunshine. Try species tulips like *Tulipa clusiana* 'Cynthia' and *T. bakeri* 'Lilac Wonder'.

182 Iris – Leaf Spot

Q: *I have brown spots on the leaves of my iris. Can you tell me how to rectify the situation?*

A: *Iris leaf spot* is a common malady of iris. The brown spots are inconspicuous until flowers appear. Afterward they may coalesce and cause the top half of the leaf to die. Though the disease does not attack flowers or roots, it can weaken the plant due to leaf loss. Since the fungus overwinters on old foliage, cut diseased leaves at ground level in October. Dispose of them in the garbage. If you are a real iris fancier, you can spray with a **fungicide**[24] when the leaves are 4 to 6 inches high. Repeat every ten days. Be sure to add ¼ teaspoon of liquid detergent to each gallon of spray to aid in wetting the waxy foliage.

183 Fire Ants – Identification

Q: *With all the advertising of fire ant poisons, I wonder how likely it is that the ants in my flower beds are really fire ants? Could they be some other kind of ant?*

A: Good question! Most fire ant poisons are effective *only* against fire ants. There are many other species of ants you might encounter. Fire ants make distinctive mounds, usually much higher and wider than native ants. If you see a mound that is more than 2 inches high and 6 inches wide, suspect fire ants.

---

24. **fungicide:** www.gardenword.com/gardenfungicide

184 Elephant Ear – Winter Care

Q: *What is the right time to dig up and store elephant ear tubers?*

A: Elephant ear is not reliably winter-hardy outdoors in north Georgia, although most will come back after a mild winter. In November, cut the stems down to 6 inches tall (*Caution*: do not let sap touch your eyes or tender skin), cover with a gallon pot, and cover everything thickly with pine straw. If you want to keep the *corm* (bulb) indoors for winter, remove the stems, dig up the corm, and let it dry for a week in a cool spot. Half-fill a large plastic box with perlite, set the corm into it, and finish covering completely. Keep it in a closet indoors. Plant the corm outdoors when nighttime temperatures are above 60 degrees F in spring.

185 Flowers – Drought-Proofing

Q: *I enjoy my flower beds, but I am concerned that we could have a total water ban. How can I garden with less water?*

A: Water use in the landscape is a big issue. Even so, I hope gardeners don't decide to avoid planting. There are plenty of plants that grow just fine with minimal water. In fact, every plant we use in our landscapes can get through a drought with little worry if some thought is given beforehand. The key for your flower beds is to prepare the soil to be water-retentive before you plant in them. It is easy to make your soil water-saving—just mix in a 2-inch layer of soil conditioner before you plant. Existing plants, like shrubs and trees, should be mulched over their *entire root zone* so water doesn't evaporate from the ground. The entire root zone is key here. Plan to cover all of the soil underneath and a bit beyond their branch spread.

186 Tiger Lily- Propagation

Q: *Is it possible to harvest the little bulbs on the stalk of a tiger lily and start new plants?*

A: Tiger lilies propagate themselves in three different ways: from *bulbils* that form between leaves and the stem; from *bulblets* that form next to the parent bulb in the soil; and from *seed*, which form in a pod behind the flower if it is successfully pollinated. These three methods insure that tiger lilies usually prosper in any spot they're planted. You can roll the bulbils out with your fingers and plant them nearby, $1/2$ inch deep, in soft soil. They will likely sprout a leaf or two by fall. Leaves will disappear with cold weather, but most bulbs will survive the winter just fine. Water and fertilize the lilies that come back next spring. I doubt any will be strong enough to flower next year, but you'll probably get flowers in the following spring.

187 Soil – Sterilization

Q: *I reuse the potting soil in my patio containers. Last year I had some type of crown rot in my impatiens. Can I sterilize the soil somehow?*

A: It's important to restore the soil's drainage capacity as well as its sterility before you reuse it. Mix the old soil 4:1 with perlite to increase drainage. To sterilize it, stir in enough water to make it quite moist but not soupy. Place in a shallow pan in a 180-degree-F oven for thirty minutes. Be aware that it will smell strongly while it is cooking. Another option is to heat the moist soil in a microwave until it steams for five minutes.

188 Daffodil – Not Blooming

Q: *How can I get my daffodils that haven't bloomed in several years to bloom again?*

A: Daffodils bloom in response to how happy they were the previous year. If you fertilized yours last spring or divided the clump and moved them to a nice new bed, yours may well bloom this coming year. If you mowed off the foliage right after they bloomed last spring, you probably won't have blooms next year either. Daffodils prefer full to dappled sunshine and an application of fertilizer in spring. Follow those instructions and you should get blooms without fail.

189 Summer Bulbs – When to Plant

Q: *When is the right time for summer bulb planting?*

A: Although summer-flowering bulbs are on nursery shelves in March, they should not be planted until the earth is *very* warm. I use 65 degrees F at a 2-inch soil depth as my rule of thumb. That temperature may be reached occasionally, but not consistently, in mid- to late April. For folks north of I-20, the first week in May is a good time to plant summer bulbs like canna, caladium, dahlia, gladiola, etc. If you plant the bulbs too early, they will likely rot in the cold earth. One way to know your local soil temperature exactly is to visit **www.georgiaweather.net**.

190 Bulbs – Planted Upside Down

Q: *In November, I planted three hundred spring bulbs in my garden. Now I am concerned that I planted them upside down. Must I dig them up and replant?*

A: You can lay to rest your fears that the leaves will grow downward until they are exhausted. Plants have a remarkable array of abilities to grow toward or away from a stimulus. Plant scientists call it *tropism.* You have probably seen indoor plants that seemed to "lean" toward a window to get sunshine. The orientation of the leaves toward the light is called *phototropism.* Plant roots grow toward gravity. That is called *geotropism.* Fortunately for you, bulb foliage is negatively geotropic. It will grow away from gravity and will emerge from the earth on schedule next spring.

In the course of researching your question, I found other interesting "tropisms." When sunflowers follow the sun as it travels across the sky each day, they exhibit *heliotropism.* Roots that grow toward water are *hydrotropic.* Vines that wrap around any surface they touch are *thigmotropic.* When a bean vine creeps along the ground toward the shadow of a vertical pole, it shows *skototropism.*

Did you know that bulbs can move themselves through the soil? Several bulbs have *contractile roots*, which pull a bulb slowly to the most favorable depth in the soil. Even if you *did* plant the bulbs upside down, they would slowly right themselves as the years pass.

120

191 Spring Bulbs – When to Plant

Q: *When is the latest I can plant bulbs for the spring?*

A: My preference is to wait to plant bulbs until night temperatures are consistently below 50 degrees F. At that time the soil is warm enough to stimulate root growth, but you won't get much foliage growth. You can successfully plant them as late as December, but the later you wait after mid-October, the less able the bulbs will be to establish themselves. You can check local air and soil temperatures at **www.georgiaweather.net**.

There are two critical times to feed your bulbs. They need nutrients in the fall when they are planted, and they need more in the spring when they have leaves. For every 10 square feet of bed, sprinkle two cups of 10-10-10 fertilizer over the soil and dig it in as you prepare the area for planting in fall. Use the same amount in March when the leaves emerge. Special bulb fertilizers are available that do not force unneeded growth in fall but give bulbs the nutrients they need.

192 Daylily – "Repeat Bloomer"

Q: *In daylily jargon, what does "repeat bloomer" actually mean? Mine are supposed to, but haven't.*

A: I'll teach you a bit of daylily vocabulary: *remontant*. This means that a daylily is genetically programmed to bloom more than once in a season. Repeat blooming occurs once a plant is well established in its garden spot. I think your daylilies are still getting comfortable in their new home. If you babied them this summer, they should have an easy time of reblooming for you next year. Remontant daylilies perform better when given optimum moisture and fertilizer, so don't let yours suffer during the heat next summer. 'Stella D'Oro' and 'Happy Returns' are good reblooming daylilies.

193 Daylily – Planting Seedpods

Q: *After blooming, I see what looks like seedpods on my daylilies. What do I do with these pods?*

A: You can plant the seed from the pods as soon as they dry and begin to split. You'll get little seedlings in fall or next spring, but they won't be ready to bloom for a few years yet. The flowers may look like the parent, or they may be a wonderful combination of the traits of daylily flowers that were near the parent plant.

194 Caladium – Storing for Spring

Q: *I have seventy caladium plants that I want to dig up and store for spring. Will it hurt the bulbs?*

A: It's fine to do this. The best time to dig caladiums is before the leaves disappear. You can use the stem as a handle to gently tug the corms free as you dig. Caladiums can be stored in a plastic tub and covered with dry perlite or peat moss. Separate the corms by leaf color and label the tubs carefully. You won't be able to tell which is which next spring without a label. Keep the caladiums in a warm, rather than cool, spot for the winter. A little-used hall closet is a good place. If kept in a cool basement or unheated garage, the roots deteriorate and do not sprout easily. Keep the lid on the container until you retrieve it in late April. Plant caladium corms when you can sit on the ground in your shorts comfortably.

195 Jack-in-the-Pulpit – Growing from Seed

Q: *I found a Jack-in-the-pulpit that produced fruit this fall. How do I gather the seeds and raise more of these flowers?*

A: The red berries covering the end of a short stalk are typical of plants in the arum family, including caladium and elephant ear. First, pick the berries from the stalk. It's good idea to wear rubber gloves because chemicals in the seeds induce an allergic reaction in some people. Wash the berries and remove the skin and pulp from the hard seed you'll feel inside. Plant them a $1/2$ inch deep and a few inches apart, in a semi-shade, moist bed. Tiny leaves will emerge in midsummer. Keep the bed moist and allow the plants to grow until next spring, when you can transplant the seedlings to their final habitat in the woods.

196 Daylily – Rust

Q: *What can you tell me about the sad, ugly rust infecting our wonderful daylilies?*

A: Daylily rust fungus requires green leaves and high humidity to germinate and causes a yellow fuzz on the underside of daylily leaves. Rub a piece of white tissue under your infected leaves. If it has lots of orange powder on it, you have daylily rust. Control is possible, but persistence is the key. Cut off all of the infected leaves and remove them from your garden. Begin spraying with a **contact fungicide**[25] to kill the visible spores and alternate every week with a **systemic fungicide**[26] to kill the fungus in the leaf tissue.

197 Canna Lily – Germination

Q: *I have tried several times to germinate canna lily seeds with no luck. Could you explain how to accomplish this?*

A: Canna seed are hard as rock and are almost impervious to water. You have to nick the seed in order for it to "imbibe" water and start the process of germinating. Some gardeners soak the seed in warm water for twenty-four hours to soften the seed coat before nicking it. You can scratch the coat by holding a seed between your fingers and rubbing it quickly on a piece of sandpaper. Or you can hold it on a damp towel with a fingertip and slice off a corner with a sharp craft knife. Plant in warm, moist soil, and sprouts should appear in three weeks.

25. **contact fungicide:** www.gardenword.com/gardenfungicide
26. **systemic fungicide:** www.gardenword.com/gardenfungicide

198 Lily-of-the-Valley – Growing in Georgia

Q: *I remember lily-of-the-valley plants growing outside my Ohio home. The fragrance was incredible. Do they grow in Atlanta?*

A: My experience with lily-of-the-valley (*Convallaria majalis*) has been mixed. I have planted and lost them twice. However, I regularly drive past a yard that I notice is covered with them every spring. My feeling is that the plant doesn't much care for Atlanta's summer heat. If you want to experiment, find a spot with bright shade most of the day. Early day sunshine would be fine, but not afternoon. Amend the proposed bed with 3 inches of soil conditioner mixed 10 inches deep. Plant the *pips* (fleshy roots) when they become available in spring at garden centers or find a bulb catalog that can ship some to you.

199 Agave – Growing

Q: *Will agave grow in Georgia?*

A: Some species of *agave* (century plant) grow well in Georgia, particularly in the southern half of the state. In metro Atlanta, most are done in by poor drainage in winter. If you want to give it a try, give the plant *extremely* well-draining soil. I'm guessing that a 3:1 mix of paver leveling sand and ground pine bark would suit an agave sited in full sunshine.

200 Dahlia – Dividing Roots

Q: *I have two dahlias that have grown well, but I need to move them. How do I do that?*

A: Keep in mind that most dahlia roots will freeze and be killed during the winter in north Georgia. The plants should be dug in October. Cut off the stems 2 inches above the swollen tuberous roots. Try not to break apart the tubers. Allow them to dry a few days in your carport or basement. Since you don't have many, just put them in a cardboard box and cover with peat moss or perlite. Put the box in a garbage bag, but do not tie the bag shut; leave the plastic loosely covering the box top. This will allow the roots to breathe but won't let them dry out badly.

Next spring, wait until night temperatures are above 60 degrees F before planting the roots. Those that have sprouts coming from them can be cut from the original clump and planted individually. You should fertilize them at planting and again in late June.

HOUSEPLANTS

Q&A

201 Rosemary – Growing Indoors

Q: *I had a very large rosemary plant that flourished outside but died of old age. The label on my replacement says they are hardy down to 20 degrees F. Should I keep it indoors or outside?*

A: Rosemary is usually hardy outdoors in Atlanta. Most gardeners leave their rosemary in the garden for winter and remove damaged limbs in spring. Some varieties, like 'Arp' and 'Athens Blue Spires', are more cold hardy than the species. Rosemary topiaries are popular gifts for the holidays, but they are problematic if kept indoors for long. Powdery mildew and root rot seem to get them every time. If you receive a potted rosemary, place it in a sunny window and keep the foliage dry. Water only when the soil begins to dry out. If the soil never seems to dry, repot the plant using a fast-draining potting soil designed for cactus. When the weather warms in April, put rosemary out in the landscape where it belongs.

202 Christmas Tree – Flocking

Q: *What is the stuff used to make Christmas trees look as if they are covered with snow? Is it poisonous?*

A: The flocking material that is applied to Christmas trees is composed of finely ground cellulose (in other words, *paper*!) and water-soluble adhesive. I don't believe it is poisonous—but I wouldn't eat it!

203 African Violet – Light Needed

Q: *My African violets are huge, but they will not bloom! What can be wrong?*

A: The most common reason for African violets to fail to bloom is lack of light. The stems and leaves of your plant have expanded to scavenge any stray photons they can absorb. It sounds like you don't have quite enough light to stimulate the flowering you want. African violets prefer a bright area that does not receive direct sunlight in the afternoon. Place your plants within 3 feet of large southeast- or southwest-facing windows. African violets can also be grown indoors under fluorescent lamps. Plants grown entirely under fluorescent lights should be placed 6 to 12 inches below a compact fluorescent fixture for fourteen hours per day.

204 Avocado – Growing Outdoors

Q: *I have grown an avocado from seed. Now it is fairly large in its pot. Can I grow it outdoors in Georgia?*

A: Welcome to the study of hardiness zones! To determine where the extremes of cold limit plant growth, the nation has been divided into ten **USDA Hardiness Zones**.[27] Zone 1 has the coldest winter temperatures; Zone 10 enjoys no frost at all. So here's the answer to your question: Georgia is located in Zones 7 & 8. Avocado trees will grow outdoors only in Zone 9, southern Florida. Pinch out the tips of all of your branches every three months, so it's kept compact enough to bring indoors each winter.

27. **USDA Hardiness Zones:** www.gardenword.com/hardiness

Amaryllis – Care

Q: *I have a holiday amaryllis in a large pot. How should I care for it?*

A: You can keep the amaryllis in a pot if you like, but it probably will not bloom again, particularly if you leave it indoors. Even if you keep the plant outdoors, the pot might restrict root growth and thereby restrict blooming.

I advise planting it in a sunny, rich bed in your landscape and letting it grow there. Remember to leave at least ¼ of the bulb (the *neck*) above-ground. Fertilize once or twice in summer. You can either leave it outdoors permanently, or you can try to force it to bloom next Christmas. To accomplish that, carefully dig up your bulb in early September. Cut off the leaves and place the bulb in a cool, dry place. In this way, you will give it the signal that fall and winter have arrived. The bulb will begin the process of preparing to bloom.

In late November, plant the bulb in a pot, allowing an inch of the neck to show above the potting soil. Feed it with half-strength houseplant fertilizer. Place it in a warm, sunny window. In two weeks, the first leaves will appear, followed by a bloom stalk. If it does not bloom for you, don't worry. Just plant it back outdoors next spring and leave it to bloom naturally each May in your garden.

HOUSEPLANTS

206 Boston Fern – Reproduction

Q: *I have perfectly round brown dots on the underside of some of my Boston fern leaves. They look like poppy seeds.*

A: The dots are called *sori*. They contain the reproductive spores of the fern. Since ferns do not have flowers, they scatter spores instead of seed. Fern enthusiasts collect the tiny spores and dust them onto the surface of a brick that has been almost totally submerged in a pan of water. They then cover the pan with a clear plastic bag. The spores sprout and form a small, heart-shaped *prothallus*. The prothallus produces two different cell masses. One produces fern sperm, and the other produces an egg. When an egg has been fertilized, it gradually grows roots and fronds, which lead to a new fern.

207 Houseplants – Fluorescent Light

Q: *Now that I've brought my Boston fern, schefflera, geranium, and ficus plants in for the winter, they only get a couple of hours afternoon sun each day. Will leaving the florescent lights on in the room be sufficient light?*

A: The fluorescent lights will help, but only if they are very close to the plant foliage. The maximum distance away is 12 inches. Otherwise the plants will lose leaves during the winter due to low light levels. One alternative is to buy a few fluorescent shop lights and hang or stand them on end close to the plants. Leave them on for sixteen hours each day.

208 Boston Fern – Winter Care

Q: *I currently have seven ferns hanging from my porch. How I can save them for next year?*

A: Assuming you have Boston ferns, as many people do, you'll have to bring them indoors for the winter. They cannot survive temperatures below 40 degrees F. Call local schools or churches and ask if they would like to have five of your plants to hang in front of sunny windows in their buildings. They will probably be thrilled to get them. Bring your two remaining ferns indoors and hang them where they get the most light possible. Keep a pair of scissors handy to prune fronds, which inevitably turn brown during the winter. Next spring, pull the ferns from their baskets and saw each rootball into eight equal pieces. Buy eight new hanging baskets and fill with potting soil. Plant each of the baskets with two fern divisions and hang them on your porch again. A month later, you'll have eight baskets filled with greenery!

209 Walking Iris – Winter Care

Q: *A friend gave me a plant he called a* **hanging iris.** *He said to put it in a hanging basket but bring it inside for winter.*

A: I'll bet you have walking iris (*Neomarica gracilis*). Some folks call it *apostle's iris* because the flower stalk arises when the plant has twelve leaves. It "walks" because the flower stem droops to the ground and roots there. The leaves and flowers look like a cross between an iris and an orchid. It's not hardy outdoors in most of Georgia but grows very well in the shade in Florida. Your friend's advice was spot on!

210 Bromeliad – Watering

Q: *A friend gave me a big bromeliad, but its leaves are beginning to shrivel. I have been pouring water into the throat of the plant. What should I be doing for it?*

A: If some leaves are still healthy, leave them on the plant but cut off the extremely limp ones. Many people know that bromeliads store water in the hollow where their leaves join, an area called the *tank*. The temptation is to pour lots of water into the tank until it runs out and soaks the soil beneath. Instead, water the soil and tank separately. Allow the soil to dry almost completely between waterings, but keep the tank constantly half-full. Every six months, flush the tank by filling it with water, inverting the plant, and then filling it again.

211 Bromeliad – Separating Pup

Q: *Two months ago I bought a large bromeliad with a spectacular pink flower. Now it has a "pup" at the base. I have been told that the pup will eventually kill my beautiful plant. How can I prevent this?*

A: The pup doesn't kill the mother plant; it is simply an attempt by the bromeliad to reproduce itself before dying, which naturally occurs after flowering. You can separate the pup now or wait until the original plant looks too bad to keep around. Use a serrated kitchen knife to cut the pup loose from the bigger plant. It may not have many roots, but push the base into a pot of moist potting soil and place it in a bright window. It will grow roots as it establishes and will eventually bloom like its mother.

212 Christmas Plants – Poison Precautions

Q: *We are looking forward to celebrating our daughter's first Christmas. One of my baby-care books said that Christmas trees are poisonous and it is safer to get a fake tree. Is this true?*

A: I have searched several poisonous plant databases and can find no mention there of the plants commonly used for Christmas trees. You possibly could be thinking of hemlock, but the hemlock tree (*Tsuga canadensis*) is not the same as poison hemlock (*Conium maculatum*), which looks like a tall, green weed. Poinsettia was once thought to be poisonous, but that turned out to be false folklore. Jerusalem Cherry (*Solanum pseudocapsicum*) is sometimes sold as a holiday houseplant and *does* have inedible, poisonous, round bright-orange or yellow fruits. Paper-white narcissus leaves are also poisonous. Red holly berries are mildly poisonous. Houseplants such as anthurium, caladium, dieffenbachia, and philodendron have poisonous leaves, so keep them out of her reach.

213 Christmas Tree – Additives in Water

Q: *I've heard a lot over the years about water additives I can put in my Christmas tree stand that will help the tree stay fresh longer. Is there anything like that commercially available?*

A: I check my tree every day and add dihydrogen oxide to the water in my stand when it gets low. Most Atlanta area municipalities sell dihydrogen oxide to citizens for a nominal fee. The cut flower industry has found certain chemical mixtures that increase the fresh life of flowers; however, research has not shown any benefit from using the floral life extenders in Christmas tree water. Aspirin, soft drinks, bleach—none are as useful as plain old H_2O (dihydrogen oxide).

214 Houseplant Pots – Covering Drain

Q: *What is the scoop on using coffee filters to cover the drain holes in pots rather than small rocks or broken pieces of pots?*

A: The coffee filter idea seems reasonable to me. If you don't cover the hole with something, potting soil will slowly dribble out. The one thing *not* to add to a pot is a layer of rocks at the bottom—it only lessens the amount of soil available for root growth.

I've said before that folks who put rocks in their pots have rocks in their head. The reason may not be obvious, but it is based on soil physics. Imagine the manner in which water moves in a pot. When you water a potted plant, the moisture initially soaks lower and lower through the soil. In a contest between gravity and the absorption capacity of the soil, some water drains out of the bottom. Most, however, stays in the soil at the bottom of the pot. The soil there becomes saturated with water.

As you know, roots suffer when they are surrounded by water-filled soil. Root rot and plant death follow when roots can't breathe their gasses into, and out of, the surrounding soil. When rocks are placed in the bottom of a pot and then covered with soil, there is less soil in which the roots of your plant *can* grow. Water still moves in the manner described above, but it now has *less* distance in which to drain away from the plant roots. The bottom line is that when you add rocks to the bottom of a pot, the result is a higher proportion of harmful, water-logged soil.

215 Desert Rose – What Is It?

Q: *I have a desert rose plant that has flowered and made a seedpod! It looks sort of like a pea pod with little wispy seeds. How do I plant them?*

A: Sometimes I feel completely overwhelmed by the number of plants that are unrelated to "real" roses but have "rose" in their name. We have confederate rose (*Hibiscus mutabilis*), rose of Sharon (*Hibiscus syriacus*), moss rose (*Portulaca grandiflora*), rose verbena (*Verbena canadensis*), and a multitude of others. Add to my list your desert rose (*Adenium obesum*), and tears come to my eyes!

Fortunately, my high school Latin teacher, Mrs. Inez Hames, made sure I would never be intimidated by Latin plant names. I was able to identify your plant and found that when the seeds are mature (pod is yellowish brown), they can be planted just on the surface of good potting soil. Put the container in a sunny window and cover the soil surface with clear plastic kitchen wrap. When the seeds germinate, remove the plastic and keep them in the window until the sprouts are an inch tall. Transplant each one into an individual small pot and raise them to full size.

216 Hanging Baskets – Evergreen

Q: *I'm looking for a plant that will stay green all year long and flourish in a hanging pot on my porch. In years past we've just bought annuals. Is there a perennial that will work under these conditions?*

A: There are no perennials that bloom or have remarkable features year-round in a hanging basket. However, to keep the outside of the basket attractive, you can duplicate a designer's trick. Fill a large, lined hanging basket with potting soil. Plant rooted cuttings of ivy (either green or variegated) side by side just inside the rim. Pin the ivy (use ferning pins bought at a craft store) to the side of the basket as the vine elongates. Plant appropriate annuals in the center, according to the season. Pansies, impatiens, petunias, and even florist hydrangeas work well. Substitute and replace the annuals as the seasons change. Your basket will at least be green year-round; flowers in the middle make it an even more attractive focal point.

217 Citrosa – Use as Mosquito Repellent

Q: *Is the citrosa plant effective against mosquitoes?*

A: The citrosa is actually a scented geranium. Many plant oils are somewhat repellent to insects. Lemon balm actually contains more citronellal oil than the citrosa does. If you rub the plant leaves on your skin, insects will be kept away for a short time. One experimenter estimated plant oils to be 40 to 60 percent as effective as DEET, the active ingredient in many mosquito repellents. If you depend on the plant to keep mosquitoes away from your patio, the results may be much less than you are hoping for.

218 Dracena – Air Layering

Q: *I have a really tall corn plant. It nearly touches my ceiling. Can I divide it somehow to save it and to make a new plant?*

A: You can't divide the corn plant unless it has a new stem that has come from the soil near the original plant. If that's not the case, you can make a new plant by *air-layering* the mother plant.

Choose a spot approximately 24 inches from the top of the plant and gently scrape away the bark in a $1/2$-inch wide band around the stem. Dust the wound with a **rooting hormone**.[28] Get some long fibered sphagnum moss (not peat moss) and soak it in water. Squeeze it until it is damp, then wrap it around the wound. Wrap thin kitchen plastic around the moss, and tie it in place with masking tape. Wrap everything with a sheet of aluminum foil. The plant will grow roots into the moist sphagnum moss, the plastic will keep things damp, and the aluminum foil will exclude light.

Check it every month until you see roots inside the plastic. You can then cut the stem just below the rootball and plant it in a pot. The rooting will go faster if the plant is outdoors in a shady spot.

---

28. **rooting hormone:** www.gardenword.com/rootinghormone

219 Houseplant – Leaf Tips Turning Brown

Q: *I have a peace lily that has leaves turning brown from the tips. Otherwise the plant seems to be healthy. What's wrong?*

A: When the tips or edges of a plant turn brown, I deduce that water is not reaching that part of the plant. Leaf diseases usually cause round spots, but water problems show up on the tips and edges. The browning could be caused by a lack of water in the soil, by too much water in the soil (leading to root rot), or by a draft on the leaves. Put on your Sherlock Holmes hat, and look for furnace vents nearby. Pull the lily from its pot to determine the health of the roots. Make sure it does not sit in a saucer full of water after you water.

220 Houseplants – Dripping Water

Q: *My corn plant is crying! Every few days I notice a drop of water clinging to several of the leaf tips. Why is it doing this?*

A: The phenomenon is called *guttation*. It happens when a tropical plant has more water around its roots than it knows how to get rid of. The roots try to push it up through the plant. The water "weeps" from the plant cells onto the leaf surface and then accumulates as a drop on the tip. Only grassy plants, like your dolorous dracaena, are able to guttate. You might also find droplets on the floor underneath. If you touch the liquid with your finger, you'll find that it is not sticky. If you do find sticky droplets on the floor, that is a sign that aphids or scale or mealybugs are feeding on your plant and secreting a sugary honeydew. Control them with an insecticidal soap.

221 Houseplants – Fungus Gnats

Q: *I have several declining houseplants that have tiny, dark flying insects in them. What are these insects, and how can I kill them?*

A: I don't think the bugs are killing your plants; I think *you* are killing them with kindness. The dark insects sound to me like fungus gnats. They grow in overly damp potting soil. The gnats are not particularly harmful, but their larvae can chew on houseplant roots. Overwatering could cause both leaf drop *and* fungus gnats. Water houseplants only when your finger, pushed 2 inches into the soil, comes back almost dry. Do not follow a calendar schedule; only water when soil is very slightly moist. In the meantime, sprinkle a ½-inch layer of dry sand on top of the potting soil. This will immediately discourage gnats from laying their eggs, and the population will be brought under control.

222 Jade Plant – Propagation

Q: *I have a jade plant that is top-heavy. Is there a way to replant some of this plant to start new plants, or is there a seed on the plant?*

A: Jade plants do have seeds, but getting them to flower prior to forming seed is a chancy proposition. The best way to propagate them is to snap off individual leaves and insert them halfway into a clay saucer full of damp sand. Given plenty of bright light, tiny foliage will form at the base of each parent leaf within eight weeks. At that point the plant can be transplanted to a 4-inch clay pot filled with "cactus mix" potting soil.

You might be interested to learn that a jade plant develops into a large shrub or small tree in its native South Africa. It can grow to quite a large plant when kept in a greenhouse, where temperatures do not drop below 50 degrees F. Once you have some small plants flourishing in April, cut back the overgrown top of your plant to a single trunk and a couple of side branches. Even though your jade plant will have few leaves at that point, place it outdoors in filtered sunshine. By the end of summer, new leaves and short stems will cover the scaffold branches, and it will resemble its kin from Africa.

223 Lucky Bamboo – Identification

Q: *I keep seeing small bunches of a plant called* **lucky bamboo.** *It is usually three to five green stems in a jar of water with glass beads or rocks. Can I cut some bamboo and do the same thing?*

A: The plant isn't bamboo at all. It's dracaena (*Dracaena sanderiana*). Practitioners of feng shui believe the plant brings calm into a room. I have seen very decorative arrangements in which the branches were contorted into fantastic shapes. I am told that it may take years to accomplish the most intricate bends and curves. You can buy this particular species of dracaena in any garden center. Wash the soil off the roots, and put the roots in a glass bowl to make your own display. Let me know if you feel any calmer after the process.

224 Norfolk Island Pine – Bark Damage

Q: *I have a Norfolk Island pine, and my dog ate away the bark on the bottom of the plant. Only the bark is gone; there is no damage to the trunk. Is the plant going to die?*

A: I don't have hopeful news about your houseplant. The bark of a Norfolk pine, and all other trees, covers the vital cambium tubes that carry water up to the foliage. If the tubes were damaged, which I'm sure they were, the plant may linger a few weeks, but it will eventually die. Try spraying the trunk of your next Norfolk Island pine with a bad-tasting **animal repellent.**[29]

29. **animal repellent:** www.gardenword.com/animalrepellent

225 'Meyer' Lemon Tree – For Georgia

Q: *I just purchased a 'Meyer' lemon tree and want to plant it in my yard. Do you see any problem with planting it here? What fertilizer should I use?*

A: I commend you for asking questions, but you're overlooking one simple fact. 'Meyer' lemon is not winter hardy where temperatures fall below 25 degrees F. That definitely includes most of Georgia. The best way to grow one is to put it in a big pot you can bring inside in winter.

Even in the sunniest spot indoors, it will lose lots of leaves. It will usually refoliate outdoors in spring when night temperatures rise above 60 degrees F. Watch out for tiny webs between leaves; they indicate spider mites, and you'll have a hard time controlling them if they become numerous.

'Meyer' lemon is a three-way cross between a lemon, an orange, and a mandarin. It was introduced in 1908 from China by Frank Meyer, an employee of the USDA. He's the same guy who discovered 'Meyer' zoysiagrass. The 'Meyer' lemon fruit is less acid than a regular lemon and makes tasty lemonade. The flowers are pleasantly fragrant, and the tree bears fruit readily when young.

The lemon is green in color until it matures. After several weeks of 90-degree F temperatures in summer, it changes to a yellow-orange color. Fertilize every six weeks while outdoors with a general-purpose houseplant fertilizer. Do not fertilize it in winter.

H
O
U
S
E
P
L
A
N
T
S

226 Pineapple – Forcing Fruit

Q: *I have heard that to make a pineapple flower you have to put a rotten apple in the middle of it. Is that right?*

A: Once a pineapple plant has thirty leaves on it, it can be forced into bloom by surrounding it with ethylene gas, a potent plant hormone. The easiest way to apply the gas is just as you've heard: put a rotten apple in the center of the pineapple and cover both with a plastic bag. Do not keep the plant in direct sunlight while the bag is on it. Remove the bag after a week and resume your normal care. If the plant is healthy, a flower spike should begin forming in two months. Once the flower spike has completed its development, a fruit will form on top of it. Three months later, when the bottom half of the fruit is golden, it's ready to pick.

227 Ants – On Houseplants

Q: *I had a nice ficus plant, but ants came in and made their home in it so I threw it away. Is there anything I can do to get rid of the ants?*

A: Sounds like you have sucking insects like mealybug, scale, or aphids in the ficus. Ants love to eat the sticky honeydew excreted by these pests. One way to control them is to wrap the trunk with a 3-inch-wide band of masking tape turned inside out. The ants get caught on the adhesive before climbing to the upper part of the tree. You could also use one of the commercial **gel ant baits**[30] under the lip of the pot.

30. **gel ant baits:** www.gardenword.com/antbait

228 Poinsettia – Care after Winter

Q: *I have successfully held over three poinsettia plants in a window greenhouse for four years. Every year they get bright red bracts. When is a good time to cut them back, and how far do I cut them?*

A: Cut off the bracts in February, leaving only the green leaves. When it is warm enough in April, set them outside on a shady patio and cut the stems back to 6 inches tall. As the plants resprout, move them gradually to even more sunshine. You may need to move them to larger pots so they don't wilt on hot days outdoors. Fertilize monthly.

As they grow bigger, shorten the longest branches a couple of times to make the plants nice and compact. On October 1, you can start the "fourteen hours of darkness, ten hours of bright light" regimen that will cause them to form colored bracts for the winter holidays once again.

229 Poinsettia – Care During Holidays

Q: *How do you take care of poinsettias at Christmas?*

A: Keep them in bright light and water only when the soil is dry to the touch. If foil surrounds the pot, remove it and place the pot on a saucer. Fertilize it in April, June, and August using houseplant fertilizer. Remove the colorful bracts as they wither. If you move it gradually into stronger light conditions, poinsettia can grow well outdoors in summer in a large pot in dappled sunshine.

Q: *I have three poinsettia plants that I've kept for four years. Last year they changed color in the summer. How can I get them to change color at Christmas?*

A: When the bracts changed color in the summer, your poinsettias were only doing what came naturally. The fact of the matter is that the bracts around a poinsettia bloom will change color ten to fourteen weeks after the bloom has appeared. You grew your poinsettia in conditions that made the plants produce blooms in March. Twelve weeks later and you had Christmas in June!

In their native Mexico, poinsettias bloom in early January. Greenhouse growers manipulate the temperature and light around their plants to make them turn color just before Christmas. You can make your plants initiate blooms by covering them each day with a cardboard box for fourteen hours beginning in early September. Water them normally and leave them outdoors until cool weather arrives.

Move them indoors, then but keep up the fourteen hours of daily darkness until late October. You should see buds appear at the end of each branch. If the plant is kept in a cool, bright window, you'll have colorful bracts just in time for the holidays!

231 Potting Soil – Reusing

Q: *I have a big pot from which I've pulled all of my summer annuals. I want to plant it with pansies, but I don't know what to do with the old soil. Do I have to dump it out and replace it with fresh potting soil?*

A: The old potting soil didn't become "used up" being home to your summer flowers. The only thing that might be wrong with it is an excess of unused fertilizer from the summer. That condition is easy to cure: saturate the soil with water, let it drain, then repeat twice more. You can do it in an afternoon. You can then plant your plants for winter color in the same pot using the same soil.

232 Schefflera – Losing Leaves

Q: *My schefflera has leaves turning brown and falling off in large numbers. It is sitting in a rather dark area. Is this the problem?*

A: As you suspect, the low light level is exactly the problem. A schefflera normally is densely covered with leaves. Your plant's leaves are probably thin and stretched out. The best thing for the plant would be to move it to a sunnier spot or to give it supplemental light. Remember, though, a fluorescent light should be no more than 12 inches from the leaves of the plant to do any good.

233 Sunroom – Plant Health

Q: *I recently built a sunroom on the south side of my house and used Low-E glass because it keeps out most of the heat from the sun. I didn't think about it at the time, but will it also keep plants from growing?*

A: Low-emissivity glass inhibits the transmission of infrared and ultraviolet solar energy. It keeps heat from coming indoors in summer and prevents heat from leaving through your windows in winter. Low-E glass is coated with a microscopically thin layer of metal. You can barely perceive any difference between regular glass and Low-E glass. Even so, Low-E glass does inhibit some of the visible light a plant could use. Most Low-E window products rate their visible light transmittance between 75 and 85 percent. All in all, your indoor plants will probably show no ill effects if you care for them properly.

234 Holiday Cactus – Care

Q: *I inherited a Christmas cactus when my mother passed away. How much light, water, and fertilizer does it need?*

A: I was delighted in October to find flower buds on the holiday cactus I've kept outdoors all summer. Yours may have swollen buds on it too. Keep it in a cool, sunny room until the flowers have opened for your enjoyment. If your mother kept it inside, it may not have stored enough energy to bloom this season. The best care for a holiday cactus is to keep it outdoors in a bright but shady spot during the summer and fall. Water if the soil becomes dry. Fertilize sparingly each month. Bring it into a cool, bright room of your house when night temperatures fall below 60 degrees F. Flower buds will form in early November and should begin opening in late November to mid-December.

235 Terrarium – Building

Q: *I would like to put together a simple terrarium with my grandchildren. Where can I get information on this?*

A: Terrariums have quite an interesting history. The original miniature glass house was invented by Nathaniel Ward in 1830 after he noticed that a fern could grow in a sealed jar containing a bit of soil and moisture. He built much larger containers for plant explorers, who found that they could transport living specimens around the world when sealed inside so-called *Wardian cases*. In garden vernacular, a Wardian case is usually straight-sided and has a hinged lid. Terrariums are any glass container in which plants are grown.

That said, you can make a terrarium from any large-mouthed glass jar or vase or cookie jar you have around the house. I recently made a terrarium from a round, 2-gallon glass canister with a glass lid. I put a 1/2-inch of charcoal on the bottom of the jar and covered it with 2 inches of damp potting soil. Small houseplants can be found at any nursery; I sometimes find it best to divide the plants in a pot to get a couple of smaller specimens. I used colored stones, Spanish moss, and driftwood to decorate around the plants. Your local library is a good source for books on this topic!

236 Venus's flytrap – Feeding

Q: *I wandered past the bog exhibit at the Atlanta Botanical Garden last weekend. Kids were putting their fingers into the Venus's flytraps to make them close. Does a Venus's flytrap get tired of opening and closing?*

A: A Venus's flytrap's jaws can reopen a few times even if a closure doesn't result in a captured insect. After being fooled five or six times, though, the trap moves slowly, and the leaf absorbs sunshine but not insects. The folk wisdom that a Venus's flytrap can be fed bits of hamburger meat is completely wrong. The plant has adapted to digest insects but not the protein and fat of animals.

237 Venus's flytrap – Care in a Bog

Q: *I bought a small Venus's flytrap in September. How should I care for this interesting plant?*

A: Carnivorous plants are indeed fascinating—in a grotesque sort of way. Venus's flytrap is more interesting than most because you can watch it grab its prey. Once spring rolls around, you should plan to keep your Venus's- flytrap outdoors permanently, in an easy-to-build bog filled with a 1:1 mixture of sand and peat moss. Keep the bog moist in winter and mark flytraps with a small stake nearby at planting since the plants are small and will lose their leaves in winter. If you give it good conditions, a flytrap will make offshoots from the base in late spring. Interestingly, Venus's flytraps do not respond very well to root fertilization. They are accustomed to getting much of their nutrition from the insects they apprehend.

LAWNS

Q&A

Q: *I have bermudagrass in the front and fescue in the back of my house. How should they be fertilized?*

A: The rule of thumb is to fertilize a lawn when it is actively growing. Here are the dates to follow for lawn feeding:

- *Bermudagrass:* Begin when grass is 50 percent green, repeat at six to eight week intervals. Last feeding should be in September.
- *Fescue:* Begin in September, repeat in mid-October, February, and April. No feeding should be done in summer.
- *Zoysiagrass:* Begin when grass is 75 to 100 percent green. Repeat only once or twice in summer. Do not feed after September.
- *Centipedegrass:* Begin when grass is 100 percent green. Repeat once in summer. Do not feed after September.
- *St. Augustine grass:* Begin when grass is 75 percent green. Repeat at eight-week intervals. Do not feed after September.

Lawn fertilizer is manufactured by many companies. Each manufacturer uses a slightly different blend of plant nutrient chemicals to arrive at a final product. In general, you can follow the recommendations on the bag to apply the correct amount of fertilizer, no matter what the "three numbers" on the bag are.

LAWNS

239 Turfgrass – Watering

Q: *My lawn maintenance guy and I have a difference of opinion. Turf experts recommend an inch of water per week, applied every seven days. My yard guy says that since the subsoil is so hard-packed below my grass that any water applied after twenty minutes just runs off. Therefore he recommends one or two twenty-minute irrigation sessions each week. What are your thoughts?*

A: I'm going to split the difference between you two. It is true that most lawns benefit from an inch of water per week during the heat of summer. It is also true that in some situations, such as compacted soil or steep slopes, water begins to run off after twenty minutes. Here's the solution: schedule your irrigation so that a total of an inch of water is applied in one day, but split the application into two or three twenty-minute sessions. In this way water has a chance to soak in rather than run off. Use a rain gauge to measure the amount applied. Be sure a total of 1 inch of water is applied during the day, preferably before noon. Most importantly, don't forget to obey local watering restrictions.

240 Lawn Irrigation – Timing

Q: *What is the best time to water my lawn?*

A: The best time is after midnight until 10:00 a.m. In this way, your grass leaves will not be wet longer than would naturally occur. This helps guard against lawn diseases like brown patch.

241 Lawn – Mowing Heights

Q: *How high should I mow my lawn?*

A: Experts agree that you should remove about a third of the height of the grass to arrive at a final height; this differs for each turfgrass.
My estimates:

Grass	Mow At (inches)	Final Height (inches)
Tall Fescue	3–4	2–3
Common Bermudagrass	3	2
Hybrid Bermudagrass	2	1.5
Zoysiagrass	2	1.5
Centipedegrass	2	1.5
St. Augustine grass	3	2–3

242 Lawn – Liming

Q: *When is the best time to lime my lawn?*

A: Lime counteracts acid in the soil and makes fertilizer more available to your grass. Because it dissolves so slowly, you can lime at any time. The amount of lime to apply can be determined by a soil test (**www.soiltest123.com**). If you can't wait for a test, apply 40 pounds of lime per 1,000 square feet every two years.

Q: *I built a new house and have bare ground in front and behind it. What lawn grass should I plant?*

A: Mr. Sun and Mother Nature will determine the best grass, not me. The biggest factor is the amount of sunshine your area gets. Let me try to specify the light levels required for the different turfgrasses.

- Bermudagrass: full sunshine to light shade
- Centipedegrass: full sunshine to partial shade
- 'Meyer' zoysiagrass: full sunshine to partial shade
- 'Emerald' zoysiagrass: full sunshine to partial shade
- St. Augustine grass: full sunshine to partial shade
- Tall fescue: light shade to partial shade

Since light levels are hard to define, use these examples:

- Full sunshine: eight hours of unfiltered sunshine sometime between sunrise and sunset
- Light shade: six hours of sunshine filtered through high pine foliage or scattered hardwood trees OR six hours of unfiltered sunshine sometime between sunrise and sunset
- Partial shade: eight hours of sunshine filtered through high pine foliage OR four hours of direct sunshine between sunrise and sunset
- Shade: all-day sunshine filtered through scattered hardwood trees OR direct sunshine at least three hours per day
- Dense shade: no direct sunshine touches the grass all day, such as the shade under a southern magnolia or the shade between two houses whose shadows prevent sunshine from hitting the earth at all

No grass will grow well in shade or dense shade. If you have a shady spot, save yourself some grief and plant ground cover or cover the spot with mulch.

L A W N S

244 Aeration – Process

Q: *When do I aerate my lawn? Can I use a spike aerator?*

A: Aeration is the process of making lots of holes in your lawn in order to soften it and to allow water and fertilizer to penetrate. The holes made by a spike aerator do not last long. The best aerator is one with hollow tines, called *spoons*. It pulls up short plugs of soil that lay on the grass until dissolved by rain. The best time to do it is when your grass is growing vigorously. For bermudagrass, zoysiagrass, centipedegrass, and St. Augustine grass, aerate in May or June. Fescue can be aerated in October or March.

245 Zoysiagrass – Overseed with Ryegrass

Q: *I have always wanted a green lawn in winter. How much will it hurt my zoysiagrass lawn to overseed with ryegrass this winter?*

A: There is no good reason to overseed any warm-season turf. I know some bermudagrass owners do it, but it's not good for the lawn. You inevitably harm the permanent turfgrass by planting ryegrass into it. Ryegrass competes for nutrients the lawn will need next spring. In addition, fertilizing the ryegrass may make the turfgrass more easily winter-damaged. Specifically in your case, zoysiagrass grows too thickly to allow ryegrass seed to fall to the soil and germinate. Enjoy the golden brown of your zoysiagrass, and don't overseed with rye.

Lawn Fertilizer – Using Beer

Q: *A friend told me about how he has a beautiful green yard. He mixes and applies one part each of ammonia, dish detergent, beer, and cola. Will it work, or is this guy being a jokester?*

A: He sounds like a jokester. Television hucksters touting lawn "formulas" made from household products come around like clockwork. The presentation is enthusiastic, but the recommendations contain only tiny nuggets of truth and effectiveness. It is *true* that household ammonia contains a small amount of nitrogen that plants need, but it evaporates before becoming available to the plants it is sprayed on. It is *true* that detergents can make other chemicals spread and stick to the leaves of plants, but the proportion of detergent should be only a few drops per gallon. Otherwise, the detergent will burn the plant leaves like an herbicide would. It is *true* that soil microorganisms consume carbohydrates, but they specialize in the complex carbohydrates found in plants, not the simple sugars and other carbohydrates found in soft drinks and beer. Leave the jokes indoors, not on your lawn.

247 Mushrooms – Control

Q: *After a big rain, I had dozens of mushrooms in my lawn. Should I remove them?*

A: Another way to think about mushrooms is to call them the "flowers" of an organism that lives underground. In your case, a common fungus has been feeding on organic debris underground. The lack of rain gave it no opportunity to send up occasional small mushrooms, so it simply waited for the right conditions. The soaking rain signaled an explosion of growth aboveground, resulting in the mushrooms you found. They will release fungus spores, but since other spores are naturally found all over your neighborhood, you won't prevent future mushrooms. Some people just pick them and put them on the compost pile.

248 Algae – Control in Lawn

Q: *Over the years, our bermudagrass has thinned out terribly. Where the soil is bare, in places where water accumulates, there is a black skin on the soil.*

A: You have algae growing on the soil. This is a common problem where poorly drained soil is exposed to sunshine. The best solution is grading to improve drainage. Mix in some good soil conditioner while you're at it, so plants other than algae can grow there.

249 Sandbur (Sandspur) – Control

Q: *Is there a weedkiller that I can use to kill sandspurs?*

A: Few things take the pleasure out of walking barefoot across a lawn like stepping on a sandbur (*Cenchrus incertus*). The plant is an annual grass that grows from seed each spring. The spur is the hard, spiny part of its flower. Fortunately, since it sprouts from a seed, the best way to control it is to prevent seed germination. Use a **grassy weed preventer**[31] in the first week of March each year, making sure to water it into the soil. Repeat twice more, at six week intervals. Follow the same schedule the following year.

250 Spurweed – Control

Q: *Around Easter a weed in my yard has little spurs on it that stick in your feet. My grandchildren and I like to go barefooted, but we can't!*

A: Spurweed (*Soliva pterosperma*) invokes all sorts of ugly words from those who step on it. Your spurweed is a broadleaf annual plant whose seeds germinate in fall and the seedlings grow slowly in winter. You could use a **broadleaf weed preventer**[32] in September to prevent the seeds from sprouting. Another time to control it is in the first week or two of March. Spray the plants a couple of times with one of the broadleaf weedkillers. If you can keep the plants from maturing and making burs for two summers, you'll have the problem licked.

31. **grassy weed preventer:** www.gardenword.com/preemergent
32. **broadleaf weed preventer:** www.gardenword.com/preemergent

251 Annual Bluegrass – Control

Q: *How do I control annual bluegrass?*

A: The annual nature of this weed supplies its most noxious habit: it reseeds itself prolifically. Annual bluegrass is outwardly attractive in the winter, but just wait until spring! The thick mat of bluegrass chokes out the better turf underneath. The old-timers call this one "po anner" due to its scientific name: *Poa annua*. That name immediately tells us that this grassy plant is an annual. Every blade (of which there are thousands) seems to be covered with seeds. These seed are carried by animals, water, and lawn mowers to other parts of the lawn.

When hot weather comes, the bluegrass dies, leaving a large bare spot and a legacy of thousands of seed for next fall. The best control for annual bluegrass is to apply a pre-emergent weed chemical in the fall. The best time is usually in mid-September and again in November. Any pre-emergent product that controls crabgrass will control annual bluegrass. The pre-emergent will prevent seeds from germinating. Of course, the pre-emergent cannot be used on a fescue lawn, which you intend to reseed!

If bluegrass is present in winter lawns, the chemical **imazaquin**[33] is labeled for use on all grasses except fescue. Since it must be absorbed by roots, control may not be evident for several weeks.

33. imazaquin: www.gardenword.com/imazaquin

252 Ashes – Adding to the Lawn

Q: *Is it harmful or beneficial to spread ashes from our fireplace on our lawn or on our azaleas?*

A: Ashes do provide a slight amount of potassium for plants. They also counteract the natural acidity of soil, so they are a substitute for garden lime. Because ashes are so very alkaline, only a small amount can be applied at a time. An application of 20 pounds of ashes per 1,000 square feet would be plenty for a lawn in one year. Apply no more than 10 pounds every six months.

253 Bermudagrass – Scalping

Q: *When should I mow my dormant bermudagrass?*

A: Removing the brown winter foliage and stubble from a bermudagrass lawn (known as "scalping") will cause it to green-up faster in spring. Since green-up is dependent on soil temperature and soil moisture, keep an eye on the weather. Plan to mow when the forecast is for sunny days ahead with night temperatures in the 50s. Scalping should be done before much green growth is showing. Mowing height depends on the smoothness of your lawn. Plan to mow low enough to remove brown stems without chewing up the dirt. Start at 1 inch and lower the height another 1/4 inch if possible.

254 Bermudagrass – Common vs. Hybrid

Q: *How can I tell if I have common or hybrid bermudagrass?*

A: Even an expert would have a hard time telling them apart if presented with just a blade or two. The difference is most obvious to me when a patch of bermudagrass is allowed to grow unmown for a week. Common bermudagrass will quickly send up seedheads that stand above the level of grass leaves. Hybrid bermudagrass will send up fewer seedheads. One way to tell them apart is to tap a seedhead from each onto a piece of black paper. Common bermudagrass will release a tiny yellow cloud of pollen on the paper. Hybrid bermudagrass is sterile; it does not produce pollen.

My personal observation is that if you can see the two growing near each other, the hybrid grass will have a deeper green color when compared to the common type. Tifgreen 328™ seems to be more prone to seedhead production than Tifway 419™. Tifgreen™ is very common in residential sodded lawns.

255 Aeration – After Pre-emergent?

Q: *I was told by a garden center employee that if I aerate after applying a pre-emergent it would be less effective. Is that true?*

A: One research source says that aerating does not lower the effectiveness of a pre-emergent applied earlier. However, it makes sense to me to avoid disturbing things after applying a pre-emergent. Your goal is to have a continuous layer of chemical dissolved in the top $1/2$-inch of soil where weed seeds lay in wait. Aerate first, then spread the pre-emergent.

256 Brown Patch – Causes

Q: *My fescue lawn looked great until June. Now there are big yellow spots that seem to get bigger each day. Is this "brown patch"?*

A: Many homeowners blame any turf dead spots on a disease called *brown patch*. It's a common fungus disease on grasses, particularly fescue lawns. Brown patch spots are small to begin with, but in warm weather they can enlarge rapidly. Seen from above, the patch will look like a doughnut—a ring of tan grass having a patch of green grass in the center. Individual grass blades will be brown down to the crown—where the blade emerges from the ground—but the crown itself will be green. Early in the morning during hot, damp weather you might see a white fungal web or dark green grass at the edge of the dead patch.

There are other conditions that cause dead spots: soggy areas, hard soil, and mower fuel spills, to name a few. Before you reach for the lawn fungicide, eliminate the other conditions. Since brown patch is associated with watering in the evening and watering too often, change your irrigation habits to one deep soaking per week. If you feel sure the spots are caused by a disease, apply a lawn fungicide. But I will warn you that it is a *lot* cheaper to manage the grass correctly in the first place.

257 Centipedegrass – Decline

Q: *Our fourteen-year-old centipedegrass yard began developing bare patches about four years ago. Now almost a third of my yard is bare and looks horrible. What did I do?*

A: A lot of centipedegrass decline can be traced to mowing too high. As you know, the grass spreads by sending out stolons across the ground. If the runners are allowed to climb on top of each other as they multiply, their roots do not engage the soil very deeply. This leads to great damage from drought and cold. Large and small dead patches appear throughout.

Centipedegrass lawns should always be mowed between 1 and 1^1/$_2$ inches high. Centipedegrass also shouldn't be given much fertilizer, since lush growth exacerbates the situation described above. High phosphorus levels can likewise lead to problems. Centipedegrass fertilizer is typically sold in a 15-0-15 nutrient ratio. In the absence of a soil test, apply 3 pounds per 1,000 square feet in May and again in July.

258 Centipedegrass – TifBlair

Q: *Will centipedegrass perform well in north Georgia?*

A: One of the great success stories of the lawn seed industry is the work of Dr. Wayne Hanna at the USDA Coastal Plains Experiment Station in Tifton. In 1977, realizing that centipedegrass doesn't tolerate cold winters very well, he began irradiating seed, planting them in cold weather conditions, and selecting the survivors. By 1985, he had developed a centipedegrass that could survive winters in Blairsville, Georgia, and as far north as Virginia. He named the seed TifBlair. I suggest you look for TifBlair seed or sod and plant it in May. It makes a superior low-maintenance turfgrass.

259 Irrigation – In Winter

Q: *I moved here from New York in September. Most of my irrigation zones are set to irrigate for forty minutes twice a week. How should I adjust it for winter?*

A: Unplug it. After October, no watering is needed by any part of your landscape except newly planted annuals or woody plants, and those beds and/or plants should be watered individually. My best advice is to turn off the system until summer arrives in June.

260 Crabgrass Preventer – When to Apply

Q: *When should I put out my crabgrass preventer?*

A: Crabgrass seeds need several days of soil temperatures higher than 55 degrees F in order to germinate. Most years in Atlanta, March 15 is the date experts recommend you apply the pre-emergent. Only the most shallowly buried crabgrass seeds will be sprouting then, but many more will germinate in April and May. That is why other weed scientists recommend applying a pre-emergent in March *and* in May. The March application prevents the early-bird weeds. A follow-up application in May keeps an active layer of chemical right on the soil surface to catch the late awakeners.

261 Creeping Charlie (Ground Ivy) – Control

Q: *I have a pesky weed with small scalloped leaves. It spreads rapidly across the ground. What is this, and where did it come from?*

A: An invader named Charlie has crept into your landscape: "Creeping Charlie" (*Glechoma hederacea*) to be exact. This common weed is also called *ground ivy* and *gill-over-the-ground*. Notice that it is pleasantly fragrant when you squeeze it. This and its square stems tell you it is a member of the mint family. The best strategy is to lightly spray every four weeks with one of the broadleaf weedkillers. You should have good control after three applications.

262 Fescue – How Long to Leave Straw

Q: *Perhaps this is a silly question, but how long do I leave the straw on my newly seeded fescue lawn?*

A: You sound like me when I call my horticulture specialist friends in Athens with an inquiry I fear is elementary to them. I don't like asking "silly" questions, but I do it on your behalf. Actually, your question is one many lawn planters ponder. If the straw was lightly applied originally (about a bale per 1,000 square feet), you can leave it in place to rot. On the other hand, if you think the straw is hindering the growth of some of the seedlings, gently remove with a leaf rake. The best way to decide what to do is to lift up some straw and look for fescue seedlings underneath. If more than 10 percent are white, the straw is keeping them too dark, and you need to take it off.

263 Lawn – Striping

Q: *How do folks cut a lawn so it has dark and light stripes?*

A: If you've rubbed velvet cloth, you've seen the difference made by having the cloth fibers lay in different directions. To make a lawn have stripes like at a ballpark, you have to roll, press, or comb it down in the opposite direction with each trip across your lawn. One way to accomplish this is to drag a store-bought welcome mat behind your mower. The cut grass gets a "nap," just as you see when you rub velvet. The opposite nap of the grass in adjacent mowed strips reflects light differently and makes the stripes you enjoy.

Q: *We've bought a house with an established bermudagrass lawn. We need to buy a lawn mower but can't agree on the type. My husband believes that we have to have a reel mower for a bermudagrass lawn. What do you think?*

A: I see plenty of bermudagrass lawns that are very attractively maintained with a rotary mower. A sharp blade is the key to a good-looking cut job. While a reel mower does give a carpet-like appearance, its initial cost and future upkeep is higher than with a rotary mower. If you choose a rotary model, let me put in a plug for buying a powerful mulching mower. Most mowers can be configured to mulch lawn clippings rather than bagging them. I favor mulching because the practice returns nutrients to the soil.

Given two similar mowers from which to choose, buy the one with the more powerful engine. The extra power is needed to finely chop the clippings. You won't be able to detect the clippings after mowing with a good-quality mulching mower. Research has proven that returning the clippings to the ground does not increase weeds or thatch or disease.

LAWNS

265 Lawn – Killed by Herbicide

Q: *I had my fescue lawn soil tested, and the report instructed me to use 15-0-15 fertilizer. While my lawn is fescue, the only 15-0-15 I could find was for centipedegrass. Thinking that it was spring and I should use a pre-emergent, I bought a weed-and-feed for centipedegrass lawns. Now my lawn is half-dead. What do I do now?*

A: In the immortal words of Homer Simpson, "Doh!!!" While most weed-and-feed products can be used on fescue, centipedegrass weed-and-feed cannot. The atrazine it contains kills fescue grass just as surely as it kills any other weed—and fescue would be a weed *if* you had a centipedegrass lawn. But you don't have a centipedegrass lawn, and now your fescue is *very* unhappy!

Unfortunately, I must convey news that will make *you* unhappy as well: turf experts recommend that you not plant seed for six months after applying atrazine. The lingering herbicidal chemical will likely prevent fescue seed from germinating this spring, but you are welcome to try planting seed to see if any comes up. Atrazine is very water-soluble, so pray for rain. If rainfall has diluted it enough, you *may* be successful with germination. You could also try laying fescue sod in the dead area, hoping that it can better survive the atrazine. Need I say it? Next time, *read the label!*

266 Zoysiagrass – Reversing Solarization

Q: *Last weekend we took the solar blanket off our pool and laid it in our yard to dry. When we came back an hour later, we found that the zoysiagrass underneath had been burned. How long will it take to recover?*

A: Now you know more about the garden practice "soil solarization" than you really meant to learn! Covering garden soil with clear plastic is a good way to kill weeds organically. It usually takes at least two weeks of sunny days to heat the soil down into the root zone to kill weed seed. I doubt you killed the zoysiagrass completely, but at this point it's just "wait and see." Water the zoysiagrass if the weather gets really dry. Do not fertilize. I predict it will come back after several weeks' wait.

267 Aeration – Cost

Q: *My lawn service aerated yesterday while I was gone for thirty minutes. All they left was a few plugs of dirt on my grass and a bill for $75. Did I get ripped off?*

A: I won't make a judgment on your circumstances, but you should consider calling the company and asking for another visit. Aeration does little good unless at least ten holes per square foot are made. You can make their visit even more effective if you irrigate the lawn thoroughly a couple of days before they come.

268 Wild Onion – Edibility

Q: *I am interested in knowing if the wild onions popping up all over my yard are edible or not. One of my friends said they are poisonous.*

A: Well, they are certainly edible, but you won't get kissed anytime soon if you eat one! Like our culinary onions and garlic, wild onions (*Allium canadense*) and wild garlic (*Allium vineale*) are members of the onion family. As a child, I discovered the pungency of these weeds when I tethered our cow to graze near them in our pasture. Her milk the next day had a decidedly Italian flavor! My mother simply made chocolate syrup to mix with the milk, and we drank it anyway.

269 Zoysiagrass – Rust

Q: *I have a zoysiagrass lawn. I have noticed an orange powder building up on the blades. What is it?*

A: Your zoysiagrass is a victim of rust. Rust disease is more common in the cool, moist conditions of late fall, but it can occur anytime. It is likely to be more severe in shady areas. Mow every four to five days, and catch the clippings if possible. There are lawn **fungicides**[34] available to control rust. Read the label carefully, and use the rate and timing that's indicated.

---

34. **fungicides:** www.gardenword.com/lawnfungicide

270 Weed-and-Feed Products – Not Recommended

Q: *I've heard you don't like weed-and-feed products. Why not?*

A: Despite the assurance on their labels that weed-and-feed products are an improvement in lawn maintenance, I have my doubts. Those that combine a weed preventer with fertilizer recommend an application earlier than I think is prudent for warm-season lawns. Those that combine a broadleaf weedkiller with fertilizer may recommend an application that is later than I think wise for fescue turf. Products that offer a "calendar schedule" of application may result in overapplication of fertilizer and weedkillers. In all cases, the implication that "one product fits all situations" grates on my knowledge that lawn conditions are highly variable.

I am a proponent of using pesticides only when a correctly identified pest is present in numbers that cannot be controlled by environmental manipulation. Proper mowing, watering, and fertilizing can combat weeds without using synthetic herbicides.

I have no problem with applying directed sprays onto occasional weed spots. I have no problem using non-selective weedkillers to wipe out weeds in an area. I simply think that we expect too much (and are promised too much) from weed-and-feed products. That's why I recommend using fertilizers and weed control products separately.

271 Fertilizing – Frequency

Q: *We have a lawn on a sloping lot. We fertilized three days before we had 4 inches of rainfall in forty-eight hours. Do we need to fertilize again?*

A: No worries. Turf fertilizers are designed to release their nutrients over several weeks. Water flowing over the fertilizer granules only dissolves a little fertilizer at a time. If the granules themselves washed down the hill, there would be a problem, but I doubt that happened. They are so small that they are likely still nestled at the base of the grass plants.

272 Fescue – Tree Leaves on New Lawn

Q: *I over-seeded my fescue lawn ten days ago, and now it's covered with leaves. How do I clean up the leaves without damaging the plants? Should I leave them for a while, blow them, or vacuum them up with my lawn mower?*

A: If the grass sprouts need mowing, let your mower shred them. If they still seem thin, use a blower to blow leaves off. You don't want leaves accumulating and shading your grass from the sunshine.

273 Marking Lawn with Dye

Q: *I have a problem spot-spraying herbicides in my lawn. It is difficult to keep up with what I've sprayed and what I haven't sprayed. Is there anything I can do to color my spray?*

A: Call a local water feature/pond supply store and ask if they have pond dye. Small pond owners use the concentrated dye to darken pond water and suppress algae growth. I would think it should be safe to use on your lawn, but read and follow the dilution instructions.

274 Irrigation System – Winter Care

Q: *Our new house has a home sprinkler system. Do we need to shut it off for the winter? How does one typically drain a system?*

A: All you really need to accomplish is to get most of the water out of the system before winter arrives. You can do this by first turning off the water valve that supplies your system. Then allow the system timer to run through all of its cycles in its normal manner. Much of the water in your pipes will run out of the lowest irrigation heads. What water remains will not be under pressure. The system should be fine when you turn it on next year.

Another alternative is to purchase a maintenance contract from an irrigation contractor. They typically will check all of your heads before draining the system in winter and check them again in spring. They may also want to shoot compressed air through the pipes to remove any remaining water.

275 Sod – Not Laying Quickly

Q: *A friend purchased ten pallets of sod. One was installed the same day. But the other nine pallets were not laid until two days later. The first sod looks great. Only 20 percent of the other sod lived. The supplier said this happened due to not laying the sod quickly. Does this sound normal?*

A: Unfortunately for your friend, the supplier is correct. Sod should always be laid within twenty-four hours of delivery. The grass and soil microorganisms trapped in the pile give off heat and "cook" the sod in short order. This is much the same way a compost pile "heats up." An increase in internal pallet temperatures can be measured within hours of harvest. In high-value environments (putting greens, Super Bowl turf, etc.), refrigerated trucks are used to transport sod.

If sod can't be laid immediately, lay the pieces on a driveway and water often enough to keep them moist. If your friend decides to lay sod again, plan on three hours per pallet (500 square feet) per person. Stock *plenty* of lemonade for the sod layers since they will be exhausted afterward!

Q: *My grass looks yellow and is gradually disappearing in a 10-foot-square area. How can I tell if this is caused by insects or by disease?*

A: Bugs in turf are very hard to find with the naked eye. You can try several methods to make them more visible.

- *Dig them out:* Japanese beetles come from C-shaped white grubs that feed on grass roots. If you had tremendous numbers of Japanese beetles, yellow grass might be caused by grub damage. Slide a flat-bladed shovel 2 inches under a patch of grass and flip it up out of the ground. Examine the roots and soil for grubs. If you find more than eight per square foot, consider killing them with an insecticide labeled for use on grubs.

- *Float them out:* If you have St. Augustine grass, chinch bugs feeding on the grass could cause it to be yellow. A good way to check for chinch bugs is to perform a float test. Cut both ends from a gallon can and press one end firmly into the grass and soil. You might need to cut a circular slit through the turf first so the can sinks an inch into the soil. Fill the can with water and try to keep it full for five minutes. Any chinch bugs present will float to the surface. The adults are approximately $1/5$ inch long and dark gray in color. Nymphs are smaller and reddish colored.

- *Wash them out:* Sod webworms chew at the base of grass plants and sometimes cause bare areas of turf. They hide in the thatch near the soil line when they are not eating. You can force them to reveal themselves by using a soapy water flush. Stir $1/4$ cup of lemon-scented dish detergent into 4 gallons of water. Pour the mixture over an area of grass and watch what happens. Any insects present will wriggle themselves to the surface where you can identify them.

277 Dog Urine Spots – Control

Q: *My husband insists that urine from female dogs will burn spots in our lawn. That sounds odd—could he possibly be right?*

A: It is true that the urine from female dogs is more likely to burn than that from male dogs. Female dogs (and toddlers) usually direct their urine to one spot. Males, on the other hand, are "sprinklers."

Concentrated dog urine burns grass due to its salt content. The only thing you can do is flood the spot with water as soon as your dog has visited there. If you provide an appropriate relief area and train your dog to use it, the lawn will be spot-free.

278 Velvet Ant – Identification

Q: *I have discovered a new insect. It looks like a big, red ant with a black stripe around the middle. My neighbor said they are "cow ants."*

A: The insect you have seen is not an ant but a female wingless wasp, called a *velvet ant*. In rural areas, it might be called a "cow killer" by the locals. Their sting is reputed to be severe enough to kill a cow! The female lays her eggs in bumblebee nests. The eggs hatch into wasp larvae, which kill and eat the bumblebee larvae. The wasp larvae then pupate in the bumblebee nest and hatch into adults. The adult cow killer can run quickly, but play it safe and don't try to catch one.

LAWNS

279 Dance Flies – Identification

Q: *What are the small flies that hover in clouds over the grass? They float in the air in swarms and sometimes follow you everywhere you go.*

A: It could be either gnats, dance flies, or midges. They can be very abundant, often near water or moist organic matter. Clouds of adults are called *leks*, aggregations of males, oriented over some small territory, thought to be visually attractive to females, which fly into the cloud for mating. Dance fly males fly up and down in a little cloud to entice females. Interesting trivial fact: in some fly species, the males bring the female a little gift of food. I cannot *imagine* how primitive a species must be if they think that a nice dinner can be a prelude to a mating ritual!

280 St. Augustine Grass – Planting from Sprigs

Q: *Will St. Augustine grass survive Atlanta winters, which seem to be getting warmer every year?*

A: I have St. Augustine grass in my own lawn in Decatur. I sprigged it into fescue grass, planting the sprigs about 8 to 10 inches apart in May. I simply bought a piece of St. Augustine sod from a nursery and washed it good in a tub of water. It was easy to pull apart the sod pieces afterward. It took two years to really cover up the fescue, but since then it's always been green and easy to take care of. The varieties 'Raleigh', 'Palmetto', and 'Mercedes' are more cold-tolerant. Although the grass can tolerate a bit of shade, it needs at least an hour or two of sun in winter to keep it healthy. If you decide to install it, bear in mind that shade, not cold, may limit the success of your lawn.

281 Cicada Killer Wasp

Q: *I have a B-52 bomber-type bee that is circling my lawn. What do you know about these bad boys?!*

A: You have a cicada killer wasp. The cicada killer wasp is about $1^1/_2$ inches long and has yellow markings on its body. The wasp burrows in the ground and mounds the soil at the entrance. The female paralyzes cicadas by stinging them, then places them in the burrow and lays an egg on them. When the egg hatches, the larva feeds on the insects. Cicada killer wasps usually appear in early July when adult cicadas are abundant. The males hover around the underground nest and buzz you, but like all male insects, they cannot sting. The female is usually off in the trees looking for a cicada to drag to the nest, where she will bury it along with one of her eggs.

Since the cicada killer wasp is generally considered harmless, I urge you to leave the nest alone. However, if you must eradicate it, a short squirt with wasp and hornet aerosol spray will do the trick. Cover the soil entrance with a rock or a brick to make sure the nest is completely fumigated.

LAWNS

177

Q: *We have armyworms in our lawn eating up the bermudagrass. What insecticide should we use, and how should it be applied?*

A: Armyworms are caterpillars that feed predominantly on grasses. They attack pastures and lawns each year. The moths that lay the eggs of your armyworms infest much of south Florida but cannot overwinter in north Georgia. Each spring, storms and windy days transport the moths northward. Their eggs develop into the black caterpillars you see in your lawn.

Liquid, not granular, insecticides are used to kill armyworms. **Lawn insecticide**[35] can be mixed with water and applied in a coarse spray over the grass. Try to wet the grass thoroughly, and do not mow for three days after application. The good news is that armyworms will not hurt your lawn permanently. Only occasionally do populations of this pest build up enough to cause concern.

L A W N S

35. **Lawn insecticide:** www.gardenword.com/lawninsecticide

SHRUBS & ORNAMENTAL GRASSES Q&A

283   Azalea – Yellow Leaves in Winter

Q: *I have several 'George L. Taber' azaleas. In winter, many leaves turn yellow, then slowly to brown, and then they drop off the plant. Is this something I should worry about?*

A: You have to keep in mind that although we think of azaleas as evergreen, they are, to varying degrees, semi-deciduous. They drop a certain percentage of leaves each winter. Large-leaved varieties, like the *Indica* clan, seem more likely to show marked yellowing than the *Kurume* group. Azalea growers struggle with leaf drop every year. Much research has been done, but varying the amounts of fertilizer seems not to have much effect. In other words, what you're seeing is normal behavior. The yellow leaves are those that were produced back in spring, when life looked good for the plant. They are more delicate than leaves produced in summer, so they are the first to drop when cold weather arrives. As long as the leaves on the tips of your azalea are green, the plant is healthy. It will fill in with more leaves in spring.

284   Crapemyrtle – Twigs Drop

Q: *After a rain, I noticed several small branches had fallen around our crapemyrtles in our yard. It seems more than is normal. What's happening?*

A: You're seeing a natural early summer phenomenon. I observe small twigs dropping from oak and pine trees also. Trees put on a lot of lush growth in spring. In early summer, they lose some of the poorly attached leaves and twigs in preparation for the summer. The small branches that drop from your crapemyrtle are long, heavy, and weakly attached. Gather and dispose of them, but don't worry that your plants are sick.

285 Wild Azaleas – Pruning

Q: *When I bought my home, I discovered some wild azaleas in my backyard. They have bloomed beautifully for years. Do they require pruning?*

A: Wild azaleas are quite a find on your property. Most of the native species bloom later than the oriental azaleas whose blossoms will begin appearing here in a few weeks. Even so, the same pruning rule applies to all rhododendrons and azaleas, native or imported: *prune after they bloom.*

If your wild azaleas are well formed, there is no particular reason to prune them. If one has been smashed by a falling limb, though, it may be necessary to prune away a great deal of what remains in order to repair damage and to help the shrub regain its shape.

286 Hydrangeas – Keeping Their True Color

Q: *I bought five 'Red and Pretty' hydrangeas this spring. They are doing well, but the blooms are hot pink, not red! What's going on?*

A: Sprinkle a cup of lime around each plant (no closer than 1 foot from the stem) each spring. That should keep the pH high and make them as red as possible.

Q: *One of the selling factors when I bought my house was the large azaleas. Since I moved in, though, one by one my azaleas are dying! Do they just die on their own after so many years?*

A: One of my primary garden rules is never to argue with Mama, whether it be your own mother or Mother Nature. Slow dieback on azaleas and rhododendrons is a common occurrence. The most common cause is the disease *Phytophthora cinnamomi*. That tongue-twisting name is usually shortened to *azalea root rot*. The fungus inhabits almost all soil; only good cultural practices and natural disease resistance of a plant keep azaleas and rhododendrons healthy.

You can help fight the disease by adding plenty of soil conditioner to clay soil before planting. Both composted hardwood and pine bark suppress root rot. If you have an azalea or rhododendron already growing in your landscape, watering deeply once per week allows the soil to dry out between times and thwarts fungal growth. Try fertilizing with organic instead of synthetic fertilizer. Scatter a ½ pound of cottonseed meal evenly under the branches of each plant in April after raking out all of the mulch.

Once you see the symptoms of leaf rolling, wilting, and limb dieback, there is little you can do for your azaleas other than prune out the diseased limbs. Mother Nature may seem cruel, but *Phytophthora* dieback is her efficient method of winnowing out the weakest and least adapted plants.

288 Trifoliate Orange – Identification

Q: *I found a small, rangy tree in the woods. It has a small, yellow fruit about the size of a golf ball. It smells like a lemon. The leaves have three dark green, soft leaflets, and the limbs have long thorns. What kind of tree is this?*

A: It's a trifoliate orange (*Poncirus trifoliata*). Also known as the Japanese Bitter Orange, it is a close relative of citrus plants. It is native to China and will survive temperatures as low as 5 degrees F. The fruit is inedible due to the presence of a bitter oil called *ponciridin*. 'Flying Dragon' is a dwarf form of trifoliate orange. Some brave gardeners grow it as a unique ornamental shrub. It is often used as an understock onto which commercial citrus species are grafted to yield more cold-hardy plants.

289 Sago Palm – Care

Q: *I'm thinking of planting eight or ten Sago palms around the outside of my pool fence. I'm looking for a palm that does not grow too high and that requires little maintenance.*

A: Just to start out on the right foot, the sago palms you are contemplating are not palms at all. Though the leaves are palm-like, they are scientifically classed as *Cycads* and are more kin to pines and ginkgo trees than to palms. Sago palm can be severely damaged by temperatures lower than 15 degrees F in the winter. They also grow so slowly that few are seen in the northern half of Georgia. That said, if your pool site is sheltered from the wind and you have a hankering for a tropical atmosphere, the sago palm is worth a try. If you're worried about spending so much money on these plants, why not try a hardy palm such as needle palm, windmill palm, or dwarf palmetto?

290 Cherokee Rose

Q: *I have to do a garden club program on our state flower: the Cherokee Rose. Do you have any historical information on its original selection and the later naming of a native azalea as Georgia's flower?*

A: The Cherokee rose (*Rosa laevigata*) is not native to Georgia but to China. A good story surrounds its introduction, though.

In 1838, native Cherokee men, women, and children were removed from their land in Georgia and forced to march a thousand miles to Oklahoma. More than four thousand of the original seventeen thousand people died along the way. The unjust and tragic relocation was called the "Trail of Tears." As the legend goes, every time a tear hit the ground, a rose, the Cherokee rose, grew in that place.

In truth, the rose already grew in the South. Renamed "Cherokee" rose, it is a common sight blooming in the spring. Cherokee rose is often confused with Macartney rose (*Rosa bracteata*), which is similar in form, but is so prolific that it is a pest. Macartney rose flowers in summer, while Cherokee rose flowers in spring.

In 1979, our esteemed state legislators wanted to honor the native azalea in some way. They named it our official state *wildflower*, while keeping the Cherokee rose as the state *flower*.

291 Sabal Palmetto Scale – Control

Q: *I have scale insects on my sabal palm trees. I have tried spraying insecticide on them, but I wonder if you could give me any more tips?*

A: Sabal palms, which are more correctly called *sabal palmettoes*, are well-known to be affected by scale. The thick, waxy shell they secrete prevents insecticides from being very effective. The good news is that a naturally occurring predatory wasp loves to lay eggs in scale, which kills the pests. For this reason, I think spraying the palmettoes with horticultural oil is the best control. Before you spray, wipe off as many insects as you can, using paper towels dampened with soapy water.

292 Azalea Caterpillars – Identification

Q: *I have caterpillars with red faces, red feet, and yellow-striped black bodies on my azaleas. They've eaten so much of one bush that you can see straight through it! What kind of caterpillars are these?*

A: The red feet give them away. You have a group of *Dantana major*, otherwise known as azalea caterpillars. If you thump a nearby branch, this caterpillar will hold both ends of its body aloft to make a *C* shape. Any product containing **B.t.**[36] will control these caterpillars safely. If you are interested in identifying caterpillars as a hobby, *Caterpillars of Eastern North America* by David Wagner (Princeton University Press, $29.95) is a marvelous reference, filled with colorful pictures.

293 Jelly Bean Plant

Q: *I was given a plant called a* **jelly bean plant.** *It has a three-lobed leaf and red flowers. A nurseryman said it was 'Red Zinger' hibiscus. Is this used to make delicious Red Zinger tea?*

A: It is indeed a hibiscus that gives Red Zinger tea its zing. Specifically, your plant is *Hibiscus sabdariffa*. Common names include roselle, red sorrel, and Florida cranberry. The seedpod of the plant is used to brew tea. They are collected, dried, and added to jellies and other foods and drinks, imparting a tart but aromatic taste. Coastal gardeners have grown it as an ornamental for years, but it will not tolerate an Atlanta winter.

36. **B.t.:** www.gardenword.com/bt

294 Aucuba – Wilting

Q: *We live on a shady lot and have a lot of aucuba plants around our small lawn. Some of the aucuba have leaves that are turning black and wilting. Does this mean they are dying?*

A: If it makes you feel any better, some of my aucubas are doing the same thing. They are suffering from *Phytophthora* root rot, a soil disease that commonly affects azalea, rhododendron, and aucuba shrubs. The fungus itself is present in most soils. There is no way to eliminate it. It attacks susceptible plants when they become vulnerable due to drought stress, winter injury to stems, or compacted clay soil.

The disease works its way up from ground level; little can be done once a plant is affected except removing wilted branches. Nonetheless, a healthy plant in the correct environment can keep the disease at bay. I plan to remove mine, thoroughly amend the soil, and plant more in the same spot.

295 Knockout Rose – How to Prune

Q: *How low I can prune a Knockout rose?*

A: Much depends on how high you want them to be in summer. I like mine 36 inches tall, so I prune to 18 inches in January. They will grow to 6 feet tall if left unpruned, but they look a bit too open and ragged for my taste at that size. Cut out any dead branches first, then any that cross through the middle. Finally, reduce the height of the rose to half the height you'd like it to be in summer.

296 'Lady Banks' Rose – Naked at Bottom

Q: *My four-year-old 'Lady Banks' rosebush climbs a west-facing brick wall. Now the bush is healthy at the top but scraggly at the bottom. How can I encourage better growth near the ground level?*

A: Pruning at the top won't make it sprout at the bottom. The best thing to do is to cut a couple of the main canes down to 12 inches tall in late February. They will sprout new growth, and these canes can be trained around the base of the plant to hide the naked lower part.

297 Hydrangea – Making Blooms Purple

Q: *I know you have covered how to make pink hydrangea flowers turn blue and vice versa. But how do people get purple blooms?*

A: You make a hydrangea have purple blooms by manipulating the pH, just as you do with the pink and blue flowers. The easiest way is to start with a hydrangea that likes to be pink, like 'Cardinal Red', 'Ami Pasquier', 'Alpenglow', or 'Pia'. Dissolve 2 tablespoons of aluminum sulfate in a gallon of water and drench the plant each spring for two years. Also scatter 1/4 cup of powdered sulfur widely under the plant for two years. The flowers will gradually turn purple in a couple of years. If not, continue adding sulfur yearly, but do not add more aluminum sulfate to the soil.

298　Hydrangea – Pruning Late in Season

Q: *I didn't have a chance to deadhead my hydrangeas in July. What will happen if I do it in October? Should I just leave them until next year?*

A: If by "deadhead" you mean removing the faded flowers, there is no reason not to remove them in October. The removal won't affect next year's blooms. If, on the other hand, you need to make the shrub smaller, there is still a way to do it and not reduce next May's flowers. The trick is to leave on the plant branches that were produced this year in June thru August. Shorten only the longest limbs of your hydrangea but leave many short branches untouched. You should be able to reduce the size of the shrub *and* have plenty of flowers next year. Consider buying an 'Endless Summer' or 'Penny Mac' hydrangea: they don't mind when they are pruned.

SHRUBS & ORNAMENTAL GRASSES

299　Hydrangea – Leaf Spot

Q: *I planted two hydrangeas a year ago. The leaves are now covered in round brown spots, and they are not blooming. What should I do?*

A: Hydrangeas commonly get a leaf disease called *Cercospora leaf spot*. It usually infects when leaves are regularly wet by rain or irrigation. It can also be a problem when the shrubs grow so densely that leaves can't completely dry. You can protect them by spraying with a **garden fungicide**[37] when damage is first seen.

---

37. **garden fungicide:** www.gardenword.com/gardenfungicide

300 Hydrangea – Identification and Pruning

Q: *I have hydrangeas with several different flower and leaf shapes. How do I tell them apart?*

A: In my garden, the color and shape of the faded bloom help me identify hydrangeas. Common *Hydrangea macrophylla* flower heads are dark tan, usually globe-like, and on the tip of stiff stems. If the brown flowers are lace-cap type, it is almost certainly a *macrophylla* hydrangea. 'Annabelle' hydrangea blooms are a very light tan, almost white, and on the end of 3-foot long arching canes. 'PeeGee' hydrangea flowers look like *Hydrangea macrophylla* blooms, but the shrub itself is much bigger . . . usually 5 to 10 feet tall. Stems are very stiff and arch gently at the top. 'Tardiva' hydrangea flowers are strongly cone-shaped, but the leaves are not oak-shaped. 'Tardiva' blooms in mid- to late summer, after oakleaf hydrangea. Oakleaf hydrangea also has cone-shaped flowers, but the bark of the stems peels attractively around the bottom third of the stem.

301 Laurel – Shot Hole Disease

Q: *My 'Otto Luyken' laurel shrubs have numerous small holes in the leaves. The guy at the nursery said the disease is called* **shot hole** *but wasn't sure how to control it. Do you know?*

A: *Shot hole* is a common bacterial disease on 'Otto Luyken', 'Zabal', and 'Schip' laurel plants. The disease's name is descriptive of the symptoms: it looks like someone shot the shrub with a shotgun! Wet leaves seem to make the disease worse, so make sure not to water your plants from overhead. If your shrubs are very close together or near a wall that prevents leaf drying, prune them to enhance airflow. Fungicides containing **fixed copper**[38] are effective against shot hole if you choose to spray a pesticide.

---

38. **fixed copper:** www.gardenword.com/copper

302　Rose – Rooting in Soil

Q: *My neighbor has a 'Lady Banks' rose on a fence. He'll let me have some to root, but I don't quite know what to do. Can you help?*

A: Rooting a 'Lady Banks' rose is easy as pie. In the first place, there may be a sprout or two already growing under your friend's plant. All you have to do is dig it up and move it to your yard. If you don't see any sprouts, you can *soil layer* one or several branches.

Start by looking in May for long shoots, which can be bent to touch the ground. Measure 8 to 12 inches back from the shoot tip and dig a narrow trench in the ground under that area. Take a dull kitchen knife and gently scrape the outer bark from the stem there for 1 or 2 inches. Sprinkle a bit of **rooting hormone**[39] on the injury and lay it in the trench. A few rose leaves should emerge from the end of the trench. Cover the stem with moist earth, and place a brick on top to keep it buried.

A length of orange ribbon tied around the brick will remind you where you were working. In August, cut the stem connecting the stem to the mother plant. By October, the stem will have fully rooted underground.

39. **rooting hormone:** www.gardenword.com/rootinghormone

303 Lilac – Growing

Q: *Which lilacs grow in our area?*

A: Just like the scent of talcum powder can transport a parent back to when their truculent teenager was tiny, the smell of lilacs reminds Midwesterners of home. Under the right conditions, lilacs are virtually indestructible. Though not a very attractive shrub, the huge trusses of flowers in spring are a sight to behold and scent to smell! The key element that we lack in the South is chilling hours during the winter. Most lilacs require over two thousand hours of temperatures below 45 degrees F in order to bloom. Atlanta receives approximately fifteen hundred hours each season. The key is to find lilac selections that do not need so much chilling in the winter. Try 'Betsy Ross', 'Lavender Lady', 'Blue Boy', 'Miss Kim', or 'Angel White' lilacs.

304 Azalea and Camellia – Leaf Gall

Q: *The leaves on the ends of some of my camellia branches are swollen and thicker than the rest of the leaves. They are also lighter green. I've seen this on azaleas but not on camellias. Is it the same thing?*

A: It is indeed the same disease: *camellia* (or *azalea*) *leaf gall*. It is caused by the fungus *Exobasidium* spp. Your plants were infected last year when spores from a similarly swollen camellia leaf were released. There is not much you can do for the problem other than pick off and destroy the effected leaves. Do it soon. Once the galls turn grayish-white, they begin to release spores that will infect your plants next spring.

Q: *Are the berries of 'Burford' holly poisonous?*

A: Auroleus Phillipus Theophrastus Bombastus von Hohenheim (known as Paracelsus to his friends) was born in Switzerland in 1493. His work as a physician and pharmacist earned him the name "The Father of Modern Medicine." One of Paracelsus's key observations was "The dose makes the poison." In other words, a substance that is harmless in small amounts can be poisonous in large doses. So it is with holly berries. One berry won't kill you—but you'd better invite the undertaker to a meal where you serve holly berry pie.

The seed or leaves of only a few landscape plants are so poisonous as to cause worry. A liriope berry, holly berry, or beauty berry seed might cause an upset stomach but would not be likely to kill a child, pet, or adult. Some exceptions include castor bean seed, lantana seed, and Carolina jessamine leaves, all of which are highly toxic.

SHRUBS & ORNAMENTAL GRASSES

306   Loropetalum – Pruning

Q: *When and how do I go about pruning a loropetalum? It has grown long limbs and is very open.*

A: Loropetalum is one of my favorite shrubs because it is drought tolerant, pest free, and blooms wonderfully in spring. In addition, loropetalum is easy to prune to any size you like. It won't stay that small for more than six months, but you can always just prune it back again as needed.

    The white-flowered form of loropetalum has been in the nursery trade for many years, but the pink-flowered form was introduced from China in 1989. Several varieties are available: 'Blush', 'Burgundy', 'Ruby', and 'Zhuzhou Fuschia' are common. Long sprouts arise from the center of the plant when it is given lots of sunshine, fertilizer, and regular watering. The best time to prune is in March. If yours is very overgrown, you could reduce it in size by 1/4 in fall and further in spring.

307   Hedge – At the University of Georgia

Q: *What is the plant surrounding the football field at Sanford Stadium in Athens? Several online sources call it English privet. As a Bulldog fan, I've got to know: what is the hedge?*

A: You are right that many online Web sites mention English privet. They are, however, wrong. The shrub is Chinese privet (*Ligustrum sinense*). I'm not sure where the confusion occurred. My guess is that a non-horticultural writer got confused with English boxwood and their misinformation has been repeated ad infinitum. Bulldog Nation would be in your debt if you'd contact the appropriate parties and have this corrected!

308 Rose – Flowers Change Color

Q: *A few years ago I planted yellow, pink, and red roses. Now the blooms are all red. Why did they change color?*

A: The most likely explanation is that you planted grafted roses and blooming sprouts have risen from below the graft union. To make a grafted rose, a twig from a beautiful rosebush is grafted onto the rootstock of an inferior rose. If you examine the trunk of your rose and find a swollen knot close to the ground, that is likely the graft union. If the branches above the graft union die for some reason, sprouts from the inferior rose will take over. If that rose was a common red one, you can see why your blooms might seem to have changed from yellow or pink to red.

309 Boxwood – Problems and Care

Q: *I have a boxwood with sections dying off. Any ideas on what I need to do?*

A: It's hard to determine a specific cause of branch dieback in boxwoods. The shrub sometimes gets a branch disease called *volutella blight*. The cure is to prune it out. The best defense against boxwood problems is to plant and care for them in the best way possible. Boxwoods *hate* waterlogged soil and *detest* dry soil. If your problem bush is growing in clay soil that was not amended very well originally, that could be a cause of decline.

In my experience, Japanese boxwood (*Buxus microphylla*) does much better than English boxwood (*Buxus sempervirens*) in the South. Perhaps the best results come from 'Green Mountain' boxwood, a hybrid of the Japanese and English species. Try fertilizing your boxwoods with Milorganite or cottonseed meal. Both release nutrients very slowly, exactly as a boxwood likes.

310 Shrubs – Fertilizing

Q: *When is the right time to fertilize shrubs?*

A: In general, you should fertilize older shrubs twice each year: once in spring after the last frost and once in early fall before the first frost. Young shrubs can be fed monthly with light doses of nutrients. It doesn't matter whether they are blooming or not. I like plain old 10-10-10, applied at one tablespoon per foot of plant height each time, but many good gardeners prefer a slow-release fertilizer like Nursery Special Osmocote, Dynamite, and others.

311 Beer – Good for Plants?

Q: *I don't disagree with your assertion that cola and ammonia don't help plants, but what about beer? I am into bonsai, and my well-learned sensei says that beer will do a tree good!*

A: One of my rules for success is *never* to argue with a sensei—particularly when he is correct! Beer does contain carbohydrates that can break down into plant nutrients. In a localized spot, like a bonsai root zone, beer could supply significant plant food. It's up to you to figure out how much beer to use without harming the roots with alcohol or attracting fungus gnats. It's when beer is suggested as a lawn tonic that I demur. Unless you use many gallons of beer per thousand square feet, the lawn won't get much benefit.

312   G. G. Gerbing Azalea – Sport

Q: *I have three large-leafed azaleas in my garden. The other day I noticed two perfect lavender-colored blossoms on an otherwise all-white 'G. G. Gerbing' azalea. How unusual is this?*

A: It's not unusual if you understand the origin of 'Mrs. G. G. Gerbing'. The 'Mrs. G. G. Gerbing' azalea is a *sport* of 'George L. Taber' azalea. Sports are caused by unexpected bud damage to a plant. An astute gardener many years ago saw a branch bearing white flowers on an 'George L. Taber' azalea. He or she decided to propagate it, name it, and introduce it to the nursery trade. The genetics of your 'Mrs. G. G. Gerbing' azalea have caused it to sport back to its parent, 'George L. Taber' azalea. Both are very popular in Georgia.

313   Azaleas – Pruning Overgrown

Q: *Can I cut my overgrown azaleas back? And, if so, how much?*

A: Yes. The best time is in early spring, even though you'll cut off most of the blooms. I cut my scraggly 5-footers down to 18 inches in February several years ago, and they are thriving now . . . 4 feet tall and covered with flowers each spring.

314 Azaleas – When to Fertilize

Q: *I continue to get mixed messages on when I should fertilize my azaleas. I have three of them, planted last spring. When is the right time to feed them?*

A: It's best to fertilize after blooms begin to fade, but there is more to it than that. Fertilizing azaleas should be based on how the plant appears and what you want to accomplish with it. Old, established shrubs don't need much food. A tablespoon of 10-10-10 per foot of height is sufficient for the year. Young plants need more food, so feed them four times, at the same rate, during the growing season. You could also use one of the "azalea-camellia" fertilizers or an **organic fertilizer**.[40] Apply the amount specified on the product label.

315 Gardenia Bush – Planting Hole

Q: *I recently planted a gardenia bush for my wife. But about 3 feet deep was a large rock that I couldn't break up. I found where the rock ended and planted the bush out therem but I worry about the rock being a hindrance to the bush's growth. Will it be okay?*

A: You dug a hole 3 feet deep??? That's going *far* beyond the call of duty! But since it was for your wife, it proves the depth of your love. Gardenia roots, and those of most shrubs, rarely go deeper than 12 inches. Any planting hole deeper than that yields nothing but good exercise . . . and sometimes a trip to the chiropractor. If you'd like to move the plant back to its originally planned site, that would be dandy. Just go easy on yourself and make the hole 3 feet wide, but no deeper than 12 inches.

40. **organic fertilizer:** www.gardenword.com/organicfertilizer

316 Gardenia, Holly, Magnolia – Yellow Leaves

Q: *Some of my gardenia bushes have yellow leaves in May. Is this an iron deficiency? What do you recommend?*

A: It is common in spring to see yellow leaves on gardenia, holly, and Southern magnolia. The phenomenon is caused by the plant moving food resources out to new growth on the branch tips, leaving interior leaves to survive as best they can. The weakened yellow leaves may get spots from fungi taking advantage of them, but the disease rarely moves to other parts of the plant. If the yellow leaves are several inches back from the branch tips, and if the tip leaves are green, your plant is reacting normally. It will look fine in a few weeks. Spraying with fungicide or fertilizing will not help the situation; it's just a part of the lifecycle of the plant.

317 Butterfly Bush – Remove Flowers

Q: *My butterfly bushes have been blooming wonderfully! Is there anything I can do to make them keep putting out the large flowers?*

A: Butterfly bush produces blooms on new stems. This means that unless new growth is constantly being formed, flower production will decrease. Hang an old pair of scissors on a stick near the bush and use them to clip off faded flowers whenever you pass by. Every three weeks, shorten a few branches by 2 feet so they will put out new growth.

318 | Flowers – Moving and Replanting

Q: *We have to move, but I have sentimental roses, daylilies, and irises. Please help with advice on proper care and replanting.*

A: Just get a bunch of cardboard boxes from a liquor store and line each with a garbage bag. Poke holes in the plastic with a pencil. Dig up your plants and put each one in a box. Cover the roots with potting soil. Take them to a shady spot at your new home and water moderately. You can keep them in boxes for a couple of weeks, but plant as soon as you can.

319 | Azaleas – Pruning

Q: *How do I prune Encore™ azaleas? Mine need pruning pretty bad, but I don't want to cut off the blooms for next spring.*

A: I had my doubts about the shrubs initially, but Encore™ azaleas have succeeded very well in Atlanta. They consistently give blooms in both spring and fall. The best time to prune them is right after they bloom in spring. In this way there will be plenty of time for buds to form for fall flowers. Spring bloom buds are at the tips of the branches from September onward. If you are forced to prune before spring, remove individual branches to reduce the shrub's size, but leave as many untouched branch tips as you can.

320   Peegee Hydrangea – Pruning

Q: *I purchased a peegee shrub and need to know how and when to prune it.*

A: With a complicated name like *Hydrangea paniculata* 'Grandiflora', it's understandable that gardeners call this plant "peegee" hydrangea. Unlike the common mophead hydrangea, peegee hydrangea produces cone-shaped blooms on new wood. In other words, you can prune it severely in winter, and it will bloom nicely the following summer. Decide how tall you want yours to be each summer, and cut it to half that height in January. It will have stocky central stems from which limber blooming branches will emerge. You can also leave it unpruned. Garden favorite *Hydrangea paniculata* 'Tardiva' produces its spectacular 12-inch long blooms in midsummer.

321   Yucca – Pruning

Q: *I have several clusters of yucca plants. Most of them are 4 or 5 feet tall. Some of the taller ones have begun to lie down along the ground. What will happen if I lop off a few feet of length from some of these plants?*

A: Yucca, also known as Spanish bayonet, is famous for its needle-sharp leaves. It can be a real health hazard if it grows too close to where you walk. The giant plumes of white flowers in summer almost make up for the need for a yearly tetanus shot if you grow it. The plant elongates as it grows; flopping is a natural way for it to spread. You can cut off whatever length seems appropriate to keep the yucca in bounds. Like most woody plants, it will resprout near the cut end. The sprouts can be left to grow until they get too long as well.

322 Winterberry Holly – Cultivars and Pollination

Q: *What are some good varieties of winterberry holly,* **Ilex verticillata?**

A: There are many varieties of winterberry holly, all of which sport masses of red berries December through March. Experts recommend that if you want a big plant, use 'Winter Red'. If you need a small, residential-sized bush, use 'Red Sprite'. The pollinators for 'Winter Red' are 'Apollo' or 'Southern Gentlemen'. For 'Red Sprite', use 'Jim Dandy', which is an early bloomer.

323 Photinia – Diseases

Q: *I have a row of red-tip photinias. The bushes at one end are losing leaves, and the leaves have dark circular spots on them. What's wrong with them?*

A: The key to raising healthy red-tip photinias is to grow them in full sunshine and to never prune them. The fungus that causes *photinia leaf spot* loves young red leaves. If you prune your photinias every spring, the new leaves are very susceptible to fungal infection. In contrast, I commonly see large, unpruned photinias that have no spots at all.

If you *must* prune your photinia, do so in midsummer. Use only hand pruners or a lopper to remove big limbs; never shear the shrub. In this way you'll avoid a flush of new growth. You can apply a **fungicide**[41] for a couple of years to arrest the spread of your disease, but try my pruning suggestions for long-term success with these shrubs.

41. fungicide: www.gardenword.com/gardenfungicide

324 Crapemyrtles – Pruning, Why?

Q: *Why is it necessary to prune crapemyrtles? What would happen if I don't prune them?*

A: There is no reason at all to prune a crapemyrtle except to make it conform to your need for size and shape. They will flower whether pruned or unpruned. To clean up my plants, I like to remove dried seed clusters and all of the small twigs along the trunk every winter. I also remove any root suckers around the base of my crapes. In a spot where the arching branches get too wide, pruning back to a limb diameter of $^1/_4$ to $^1/_2$ inch will maintain the vase shape of a tree-form crapemyrtle. I dislike intensely the wholesale, murderous "whack back" that ill-trained maintenance crews perform. The resulting dense mass of foliage makes powdery mildew and aphid problems almost a certainty.

325 Plants – Heeling In

Q: *We will be moving soon, and I have several plants that I would like to take with me. There are several rosebushes, Indian hawthorn, rhodo-dendrons, azaleas, bulbs, and a red twig dogwood. They are healthy and did quite well this past summer. What would be the best way to keep these until they can be planted?*

A: You'll have to *heel in* your plants where they will not be disturbed until you are ready to plant at your new home. Basically all you do is dig a trench 3 feet wide and 12 inches deep. Pile the removed soil beside the trench, which can be as long as you like. Dig up your individual plants and put the rootballs side by side in the trench. It is fine to crowd them a bit if you have to. Try to keep the roots buried at the same level at which they were growing originally. Once the plants are all lined up in the trench, cover the rootballs with the soil you originally removed. Water them thoroughly to get good root to soil contact. All of your plants should be perfectly happy waiting there until planting time.

326 Boxwoods

Q: *My boxwoods are covered in spiderwebs. Is there something I can spray on them to get rid of the spiderwebs without hurting the boxwoods?*

A: I believe you should leave the spiderwebs alone. They are likely just the first webs of spiders that have recently hatched. Most will die over the next few weeks. More importantly, spiders catch boxwood leaf miners, a destructive insect that tunnels in the leaves of boxwood shrubs. The spiders are friends, not foes.

327 Boxwood – Pruning

Q: *What is the best way to prune boxwoods?*

A: Electric hedge trimmers are the devil's tool when it comes to boxwoods. The trimmers are so easy to use, it is tempting to make green meatballs out of your landscape shrubs. That's exactly the wrong way to keep a boxwood healthy. A healthy boxwood should have leaves growing along the outermost third of each branch. Sheared boxwoods only have leaves on the outer few inches of each branch. If a limb dies, the result is a huge "hole" in the side of the shrub. If the shrub needs its size reduced, only bare limbs are left and recovery is slow.

The best pruning technique is to use hand pruners to take out individual limbs to reduce the size of the plant over a couple of years. If you have a big boxwood, reduce its size by $1/4$ this year and remove another $1/4$ next spring. Even if your limb removal makes a few holes in the foliage, the nearby limbs will quickly make sprouts to fill the empty spaces.

328 Boxwood – Winter Discoloration

Q: *Every year my boxwoods change from a nice green color to a purple-bronze color in the winter. Is there any way to prevent this?*

A: Boxwoods are beautiful shrubs, but the bronzy discoloration you describe is common. Usually it has something to do with the shrub's root system. Boxwoods have a shallow root system. That means that they are very susceptible to both too much and too little water during the growing season. If the roots have been weakened during the summer, discoloration in the winter is the result.

Another cause could be an infestation by nematodes. These microscopic worms feed on boxwood roots, causing weakness and a change in leaf color. You should examine the soil around your boxwoods to see if water problems could be causing your problem. Nematodes can be detected by bringing a sample of the soil to your county Extension service office (1-800-ASKUGA-1) in the summer for a nematode assay.

If you decide that these shrubs are beyond saving, replace them with 'Green Velvet' or 'Green Mountain' boxwoods. These selections are resistant to root problems, and they do not change color when stressed. Make sure to plant them in well-drained soil to avoid future difficulties.

SHRUBS & ORNAMENTAL GRASSES

329 Privet Hedge – Transplanting

Q: *I have some of the famous University of Georgia hedges (salvaged after the Auburn game in '95) that I would like to transplant to a new house. My plant is 30 inches wide and 5 feet tall. What should I do to prepare it for the move?*

A: I spent much of my childhood resenting the privet hedge that you hold in such high regard. On chilly December days, my father would detail me to drag a small chain behind his tractor through a thicket of privet and wrap it 'round a privet trunk. With a yell from me, the tractor would lurch forward and pull the privet from the underbrush. I would crawl back out, limber twigs snapping me in the face, to unwrap the chain, drag it back to another trunk, and repeat the process. For a boy who would rather be watching *The Popeye Club* on television, privet hedge was not my favorite plant, not by a long shot.

The hedge that has intimidated hundreds of opposing football teams is nothing but Chinese privet (*Ligustrum sinense*). Horticulturist Mike Dirr remarks that it grows anywhere that birds fly. It is high on the Invasive Plants lists kept by most naturalists. This explains why my father and I never obliterated it from the farm and why 200-pound linebackers can hardly dent it. I would prepare your trophy by standing in front of it and announcing, "I'm going to move you!" Immediately grab a shovel and dig it out, keeping on the plant as many roots as you can. Plant it in full sun at your new abode and yell, "Go Dawgs!" as you water it.

SHRUBS & ORNAMENTAL GRASSES

330 Gardenia – Wax Scale

Q: *I have a gardenia bush and have noticed whitish, waxy-feeling deposits on the branches. What should, or can, I do about them?*

A: You have an infestation of *wax scale*. The insects suck sap from the small branches of holly, quince, camellia, and several other shrubs. The waxy covering they secrete looks like bits of white chewing gum stuck to the twigs. The females (there are no males) lay their eggs in March. Tiny "crawlers" emerge in May, all looking for a spot to settle and begin drinking from their host. Control is twofold: Pick off and destroy all of the waxy adults you can find. In June, spray the gardenia with **garden insecticide**[42] or **horticultural oil**.[43] This will kill the defenseless crawlers. Do this for two years, and you'll eliminate the scale population.

331 Abelia – Dwarf

Q: *I bought a dwarf 'Little Richard' abelia two years ago. The shrub now has several 4-foot-tall shoots in the middle. Why did this happen?*

A: 'Little Richard' is a selected sport of *Abelia grandiflora* 'Sherwoodii'. It has dense, lustrous green leaves. 'Sherwoodii' occasionally sends up limbs that are reversions to the species abelia, which can grow to 8 feet tall. With this in mind, my guess is that your 'Little Richard' has sported a couple of tall limbs like its 'Sherwoodii' parent does. If the rest of the plant is growing compactly, just remove the sprouts at their origination point.

42. **garden insecticide:** www.gardenword.com/gardeninsecticide
43. **horticultural oil:** www.gardenword.com/hortoil

SHRUBS & ORNAMENTAL GRASSES

332 Holly – Insects among Blooms in Spring

Q: *We have some very mature holly bushes right in front of our house. In spring they are full of flying insects. How can I get rid of them?*

A: Holly blooms have lots of nectar in them. My bet is that you're seeing crowds of different pollinating insects looking for a good springtime meal. Even though you may see honeybees in the crowd, don't worry. They are *much* more interested in food than in stinging. More slender insects are probably harmless thread-waisted wasps seeking nectar from the flowers or perhaps honeydew from aphids or scale insects. They rarely sting, are not aggressive, and help the environment too. I recommend you enjoy all of the pollinators and let them go about their business.

333 Euonymous Scale – Control

Q: *My variegated euonymous has lots of little white dots under the leaves, and it doesn't look very healthy. Can you diagnose this?*

A: In my experience, a heavy infestation of scale on euonymous is almost impossible to control without major pruning to remove the majority of the insects first. Euonymous grows vigorously, so pruning any time between spring and early fall won't hurt it terribly. You'll get some regrowth before winter but lots more next spring. I recommend applying systemic insecticide in spring and also spraying what's left of the shrub with horticultural oil immediately (be sure to follow label directions for hot-weather application).

334 Planaria (Flatworm)

Q: *I turned over a rock in my backyard and found the ugliest creature I've ever seen! It looked like a slimy earthworm, about 8 inches long, and had a flat head shaped like a hammerhead shark. Is it dangerous?*

A: The creature you found is called a *soil planaria*, probably *Bipalium kewense*. It is harmless to animals but is a predator of beneficial earthworms. Back in high school biology, you studied planaria and learned that they are uniquely able to reproduce themselves after being cut in half. Most planaria live in water or swampy areas, but this one can survive on land if it stays moist. This particular flatworm is commonly discovered under rocks and clay pots when there has been lots of rain recently. Show your planaria to the neighbors as a curiosity, but my recommendation is to destroy it by wrapping it in tissue paper, which will dry it out completely. Do not "stomp it," since severed pieces can regenerate.

335 'Foster' Holly – Spittlebug Control

Q: *My 'Foster' holly is covered with black bugs. They are about a 1/2 inch long, with orange stripes running across the body. What are these creatures?*

A: Your holly is hosting adult spittlebugs. 'Foster' and 'Nellie Stevens' hollies are attractive to them, but 'Burford' and yaupon holly are resistant. You probably saw the "spit globs" of spittlebug nymphs at the base of your turfgrass and garden plants in late spring. Although adult spittlebugs can feed heavily on holly leaves, the hollies don't seem to be hurt much. If you see lots of yellow leaves, spray with a **garden insecticide**.[44]

44. **garden insecticide:** www.gardenword.com/gardeninsecticide

336 Azalea Lacebug – Control in Spring

Q: *Last summer the leaves on my azalea lost their bright green color. The back of the leaves looked like they had bugs on them. Any advice?*

A: I feel sure you have/had *azalea lacebugs* sucking sap from the leaves. Each tiny white spot you see is a cell that no longer contains chlorophyll. Obviously, that's not good for the azalea! The best way to combat these bugs is to drench the soil with a **systemic insecticide**[45] in the spring. I like systemic insecticide drenches. The chemical poisons the sap but does no harm to beneficial insects. If you notice azalea lacebugs in summer, spray the shrubs with **garden insecticide**[46] in the evening, so as to protect bees and other beneficial insects.

337 Bagworm

Q: *My Leyland cypresses all have little pods, containing some sort of worm, hanging from almost every branch. What should I do now?*

A: Junipers, Leyland cypress, and cedar trees can be skeletonized by *bagworms* in late summer. Examination of a rapidly disappearing shrub reveals dozens of brown "bags" hanging from the limbs. The bags are made from the plant's needles. They contain a wingless moth, who feasts on the plant's greenery. Unfortunately, once the bag is easily noticeable, it is too late to control the pest with insecticides. At this point, there is no solution except hand removal.

Wear a long sleeved shirt to avoid being scratched by the needles and scales of the host plant. Make a note to spray **B.t.**[47] or a **landscape insecticide**[48] three times at weekly intervals next June, when the caterpillars have not yet formed their protective bags.

45. **systemic insecticide:** www.gardenword.com/systemicinsecticide

46. **garden insecticide:** www.gardenword.com/gardeninsecticide

47. **B.t.:** www.gardenword.com/bt

48. **landscape insecticide:** www.gardenword.com/gardeninsecticide

338 Boxwood – Leaf Miner

Q: *Last year's growth on my boxwoods is mottled looking. Is this a disease?*

A: Your boxwoods are most probably infested with *boxwood leaf miner*. August is the month when gardeners notice the splotchy brown and yellow leaves caused by the pests. A fly-like adult insect laid eggs on the boxwood leaves in late spring. When the eggs hatched, the larvae chewed into the center of the leaf and happily munched away, protected from predators and the elements. Now you easily notice the mottled appearance of the damaged leaves. Leaf miners are very difficult to control once they are inside the leaves. The best way to reduce their numbers is to spray when the adults are present in April and May. **Insecticidal soap**[49] or **horticultural oil**[50] will kill them if the shrubs are sprayed thoroughly. Make three applications at weekly intervals beginning three weeks after new spring foliage appears. **Systemic pesticides**[51] offer another choice. They are absorbed by plant tissue, making it deadly to chewing insects.

339 Asian Ambrosia Beetle – On Crapemyrtle

Q: *I have "toothpicks" of sawdust sticking out of my crapemyrtle tree. I've heard that a beetle causes this. Is that true?*

A: *Asian ambrosia beetles* bore into the limbs and trunks of crapemyrtle, ornamental cherry, Japanese maple, Siberian elm, red bud, and several other ornamental plants. They prefer drought-stressed plants, but they also attack perfectly healthy plants. The female beetles introduce a fungus under the bark. The fungus infects the plant, which rapidly dies. Specific controls for ambrosia beetle are scarce. If holes and sawdust are found, they are already inside and immune from poisons.

Apply an insecticide labeled for use on borers on susceptible plants in March and in April every year. If you notice dozens of sawdust toothpicks in the trunk of a plant, it will likely not survive.

49. **insecticidal soap:** www.gardenword.com/soap

50. **horticulural oil:** www.gardenword.com/hortoil

51. **systemic pesticides:** www.gardenword.com/systemicinsecticide

210

SHRUBS & ORNAMENTAL GRASSES

340 Pampas Grass – Pruning

Q: *I have a pampas grass plant. When should it be pruned?*

A: January is the right time, before any growth starts. Cut pampas grass clumps down to 10 inches tall. I've done it with a carpenter's saw, but I've found a chain saw to be very handy too. The process is easy to manage if you cinch the clump up tight with a rope so you can saw away at the base. Be sure to wear a long-sleeved shirt and gloves when you work: the grass leaves are razor sharp. Remove any dead stems in the center of the clump. After ten years, dig up and remove ⅔ of the clump to rejuvenate it.

341 Banana Shrub

Q: *I remember a shrub in my cousin's yard they called a **fresketti**. It had small yellow blossoms, and the fragrance reminds you of a banana. Are you familiar with such a plant?*

A: I think you are remembering the sweet scent of a banana shrub (*Michelia figo*). It has yellowish blossoms and its fragrance is similar to banana. Its original name was *Magnolia fuscata*. That's probably where your "fresketti" comes from. Banana shrub should grow wherever figs thrive. In north Georgia, it will need winter protection.

342 Blue Fescue – Care

Q: *I have an area where I have planted blue fescue. There is dead and brown grass on the underside of the plant. Is there a proper time to trim back the plant?*

A: Blue fescue is an interesting focal point for a garden. It grows only 12 inches tall, but the foliage is a striking blue-green color. 'Elijah Blue' is a common cultivar. It was not named after Elijah Blue Allman, the son of Gregg Allman and Cher, but for the street (Elijah Lane) on which the cultivar's breeder lived.

You can remove brown leaves anytime. If the whole plant looks ratty after a hard winter, cut it back to 3 inches tall. Don't forget, blue fescue cannot stand poorly drained clay-filled soil. If your plants die, try again, but plant in an area containing native soil, gritty sand, and soil conditioner in a 1:1:1 ratio.

343 Purple Fountain Grass – Overwintering

Q: *I planted purple fountain grass this year. Will it come back next year?*

A: Purple fountain grass is a perennial in south Florida, but it doesn't have a chance of surviving most Georgia winters outdoors. That is actually a good thing, because the grass is considered mildly invasive in places where it can reseed itself and grow from year to year. I have heard of Georgia gardeners who have attempted to keep it alive indoors, but their efforts have mostly ended in failure. The plant is so inexpensive that it makes more sense to buy a new one each spring.

TREES
Q&A

344 Birch – Planting

Q: *I am new to Georgia. Is there any reason why I shouldn't plant birch trees?*

A: I am pleased to welcome you to our fair region! Only one birch tree grows well here. The river birch (*Betula nigra*) loves the sun, grows rapidly, and has attractive peeling bark. Look particularly for the 'Heritage' variety and purchase it from a grower who can guarantee that it is a real 'Heritage' river birch. I have seen many birches being sold as 'Heritage' that seemed to be common river birch instead. 'Dura-Heat' is another superior cultivar.

345 Mulberry Tree

Q: *My friend has a beautiful mulberry tree. I would love to grow a mulberry! What advice can you give?*

A: Look for small mulberry seedlings growing near your friend's tree. Before you transplant, make sure you've thought about what you're getting into. The mulberry was originally imported from China in the 1600s to feed silkworms in an effort to start the silk industry in the Americas. Silkworms wouldn't grow here—but the mulberry tree certainly does. It is generally considered a weed tree because of the mess birds make after eating the fruit. Buy a cover for all your vehicles when you plant mulberries! The wild fruit is edible by humans but in my opinion is a poor substitute for a July-ripe blackberry.

346 Blue Spruce – Planting

Q: *Would a blue spruce tree live in Georgia? How much attention do they need?*

A: Although they are not at all well adapted to our heat and humidity, enough blue spruce trees survive to make me a liar when I state that gardeners should not plant them. If you want to try growing one, remember that site selection and preparation is paramount. Plant your spruce in a spot that gets some afternoon shade. More than a couple of hours of hot summer sunshine in a day is usually too much.

The area in which it is planted *must* be well drained around the roots. Loosen an area 10 feet in diameter, add three bags of soil conditioner and three bags of paver underlayment sand, and mix the soil and amendments together thoroughly. Plant the tree in the middle, spreading the roots outward. Do not let the planting area dry out for the first year (although the soil should never be soggy either). If all goes well, your spruce will last for twenty or thirty years. If not, the wood adds a nice scent to your fireplace.

T R E E S

347 Hammock – Hanging from Tree

Q: *I want to hang a hammock between two sweetgum trees with trunks approximately 12 inches thick. If I put a screweye into the trunk, will it cause damage to the trees?*

A: Will it cause damage to the tree? Well, I see young people with pierced tongues and wonder if the wound causes permanent damage. But some kids like them . . . and since I unknowingly wore a T-shirt inside out all day recently, who am I to criticize fashion? But to answer your question, *yes*, the pierced tree will be somewhat more prone to disease or insect invasion, but, in a practical sense, it likely won't be hurt by the screweye.

I do have a mechanical suggestion. Screw eyes can pull loose. I'd recommend a long, $1/2$-inch thread diameter eyebolt. Companies that serve arborists sell these big eyebolts for tree repair work. Use an extended-shaft, $5/8$-inch spade bit to drill a hole at the proper height through the tree. Put a big washer under the nut on the far side of the tree. Hook your hammock to the eye of the bolt, and swing the summer away.

348 Japanese Maple – Sports

Q: *I have some unusual new growth in my Japanese maple. The green leaves are on two stems, one of which is growing from the main trunk about 12 inches above ground level, and another small branch is growing from a branch that has dissected purple leaves. No one can tell me what I have, or if I should just cut this growth out.*

A: Japanese maple trees are often grafted onto less-decorative rootstocks, so examine it closely to see if the first sprout has emerged from below a graft union. The union is usually swollen slightly, making it easy to see. These understock sprouts should be pruned out.

If the branch with green leaves truly comes from a branch having the purple leaves, you have what's called a *sport*. This is just a reversion to the original parent tree of the purple-leaved plant. This phenomenon is not particularly unusual, but if the sport has attractive leaves, you could take cuttings and propagate it for your pleasure. Since the green leaves of the sport don't seem very attractive, simply prune it out at the origination point.

349 Kousa Dogwood – Identifying

Q: *We have a tree that looks very much like a dogwood, yet it has a fruit that looks like a medium-sized plum with spikes on it. In fall they become soft with a pleasant fruity smell. What kind of tree is this?*

A: That sounds like a kousa dogwood. I've grown kousa dogwood (*Cornus kousa*) but had never seen the fruit until I visited the fine dogwood collection at the Biltmore Estate in Asheville, North Carolina. One kousa dogwood there was loaded with the odd-looking edible pink fruit you saw. I sampled several of them. "Lightly sweetened vanilla custard" is my memory of the taste.

TREES

217

350 Magnolia – Algal Leaf Spot

Q: *We have a number of magnolia trees in our yard. On some of them the leaves are heavily infested with circular brown spots, about ¹/₄ of an inch in diameter. Any thoughts?*

A: It's probably *algal leaf spot*. This leaf disease usually follows rainy, wet weather in the fall or spring. Management can be achieved primarily by sanitation. Remove infected attached and fallen leaves, and destroy them. Increasing air circulation around the trees and improving soil drainage will help prevent future infections. **Copper sprays**[52] can be used preventively but are usually unnecessary.

351 Magnolia – Moving

Q: *I have a volunteer magnolia growing 3 feet away from a huge red oak. This magnolia is about 6¹/₂ feet tall. Am I wasting my time in trying to relocate the magnolia to my girlfriend's home?*

A: Even if the magnolia doesn't live, you still have to make the attempt. This will bring you uncounted favor in your girlfriend's estimation . . . plus you may be lucky and have the tree live after all. Six feet tall isn't too big to attempt. Be sure to take a picture of you two together by the tree after you plant it.

52. **copper sprays:** www.gardenword.com/copper

218

352 Maple – Epicormic Branches

Q: *I planted a sugar maple a year ago. The buds on it never opened. I only see one small group of leaves near the base of the tree. My husband wants me to replace it with a new tree. What do you think?*

A: Sorry to say, your tree is as close to dead as it can be and still have leaves. The leaves that appeared close to the base are called *epicormic branches*. They are a tree's last gasp when it is under tremendous stress. I often see trees around newly built homes whose trunks are covered with epicormic branches. They have many dead limbs and will soon die due to root damage during construction. Give your husband the challenge of planting and caring for a new tree. He'll be delighted to dig a wide rootball and to baby it this summer.

353 Tree Stump – Killing

Q: *I want to kill a sweetgum stump. Every time I cut it down, sprouts reappear. How should I do it?*

A: Some trees and vines are impossible to kill just by cutting them down. Their roots and stump are primed to sprout after you cut off the main part of the plant. To prevent resprouting of mimosa, sweetgum, privet, or 'Bradford' pear, buy **glyphosate**[53] or **triclopyr**.[54] Immediately after cutting a sprout, use a disposable paint brush to paint undiluted herbicide on the cut stub. For large stumps, chop around the edge of the stump with a hatchet and paint the chemical there as well.

53. **glyphosate:** www.gardenword.com/glyphosate
54. **triclopyr:** www.gardenword.com/triclopyr

354 Plum – Black Knot

Q: *Many of the limbs and branches on my plum and cherry trees have hard, scaly cases encircling them. I've tried to cut into them, but it takes a strong knife. It's almost like they're part of the tree. What do you think it is?*

A: Your description sounds like the disease *black knot*. It is common on plums in Georgia. The fungus causes a hard, black crust around twigs. Infection occurs from April through June, especially on the current season's growth. Remove all knots and swellings by pruning 3 to 4 inches below the knot during the dormant season before April 1. Plan on using a preventative spray of lime-sulfur each year in winter. If more than half the tree limbs are infected, remove the tree.

355 Norway Spruce – Planting

Q: *I planted a 5-foot tall Norway spruce in my backyard in December. In the last few months, needles on some branches have turned brown and fallen off. Do you have any ideas on preventing further damage?*

A: When you purchased the tree, did the name "Norway spruce" not raise any questions in your mind about how well it would grow here? In my experience, all of the spruces, including Colorado blue spruce, Alberta spruce, and Norway spruce do not prosper except in the mountains of north Georgia.

356 Oak Sower Gall

Q: *We found a fuzzy, gall-like thing on an oak tree. It was white with brownish-red spots. Upon breaking it open, it has seeds inside and appears to have pierced the bark of the tree branch that it was surrounding. Any ideas?*

A: You found an *oak sower gall*. It formed in reaction to a tiny wasp laying her eggs on the bark of the oak twig. Tree tissue grew around the eggs, protecting them from predators. The seed-like things are actually capsules where the wasps develop. You can put the gall in a glass jar and wait for the wasps to hatch in a week or so. Since they are harmless to both humans and trees, simply release them when your curiosity is satisfied.

357 Oak – Slime Flux

Q: *My husband and I noticed some type of oozing lesion on our oak tree. Is there any way to protect other trees from this disease?*

A: My bet is that the tree has a common malady of oaks: *slime flux*. This bacterial infection of the trunk causes sap to ferment, leading to oozing goo on the bark. There are actually two types of slime flux: *alcoholic* and *acidic*. The acidic flux smells like vinegar. The alcoholic flux smells like beer. Other times you might find the foaming ooze by the large number of insects attracted to the sweet liquid. An infection can be caused by a wound on the trunk surface years ago.

There is no external treatment for the condition. The tree will attempt to "wall off" the damage internally. The best thing to do is to wash off the trunk to discourage bugs. Mix a pint of chlorine bleach in a gallon of water to make a final rinse. The flow of sap is often periodic; it may disappear and not reoccur or you may see it every year.

358   Pine – Fusiform Rust

Q: *My wife noticed orange powder dripping from a swollen limb on one of our pine trees. Do you have any idea what it is and how to treat it?*

A: The knots and orange powder are signs of *fusiform rust disease*. The orange spores will be blown by the wind to nearby oak tree leaves, where they will mature for a year. The developed spores infect young pine shoots or wounds on a limb or trunk. There are no fungicides available to treat fusiform rust. Your best course of action is to remove the infected limbs. Orange powder coming from the main trunk of a pine tree indicates an infection there. The trunk will be weakened at that point, and the whole tree will need to be removed in the future.

359   Pine Beetle – In Mulch

Q: *I had some pines cut down because they had pine beetles. Should the tree be sprayed with insecticide? Is it safe to use the shredded limbs and chips as mulch?*

A: The infested pine tree trunks should be removed from your property. If they are left on the ground, some of the beetles will continue to hatch and may attack other trees in your yard. Spraying an insecticide does not guarantee that all of the beetles will be killed. On the other hand, the shredded chips are safe to use. Pine beetles prefer feeding on the trunk, not on limbs. Even if some beetles are under the limb bark, the chipper machine will make short work of them.

360 Pine Needles – Excessive Acidity

Q: *I'm confused about mulching with pine straw. Don't pine needles acidify the soil?*

A: You're confusing causation with association. It's a common misconception that pine needles acidify the soil. Because pine trees can tolerate poor growing conditions, folks assume that their needles made the soil bad in the first place. I've known gardeners who fear that using pine straw as mulch under shrubs and trees will make the soil too acidic. Neither pine trees nor pine straw make soil unduly acid. It's true that decomposing leaves from *any* tree naturally release a small amount of organic acid. But soil chemistry is such that the effect of leaves on soil pH is not noticeable except over many, many years.

361 Tree – Reviving after Lightning Strike

Q: *A big pine tree next to my house was hit by lightning. It blew the bark off in a line 1 to 2 inches wide from the top to the bottom of the tree. Is there some hope it will live?*

A: It all depends on how much damage the exploding sap did under the bark. The damaged strip may not be all of the harm done since some may not be visible. Water deeply once per week during the summer. Trees respond to burns like humans do: they ooze constantly. You don't want your tree to dry up. In my experience, pines have a 50-50 chance of dying from a lightning strike, so you'll just have to wait and see what happens.

362 Pruning Trees in Fall

Q: *We have several limbs on big oak and pine trees that need to be cut off. My husband says it shouldn't be done until the sap is out of the limbs in December. I think it needs to be done now in August. What is your opinion?*

A: In my opinion, your husband is a smart man. Having spent a weekend cutting and hauling tree limbs to the curb in July, I can testify that cutting limbs in December would be a much more pleasant experience.

On the other hand, there is no reason that the job can't be accomplished in summer. A rule of thumb is that no more than $1/4$ of the total foliage on a woody plant should be taken away during the growing season. Your trees seem large enough that this should not be a problem. If you pledge to make plenty of lemonade for him and to position a big fan near his sawing area, I feel sure he will remove the limbs expeditiously.

363 Red Dogwood – Blooming White

Q: *Four years ago I planted a red dogwood. The first year it bloomed red, but afterward it has bloomed white. What's up?*

A: I'll bet the red dogwood was originally grafted onto a white dogwood rootstock. In the intervening years, branches from the white dogwood have vigorously sprouted and overwhelmed the red-flowering branches.

If you still have some red blooms, you can remove all of the white flowering branches now and encourage the tree to sprout more red blooming branches above the graft union. Fertilize in April, June, and September to maximize growth. Mulch widely under the tree, and don't neglect watering during drought.

TREES

364 River Birch – Bleeding

Q: *I asked a crew to remove a large branch from a river birch. The stump where the branch was removed has been "weeping" since it was cut. How am I to stop this tree from losing water or sap before it dries out and dies?*

A: Bless your heart, you can look for something else to worry about! The bleeding does absolutely no harm to the tree—it just upsets the owner. Several kinds of trees are famous for bleeding copious amounts of sap when pruned in the spring. Vermont farmers intentionally cut their trees to collect the sap that's made into maple syrup. The bleeding will stop in a few weeks and will not harm the tree.

365 River Birch – Leaf Drop

Q: *I have two river birch trees. Every summer most of the leaves turn yellow and fall off. They regrow but fall off again later in the summer.*

A: The name "river birch" indicates the environment this tree loves: moist riverbanks. When the soil around its roots gets dry, the tree quickly shows its unhappiness by dropping leaves. I see plenty of healthy river birches in full sunshine, but I also see many that respond like yours every summer. My guess is that the ones that drop leaves early have been planted in a soil situation that limits healthy root growth. The good news is that early leaf drop never seems to hurt a birch permanently. Next summer try soaking the soil under the drip line every week unless you get adequate rainfall.

366 Tree Planting – Remove Burlap

Q: *Should I totally remove the burlap around "balled and burlapped" tree rootballs?*

A: It's best to totally remove it. Burlap is often chemically treated to prevent it from rotting too soon at a nursery. Although it eventually deteriorates in the ground, it inhibits root growth. The best technique is to put the tree in its final position, then excavate far enough around the rootball so you can cut away all the burlap you possibly can. The same goes for wire caging, if present. You may need a hacksaw or bolt cutters to clip the thick wire, but research has shown that wire cages can damage roots as they grow through.

367 Royal Paulownia

Q: *I saw a newspaper ad for a royal paulownia that said, "Super-growing Flowering Shade Tree—Grows Roof High in Just One Year!" Is it a good tree for Georgia?*

A: The tree known as royal paulownia (*Paulownia tomentosa*) is a common, weedy, roadside tree with big hairy leaves. An acquaintance bought one a few years ago; on arrival it was barely 24 inches long. In twelve months it shot up to 15 feet tall. Because its limbs break easily, it isn't recommended as a landscape tree.

TREES

368 Sassafras

Q: *What do you know about sassafras tea? Is it safe to drink?*

A: I drank gallons of sassafras tea when I was a kid. I'd go up to a thicket of small trees we called "The Hut" and dig the roots of two or three sassafras saplings. Once home, I'd scour the roots with a brush to remove soil, then chop them into pieces that would fit in my mother's large boiler. We'd simmer the fragrant roots for an hour, then cool the liquor and add sugar to make a bracing springtime tonic. Unfortunately, scientists found that *safrole*, the main ingredient of the tea, caused cancer in animal tests. I don't drink it anymore, but I'm glad I had the experience when I was a kid.

369 Sycamore – Dead

Q: *I have a three-year-old sycamore tree. No leaves have appeared this spring; should I be concerned?*

A: In the words of the Monty Python parrot skit, your tree has "kicked the bucket"; it has "shuffled off its mortal coil"; it has "joined the choir invisible." In fact, it is "deceased!" That said, it's hard to know why it died. It could have been planted too deeply originally, or perhaps it dried out during the summer after planting. You'll have to replace it. May I suggest a nice red maple?

370 Tree – Planting on Steep Slope

Q: *I will be planting a tree on a steep slope. How much of the rootball should be exposed on the up and down sides of the hill?*

A: None! Planting a tree on a slope correctly is a laborious process because the rootball must be kept level with the surrounding soil. The soil where you are planting is sloped—but that doesn't mean you should plant the tree at an angle into the slope. Nor does it mean the rootball can be left "halfway in, halfway out" as you have suggested.

You have to terrace the slope to make it flat for an area 5 feet in diameter. The tree can be planted in the center of this flat area. Since you'll have to "cut in" to the slope to form the terrace, use a couple of firmly anchored treated timbers to hold back the upper slope. It would be a good idea to use more timbers below the terrace to hold it back and to protect the lower side from erosion.

T R E E S

371 Tree Roots – When Do They Grow?

Q: *During mild Atlanta winters are the roots of my young oak trees active, or does the entire tree shut down?*

A: Anytime the soil temperature is above 50 degrees F, a tree's roots can grow and absorb nutrients and moisture if it needs any. That said, since there are no leaves on your trees in winter, not much is needed by the trees, so the effect of winter moisture on tree growth is minimal.

372 Tree – Roots in Pipes

Q: *I have a river birch approximately three years old growing over the water pipes leading to my house. Are the roots of great concern?*

A: All trees act the same regarding water supply pipes: they ignore them unless the pipe leaks. Even then, the pressurized water in the pipe would not allow roots to invade. A tree root cannot tell the difference between a pipe, a stone, or a buried cannonball. A plumber can easily discover whether there is a slow leak between your source and your house.

Supply pipes are not usually the problem when tree roots are discussed. It is typically leaking sewage pipes that they invade. You have little to worry about if your sewage pipes are sealed PVC plastic or well-installed cast iron. Unless you suspect leaking pipes, leave the river birch in place.

TREES

373 | Tree Cavities – To Fill or Not to Fill?

Q: *An arborist has recommended inserting a pipe at an angle through the cavities in a large oak so that any water will exit the tree. Is this good for the tree?*

A: Current arboricultural thought is that drilling a cavity to drain it causes more problems than allowing the cavity to fill with water. Trees compartmentalize all wounds and openings with a thick, internal layer of hard-to-damage cells. Inserting a tube will break through the cell barrier the tree has already made, forcing the tree to further "wall off" the damage done by the drill. Standing water actually protects the wood because rot fungi cannot grow rapidly in an oxygen-poor environment.

On the other hand, water-filled tree cavities are very good homes to mosquitoes. If the cavities are far up the tree where you cannot treat them for mosquito larvae, an argument could be made to drain the cavities. However, if they are near the ground, you can put **mosquito larvicide**[55] in each one.

55. **mosquito larvicide:** www.gardenword.com/mosquito

374 Tree Wound Dressings

Q: *We have a large white oak that had a large chunk of bark knocked off. The wound is 12 inches wide × 30 inches high. What is the best way to treat this wound?*

A: A number of products are touted as "wound dressings" for trees. I believe that research has shown that tar, paint, and other sealants offer no help for a damaged tree. They retard the tree's own defenses, and they eventually crack and allow rot and insects to invade once again. A mature white oak would be very slow to heal over any wound on its trunk. It simply isn't growing very fast at trunk level and would not produce much callus wood. My recommendation is to clean loose bark from the wound area, perhaps spray the wound with gray paint to conceal it, and leave the tree to its own devices.

375 Trees – Fertilizing

Q: *How should I fertilize my trees—and when?*

A: In general, ornamental trees should be fertilized only when you want to stimulate them to grow larger. If a tree has reached the size you want, no fertilizer is necessary if you are regularly fertilizing the lawn beneath or near the tree. To help young trees grow faster, give them 1 tablespoon of 12-4-8 (or 16-4-8) per foot of height in March and again in July. Apply $1/3$ of the fertilizer beyond the drip line of the foliage since the roots of established trees extend out into this area.

376 Trees – For Screening

Q: *We need some evergreen bushes or trees for privacy and noise blocking from a roadside. They would be planted in an area that is shady most of the year. Any suggestions?*

A: Two candidates that come to mind are Carolina cherrylaurel and Canadian hemlock. Both are shade tolerant and will eventually grow tall enough to screen the roadway. Also consider wax myrtle, 'Nellie Stevens' holly, and perhaps a few camellias for color. If planted in a row along a property line, don't dig a hole for each plant. Instead, till a band of soil 4-feet wide for the length of the line. Plant at appropriate intervals in the tilled area. They will grow much faster in this way. Otherwise each plant needs a loosened area 6 feet in diameter.

377 Tulip Tree – Topping

Q: *I have a tall tulip poplar in my backyard that constantly drops limbs. I don't want to cut it down, so I'm thinking about topping it. Would this help the limb breakage problem?*

A: Topping your tree is a bad idea. Once you cut out the top of your tree, it will quickly sprout new branches near the cut and they will head for the sky. Since they are only weakly attached to the bark of the treetop, any future wind-, ice- or snowstorm has the potential to bring the limb crashing down. That's just what you are trying to avoid by topping the tree! In fact, you are caught between a rock and a hard place. You don't want to lose the tree's shade, but you're frustrated with a messy tree. All in all, your best course of action might be to keep the tree untopped and remember not to park or picnic underneath.

378 Cherry – Damaged Bark

Q: *I've had a weeping cherry for six years. It bloomed beautifully for three years, but the bark split wide last summer. It never bloomed and did not produce leaves until June.*

A: Remember the Black Knight in *Monty Python and the Holy Grail*? Even when both of his arms, and both legs, were cut off by Arthur, he was adamant that he would not die. "I'll bite your legs off!" he shouted as Arthur and Pansy passed. Your cherry reminds me of the Black Knight. Even with grievous wounds, it has refused to die so far. We aren't told the fate of the Black Knight, but I'd bet his end came soon after his appendages were removed. So it is for your tree: once the bark is severely damaged, the end comes rapidly. Your best course is to remove it and replace it with a healthy tree.

379 Weeping Cherry Tree – Propagation

Q: *I have been digging up the seedlings under a weeping cherry tree and giving them to friends and family. Will the seedlings be weeping cherry trees or just plain cherry trees?*

A: Since cherries don't often come up from seed, I believe you are digging root sprouts rather than seedlings. Weeping cherry trees are most often made by grafting Higan cherry (*Prunus subhirtella* var *pendula*) onto the trunk of another species. One of my friends has a gorgeous specimen formed by grafting weeping cherry branches onto a paperbark cherry (*Prunus serrula*) trunk. Paperbark cherry has glistening mahogany bark that peels into thin sheets of tissue. What a sight! Unless your tree is a true ungrafted weeping Higan cherry, I believe your plant gifts will grow into "cheerful" cherry trees.

380 Windmill Palm – Flower

Q: *I have a ten-year-old windmill palm that has gotten a bloom on it for the first time. In fact it has three separate airy masses. Are these seeds or what?*

A: The yellow sprays are not seed; they are flowers. A mature windmill palm will bloom each year. *If* your palm is female and *if* there is a male palm nearby, you'll get round, blue seeds in August. The seed can be collected and germinated by placing a few in a resealable plastic bag containing a 1:1 mixture of peat moss and perlite. Moisten the mixture slightly, seal the bag, keep it between 75 and 90 degrees F, and wait. If they're going to germinate, they will do so within a couple of months. Plant them in a protected spot while they are young, and you'll have a forest of windmills pretty soon!

381 Chinese Elm

Q: *I recently planted a large Chinese elm. When I was mulching afterward, I spotted a rope sticking out of the ground near the trunk. It looks like the rope was originally wrapped around the trunk and has strangled it. What should I do now?*

A: You should call the nursery where you purchased the tree and tell them to come pick it up and drop off a replacement. Your tree will never recover from the damage to the lower trunk. The rope should have been removed years ago. Unfortunately, it was hidden by soil when the tree was dug. Besides strangling the tree, the trunk will be weak at ground level. Your elm will snap off there sometime in the near future.

382 Austree (Aus-Tree)

Q: *Have you ever heard of Aus-trees? They are a hybrid and are supposed to be super fast-growing and good for shade and windbreaks. Will they do well here in Georgia?*

A: The Austree is heavily promoted through the mail and by magazine advertisements as being the solution to shade problems. They are actually a hybrid willow and, as such, do grow rapidly. However, rapid growth usually produces weak branches, and hybrid willows are no exception. These trees can grow 6 feet per year, but they are messy. They constantly drop small and large twigs, and the roots constantly send up sprouts under the tree.

Willows are a favorite food of tent caterpillars, and they are susceptible to canker diseases. They have some potential as a windbreak or a privacy screen if you have a very large property, but they are definitely not good landscape shade trees.

383 River Birch – Puckering Leaves

Q: *Each year the leaves on my river birch begin to pucker up like a ruffled potato chip. Is there anything I can do to get rid of this?*

A: I'll bet there are witchhazel shrubs somewhere in the neighborhood. *Witchhazel gall aphids* cause conical protrusions on witchhazel leaves. Winged aphids develop inside the galls, then leave and fly to birch trees. There, they give birth to scale-like insects, which feed and induce the birch to form corrugated galls on the leaves. This "potato-chip effect" is what you are seeing. This is mostly a cosmetic problem, but if it really bothers you, spray the birch leaves with landscape insecticide just as the leaves open each spring.

384 Osage Orange – Fruit

Q: *We picked up a strange fruit from the Confederate cemetery in Jonesboro. It is bright green and corrugated like a human brain. Could you identify it for us?*

A: When I worked for the Extension office in Clayton county, I could count on getting calls about this fruit/tree every fall. It is Osage orange (*Maclura pomifera*), aka bois d'arc (bodark), hedge apple, or monkey-brain tree. The fruit is not poisonous, but I wouldn't recommend that you eat it. Horses graze on them occasionally, and squirrels rip the centers out, but I don't think the pulp has much taste.

385 Leyland Cypress – Trimming

Q: *Twelve years ago we planted two Leyland cypress trees near a swimming pool. They are now approximately 25 to 30 feet tall. Can we trim these trees?*

A: Leyland cypress is trimmed to all shapes and sizes in England so you can certainly do the same here. The key is to do it gradually, no more than ¼ per year. The very best time would be in March, but you can safely do it any time, within reason. The top will look brown and flat for a few months, but it will green up again next year.

236

386 Leyland Cypress – Substitutes

Q: *What are some substitutes for Leyland cypress?*

A: I like plants that have a similar appearance and growth habit. My list would include:

- Japanese cedar (*Cryptomeria japonica*)
- Eastern red cedar (*Juniperus virginiana*)
- 'Green Giant' arborvitae (*Thuja standishii* × *plicata*)
- 'Emerald Green' arborvitae (*Thuja occidentalis*)

387 Leyland Cypress – Burned

Q: *Some meathead tossed a lit cigar onto my dormant bermudagrass lawn. It burned some of my grass and spread into the mulch under my Leyland cypresses. Some lower limbs of these trees burned before the fire was extinguished. Will they recover?*

A: You're lucky you have any Leyland cypresses left! These needled evergreens can go up in flames with a *whoosh!* if they are dry in summer. My guess is that the burned branches will not green up. You'll have an open spot where the damaged limbs once were. However, over the next few years, nearby limbs may send fresh greenery into the open area, looking for sunshine. My prediction is that unless the fire hurt the main trunk, the Leylands will gradually look less and less bad, and in a few years, you'll barely notice the damage.

388 Cedar Apple Rust

Q: *I have two 7-foot-tall Eastern red cedar trees. Both have growths that look like walnut meats on them. Is this cedar apple rust?*

A: Orange, jelly-like spore "gobs" were on the trees last spring, but you didn't notice them. The gall you notice now will be at the center of the fist-sized jelly mass in April/May. This particular disease travels back and forth between red cedar and apple trees. Both hosts are required for it to develop. Cedar apple rust is less harmful to cedars than apples, on which it causes leaf and fruit drop. If you value landscape apples and crabapples, remove all of the dried galls now.

389 Cherry – Autumnalis

Q: *We have an everblooming cherry tree in our front yard. This crazy tree will bloom in the winter, fall, and spring months. Any idea what it is?*

A: It's an 'Autumnalis' cherry (*Prunus subhirtella* 'Autumnalis'), which is well known to bloom in warm weather in the winter. I have one in my backyard, and it blooms merrily in January. 'Okame' cherry (*Prunus* 'Okame') is vaguely similar to 'Autumnalis' and blooms in early spring but doesn't seem as prone to blooming throughout the winter.

390 Cherry – Quick Death

Q: *In June we purchased an 8-foot-tall flowering cherry tree. When I unloaded it from my truck, the leaves had burned edges. I watered it daily after planting. It really took off and filled in nicely, but four weeks ago it started to turn brown and is now completely brown: no green at all. What's wrong?*

A: You've learned a painful lesson, I'm afraid. My guess is that the tree was weak when you bought it. It had been at the nursery too long, and they were probably glad to get rid of it. The windy trip home in your truck partially dried all the leaves and they fell off. The tree then used its last bit of energy to leaf out again. However, you were watering so much the roots rotted off. So it died . . . and that's the end of the story for your tree.

However, now you are wiser, and from this I hope you learn four things: (1) The best time to plant trees is in the fall, not early summer. (2) Never transport shrubs or trees uncovered in your truck. Cover them with burlap for the trip home. (3) Watering is a matter of good judgment. Soggy soil can kill a plant just like dry soil can. (4) Good gardeners become that way by learning from their mistakes. Wisdom comes from experience. One day you and I both will be very wise indeed!

TREES

391 Goldenrain Tree – Not Blooming

Q: *I planted a goldenrain tree four years ago. The bright yellow blooms I expected in June never happened. Will it ever bloom?*

A: My wife is an elementary school reading specialist. Practically every week she meets with parents who are concerned that their child is not reading yet. She carefully explains to them that there are several skills children must master before they are able to read. She reassures the parents that their child "will read when he/she is ready to read" and that different children finally acquire all the skills at different ages. In just the same way, plants have to acquire several different resources before they are ready to bloom.

Roots must be well established so they can send hormonal signals to the limbs to produce sufficient leaves. Limbs must be abundant enough to collect sunshine to create excess energy to supply to flowers and seeds. Soil moisture and nutrients have to be present in the correct amounts to maintain plant health.

Your goldenrain tree hasn't bloomed yet because it has not matured into a state that produces flowers on the limbs. Just as you can't force a child to read when they are not ready, you can't make a plant bloom before it is well prepared. Water your tree when the soil is dry, give it a few handfuls of fertilizer each spring, and wait for the inevitable. It *will* bloom when it is ready.

392 Dogwoods – No Blooms

Q: *I have some wild dogwoods in my yard that don't bloom very well. How can I make them bloom better?*

A: Have you ever marveled at reports that a Kentucky Derby winner is worth millions of dollars? Why would people pay millions for a horse that looks basically the same as those you see dotting the pastures of rural areas? The answer, of course, is that the genes of two similar appearing horses are completely different. The offspring of the race winner are likely to inherit speedy genes. The offspring of a rural horse might only inherit the ability to consume large amounts of hay and cracked corn.

Your wild dogwoods might be performing to the limits of their genetic potential and still only give you a few blooms each year. If they are growing in bright shade, have mulch spread widely around their trunks, and are fertilized lightly each year, you have done all you can do to *make* them bloom. That's why "named" dogwoods like 'Cloud 9', 'Cherokee Chief', and others make such superior plants in the long run. As with children, enjoy your wild dogwoods for what they are and don't try to make them what they're not!

393 Dogwood – Peak Bloom

Q: *Can you tell me when the dogwoods will be blooming in Atlanta? I have friends who want to come when they are at their height.*

A: My retired horticulturist friend Newton Hogg has forgotten more information about plants than I will ever know. One of the ways he stays so current is to make notes about garden phenomena each year. He has kept records of the dogwood flowers in his Decatur landscape since 1982. That year his dogwoods began opening on March 20 and were pretty well finished two weeks later. Studying his notes for every year since then, Newton concludes that somewhere between April 5 and April 15 you should have a dogwood display worthy of showing to your friends. If you are lucky, the azaleas will be flowering at the same time, and you'll knock their blooming socks off!

394 Leyland Cypress – Origin

Q: *Where did Leyland cypress come from? Is it a native plant?*

A: Leyland cypress isn't native anywhere! It originated as an unexpected cross between Alaska cedar (*Chamaecyparis nootkatensis*) and Monterey cypress (*Cupressus macrocarpa*). The parent trees are native to the North American Pacific coast. The seedlings were collected in Wales at the Leighton Hall arboretum in 1888. The beauty and rapid growth of these new hybrids caused them to be planted throughout England and Europe earlier this century. Leylands were first introduced in the South in 1965 at Brookgreen Gardens, South Carolina, and Clemson University. They are so easy to propagate and grow that nurseries have sold millions of them since. It's hard to believe these ubiquitous trees have been available less than fifty years in our part of the world.

395 Italian Cypress – Substitution For

Q: *We love the look of Italian cypress but not Leyland cypress. Is there a tall and cylindrical substitute that will grow here?*

A: Italian cypress (*Cupressus sempervirens*) is an extremely columnar tree. It can grow 30 to 50 feet tall while remaining only 3 feet wide. It often has problems with root rot and spider mites. I don't see many attractive ones. Look instead for 'Skyrocket' juniper or even 'Green Spire' Leyland cypress, which is much narrower than the Leylands you see so commonly planted.

396 Deodar Cedar – Dying

Q: *I have two large deodar cedars, planted around three years ago. One of the trees is beautiful, but the other one has slowly turned yellow, and the needles are dropping. What can you tell me?*

A: On my dad's chicken farm, we had only two kinds of hens: alive and dead. We rarely saw a sick chicken, because they went from happy clucking to stone cold stillness in just a few hours. Yellowing throughout a tree indicates a root or lower stem problem. If the sick deodar is planted where the root system stays wet all of the time, that would explain the problem: they don't care for wet feet. Conversely, summer heat and drought can also be fatal. Sadly, I don't hold much hope for your tree. I think it has uttered its last *cluck*.

TREES

243

397 Bradford Pear – Fruit and Thorns

Q: *There is a tree in our front yard that I always assumed was a Bradford pear. It blooms the same time, has a similar look, but it has berries. It also has thorns on it! Do Bradford pear trees have berries? If not . . . what do I have in my yard?*

A: 'Bradford' pear is a selection of a wild Asian pear (*Pyrus calleryana*) that has thorns. 'Bradford' usually has berries—some trees more than others. My bet is that your pear is a seedling that came up from a 'Bradford' fruit planted by a squirrel years ago. The seed's genetics were closer to its wild parent than to the 'Bradford', so it has thorns and berries and an unattractive shape. Remove it or enjoy it—your choice.

398 'Bradford' Pear Suckers – Controlling

Q: *A departed 'Bradford' pear tree valiantly clings to life by continuously sending up insidious suckers from the roots. How can I control them, short of a flamethrower?*

A: Get some **triclopyr**.[56] Paint it on the freshly cut stubs of the pear suckers. They won't resprout there again, but one or two might do so several feet away. This method is quick, easy, and effective. And triclopyr smells so much better than napalm in the morning!

---

56. **triclopyr:** www.gardenword.com/triclopyr

TREES

399 Redwood – Growing

Q: *Can I grow a redwood tree here?*

A: The coast redwood requires constant moisture from the fog banks along the California coast, so it would not grow here for very long. On the other hand, the dawn redwood grows just fine in Atlanta, if given moisture in the summer. It is a rapid grower, 80 to 100 feet tall, so plant it well back from the house. It is deciduous, but its form and color are beautiful in winter or summer. The tree is sometimes called a living fossil, since its leaf prints have been found along with fossilized animal remains. The first living tree was found in 1948!

400 Wooly Alder Aphid – Control

Q: *I have an elm tree that is covered with white stringy-looking things that move slowly. Do you know what they are?*

A: Some years there is a tremendous population explosion of small, white, wooly insects covering leaves and stems of maple, birch, and elm trees. These are *wooly alder aphids*. Profuse amounts of sticky liquid fall from the insects crawling in a tree. It covers walks, cars, and decks below. The aphids suck sap from the tree and excrete "honeydew." Surfaces on which the honeydew falls may turn black, as sooty mold grows on the sweet liquid. If they are really a problem for you, blast them out of the tree with a hose or spray with insecticidal soap, following label directions.

401 Noble Fir – For Christmas Tree

Q: *My favorite Christmas tree is the beautiful Noble fir. They are next to impossible to find. I want to grow my own in my backyard. Could you give me a suggestion where I could purchase a live one?*

A: Noble fir (*Abies procera*) is a gorgeous tree. It is densely evergreen and very symmetrical, but slow-growing, reaching 50 feet in fifty years. Unfortunately, its native range is almost exclusively the maritime forests of Oregon. You can occasionally find cut Noble fir trees for Christmas, but they are expensive because they have to be shipped from the West Coast. Fraser fir (*Abies fraseri*) is a popular Southern Christmas tree, but it only grows at elevations above 4,500 feet in the Southern Appalachians. Investigate cryptomeria (*Cryptomeria japonica*) or Canadian hemlock (*Tsuga canadensis*) as substitutes for Noble fir outdoors.

TREES

402 Tree Roots

Q: *Do tree roots come to the surface for air?*

A: Not exactly, but close. The best way to describe it is that roots grow in areas where there is sufficient air. If a young tree's roots can't penetrate hard clay soil, they creep along the surface nearby. As the tree matures, the roots grow bigger in diameter. The upper surface of major roots then slowly rises above the soil. Erosion washes soil away from the roots as well. Feeder roots at the end of the major roots, though, remain below the soil. So, roots *do* look for aerated soil, but I can't say they "come up for air." You can prevent surface roots by thoroughly loosening a 10-foot diameter circle of soil around the spot where you initially plant a tree.

403 Trees – Topping

Q: *I have three young maple trees that are very tall and skinny. Should I cut some of the top off to make the trees more full?*

A: Pruning the tops of the trees won't make them become fuller. The reason isn't intuitive, so a short explanation is in order. When you remove branch tips, you remove the source of hormones that regulate the growth of twigs nearby. If you top your trees, you'll see lots of little branches growing next summer within 12 inches of the cut. But the hormonal regulation doesn't extend down very far. Cutting the treetops will have no effect on lower, already growing branches. It is simply the nature of maples to grow tall first, and then more slowly fill out to become oval in shape. Leave the maples alone and let time make them full.

404 Tree Seedlings – Inexpensive

Q: *Does Georgia have a program to provide tree seedlings to residents?*

A: The Georgia Forestry Commission Reforestation Department sells several species of seedling trees, including dogwood, crabapple, red maple, and persimmon to suburban homeowners. Hardwood seedlings cost only a few dollars, plus shipping. Find out more by calling 1-800-GATREES.

TREES

405 Trees – Root Stability

Q: *Four years ago I transplanted some oaks from the woods into my yard. How long does it take for their roots to anchor the trees?*

A: I think four years is plenty of time. Vigorous new growth on the branches this year would be evidence that the roots have spread and started making new anchor roots. If the trees look healthy but have not grown much, keep a guying system in place another year. Remember that any time you guy a tree, it should be a loose system, not tight. The gentle swaying of the tree trunk stimulates root growth. Also, never use wire (even padded wire) or chain around the trunk. Nylon straps an inch wide are best to avoid trunk damage.

406 Tree – Bark Damage

Q: *My two-week-old 'Yoshino' cherry was doing great until the neighbor's goat scraped 2 feet of bark halfway around the trunk with his horns. What should I do?*

A: This is a case where you would be better off replacing the tree than trying to nurse it through the damage. The bark wound is so extensive that no amount of treatment will ever fix it. The tree will be permanently weakened above the damaged area. 'Yoshino' cherry is easy to find at garden centers. Do yourself a favor and plant another . . . and put a fence around it!

407 Tree – Survival Watering

Q: *I have several dogwood trees that lost their leaves during the drought. Are they going to be dead next year?*

A: It's never good when a tree loses its leaves during the growing season. If your dogwoods were healthy this spring and defoliated simply due to no water during high heat, they may come back just fine next spring. Scrape twigs with your fingernail to see if there is green underneath. Practice *survival watering* during times of drought by applying 2 gallons of water for every inch of trunk diameter (measured at $4^{1}/_{2}$ feet above the ground) for each day between individual waterings. Example: a 10-inch-diameter tree watered three days ago would need 60 gallons of water slowly applied at the drip line.

408 'Bloodgood' Maple – Turning Green

Q: *I planted a 'Bloodgood' Japanese maple in spring. The tree made it through the summer in fine shape, except the red leaves faded to green. What gives?*

A: 'Bloodgood' typically fades to a combination of red and green by July. The amount of fade depends on where the tree is sited in your landscape. More shade equals more of a green tint to the leaves. Learn to expect this each year; the leaves will still turn bright crimson each fall.

409   Hemlock – Wooly Adelgid

Q: *We have property in north Georgia with quite a few hemlock trees. We noticed some of the branches dying in a few of the trees, and now a lot of the trees are in decline. What's happening?*

A: I'm afraid your hemlocks may be afflicted with hemlock wooly adelgid, an invasive aphid-like insect native to Japan. Thousands of Appalachian hemlocks have been killed by this pest. Hemlock stands are among the only old growth forests in the East, and are of great importance to wildlife and water quality. Research has shown that a tiny Japanese ladybug has a huge appetite for adelgids. Activists are raising money to fund a laboratory for raising the predator beetles. You can protect individual trees by spraying with **horticultural oil**[57] in April or by drenching the roots with a **systemic insecticide**.[58]

410   Sawtooth Oak – Not Recommended

Q: *We have some oak trees that drop a plethora of acorns. The caps on these acorns are like "mop heads"; they have bristles sprouting out. What kind of oaks are these?*

A: The trees are probably sawtooth oak (*Quercus acutissima*). It is native to Asia and has been planted in numerous places for ornament and to attract wildlife. Unfortunately, the "mop-head" acorns sprout so vigorously that this invasive tree has the potential to drive out native plants. The native chestnut oak (*Quercus prinus*) would be a better choice.

57. **horticultural oil:** www.gardenword.com/hortoil
58. **systemic insecticide:** www.gardenword.com/systemicinsecticide

411 Bark Damage – Care

Q: *A grading machine backed into our poplar tree and scraped a section of the bark off. The interior of the tree was not damaged, but loose bark is left hanging. What should I do now?*

A: Use a razor knife to cut the shredded bark back to where it adheres tightly to the trunk. Sensing the exposure to air, the tree will "wall off" the wound and begin trying to seal over the damage. Do not coat the injury with tar. Thick coatings eventually allow insects and fungus to hide next to the sapwood. You can use brown spray paint to make the inner wood less noticeable.

412 Catalpa – Control Caterpillars

Q: *We have a 25-foot-tall catalpa tree that we want to use as shade and not as a source of fish bait. Each year it has thousands of worms that eat all the leaves and leave a nasty mess under it. What will control them?*

A: The easiest way to kill any type of caterpillar is with products that contain **B.t.**[59] Your biggest problem is how you'll get the spray up in the tree. If you have good water pressure, use one of the long-necked, hose-end sprayers designed for trees. Apply insecticide to the catalpa in late June and repeat every two weeks until late August.

59. **B.t.:** www.gardenword.com/bt

413 Longleaf Pine – Identification

Q: *I was at Callaway Gardens recently and noticed distinctive pine trees growing near the road. It has long needles but is short, just a couple of feet tall, and looks like a bottlebrush. Do you know it?*

A: You saw longleaf pines (*Pinus palustris*). Garden designers have been using the young form—which looks sort of like Cousin Itt from *The Addams Family*—as a design element for several years now.

Hundreds of years ago, the southern half of Georgia was covered with longleaf pine, in association with wiregrass. The pine/wiregrass prairies supported an incredibly complex and productive ecosystem. The pines have been extensively harvested, such that there are now few pine-wiregrass examples in the state. Left to grow naturally, the seedlings you saw will eventually grow 50 to 100 feet tall.

414 Mock Orange – Identification

Q: *I have a bush in my yard that produces dogwood-tree-type flowers in the spring. The elderly lady who propagated it years ago told me that it is an English dogwood. What do you think?*

A: You have a mock orange (*Philadelphus coronarius*). It grows into a large shrub, 8 to 10 feet tall with lots of stiff, upright branches. The fragrant flowers in spring draw attention to it, but the plant is relatively nondescript for the rest of the year. Mock orange rarely needs pruning except to remove dead branches. It doesn't require much fertilizer after maturity. Throw a handful of 10-10-10 under it every couple of years and it will be happy.

415 Sweetgum – Eliminating Balls

Q: *I heard there is a way to stop sweetgum trees from dropping their spiny balls. What is it?*

A: The spiky seed pods of the sweetgum tree are a nuisance to many gardeners. It is theoretically possible to eliminate the balls each year, but it is a difficult process. The chemical **ethepon**[60] releases ethylene gas when it is sprayed onto the tree branches. Ethylene gas is a powerful plant hormone. If the tree is flowering when the chemical is applied, the gas will cause the flowers to drop off. Voila! The tree will be neutered for the year.

Unfortunately, the entire tree must be sprayed each year, and spraying at the right flower stage is critical. Most people find the effort too difficult.

Another alternative for you is to cut down the offending tree and plant a fruitless sweetgum, *Liquidambar styraciflua* 'Rotundiloba', in its place. As you know, the tree is fast-growing, and it offers lots of summer shade when mature.

T
R
E
E
S

60. **ethepon:** www.gardenword.com/ethepon

416 Arbor Day – Celebrating

Q: *Would you please give me the date for Arbor Day?*

A: Arbor Day is celebrated in Georgia on the third Friday of February.

Besides local schoolyard celebrations, Trees Atlanta (**www.treesatlanta.org**) usually hosts several activities. National Arbor Day is the last Friday in April, but several states, like Georgia, celebrate in accordance with their own spring season. You can get more information at **www.arborday.org**.

417 Tree – For a Memorial

Q: *In January, my wife and I suffered a fetal demise in the middle of our pregnancy. We want to plant a tree as a memorial to our unborn child. Could you suggest a tree that would symbolize both strength and beauty?*

A: I'm truly sorry to hear your news. I'll pray for courage for you both. I don't know whether you'd rather honor the date of passing or the planned date of birth. Not many things are blooming in January, but a coral bark maple has intense red bark in winter. White is often used for memorials. I'm sure you've thought of dogwood, but you might also look at Kousa dogwood ('Celestial', 'Constellation', etc). It blooms in May/June as opposed to our common flowering dogwood in April. Another small tree I like is fringe tree (*Chionanthus virginicus*). It is covered with white flowers in May. I gave one to my mother for Mother's Day.

VINES & GROUND COVERS

Q&A

418 Clematis – Wilt

Q: *I have a two-year-old evergreen clematis that is climbing on my garage. In the last couple of months, it has started to turn brown at the ends of the vine, and the leaves are turning yellow. What could be wrong?*

A: My experience with evergreen clematis (*Clematis armandii*) is the same as yours: sometimes parts of it die for no apparent reason. The good news is that mine has come back faithfully after each of these harrowing episodes. There is no fungicide registered for control of the wilt. If your vine is healthy, it will very likely come back again like mine does. If you plant another one, install it deeply, with 2 or 3 inches of the lower vine covered in well-draining, loose soil. In this way, if the top of the plant dies, there will be healthy nodes belowground, which will sprout anew.

419 Clematis – Pruning

Q: *When and how should I prune my two clematis? Both are older vines, one purple and the other white.*

A: The question of when to prune is determined by whether the particular clematis blooms on *second-year wood* (growth from the previous season) or on new growth and, further, if it blooms early or late. *Early-blooming clematis:* Prune lightly in early spring so as not to destroy the dormant flower buds. *Late-blooming clematis:* Prune hard in early spring so the plant can produce strong growth on which blooms will develop later.

If an early-blooming clematis has developed into a tangled mess, cut it down to below the tangle in spring. Close to the ground is fine, but don't cut into the larger woody stems. Your clematis should recover by the end of the growing season and produce good blooms next year.

420 Cypress Vine – Invasiveness

Q: *Can you tell me anything about cypress vine? I have some seed but want to know how invasive it is before planting.*

A: Cypress vine (*Ipomoea quamoclit*) is one of the "nicer" invasive vines. You can readily identify the airplane-shaped leaves when they come up in spring. They are easy to spot and pull. The tubular red flowers of summer are very attractive to hummingbirds. In my experience, you can grow them in one spot, where they will reseed each year, and eliminate escapees as they are seen.

421 Porcelain Berry Vine

Q: *We have a vine that has killed a dogwood tree in our yard. The leaves look like grape leaves (but smaller), and it has small blue-black berries. What is it?*

A: I'll bet you have a porcelain berry vine (*Ampelopsis brevipedunculata*). Don't the blue berries look like porcelain to you? I've seen it sold in nurseries, but as you have discovered, it quickly escapes and becomes a pest. Birds love the seed and scatter them far and wide. The variety 'Elegans' has green leaves splashed with pink and white, but it is just as invasive as its solid green parent. Cut the vine at its base and paint the stump with non-selective herbicide. The roots will sprout again nearby so keep an eye out for them and treat similarly until all are dead.

Q: *Skunk vine is becoming a real gardening problem in south Georgia. It is spreading from the woods into and over our azaleas, Indian hawthorn, and others. What can we do?*

A: Skunk vine (*Paederia foetida*) is a serious problem in Florida and south Georgia, and is spreading elsewhere. It smells so bad that some have nicknamed it the "human gas vine." A **non-selective herbicide**[61] will kill it, but this will kill ornamental plants living under the vine too.

    If you don't have too much of the stinky weed, you could clip it at the soil line and dab non-selective herbicide on the stump so it doesn't resprout. Otherwise, take a tour of your property every week with a sprayer of herbicide in hand. Natural controls eventually may be found . . . but for right now, only *you* are skunk vine's enemy.

423 **Tater Vine (Air Potato) – Identification and Control**

Q: *I have a problem with a lovely but horribly invasive vine that grows little potatoes on its stem. It sprouts and spreads like a demon! What is it, and what can I do about it?*

A: Most folks afflicted with this pest call it "tater vine" or "air potato." It is actually a variety of yam, scientifically identified as *Dioscorea bulbifera*. The glossy green leaves are certainly ornamental, but the vine's intrusive nature has placed it very near the top of my invasive plant list.

    Like kudzu, air potato has a large starchy root. The root stores plenty of energy for resprouting if the leaves are cut off. A non-selective herbicide would give you fair results immediately, but you'll need to reapply the chemical every time the leaves reappear. You will have to protect other plants from the chemical spray, but I think this is the best choice you have.

61. **non-selective herbicide:** www.gardenword.com/nonselective

424 Fence – Hiding with Vines

Q: *My next-door neighbor has put up a chain-link fence, which I find hideous! I really want to hide it; what do you suggest?*

A: I use evergreen clematis (*Clematis armandii*) for this purpose, and it has done very well over several years. Severe cold has damaged it a couple of times, but it sprouted back immediately and vigorously. It sports white, slightly vanilla-scented flowers in April. Another suggestion is cross vine (*Bignonia capreolata* 'Tangerine Beauty'). It is generally evergreen in Georgia and has red-orange flowers in late April. Still another choice is Confederate jasmine (*Trachelospermum jasminoides*). Its fragrant white flowers in May are pure heaven to smell.

425 Hyacinth Bean – Saving Seed

Q: *I bought some grape hyacinth seeds when I visited Monticello because I liked the color of the flowers. I planted them, and now the plant has produced a large, purple bean pod. Can I save the seed and plant them next year?*

A: I think you misspoke when you called them "grape hyacinth seeds." Monticello is famous for the arbors covered with hyacinth bean (*Dolichos lablab*) vines. The same plant is sometimes called *Thomas Jefferson bean*. The seeds are quite attractive: black with a white stripe along the top. The vines bloom from July through October and produce bright purple bean pods containing three or four seeds. You can certainly save the seeds once the pods have turned brown after the first frost. Keep them in a cool place until next May, then plant them where you can enjoy them once again outdoors.

426 Ivy – Removing from Brick

Q: *We recently purchased a house that has a wild covering of ivy on the brick walls and siding. How can I remove the ivy without damaging the restored masonry underneath?*

A: Allowing ivy to grow on walls is a bad idea. The foliage holds damaging moisture close to the wall and allows critters to crawl into windows. My best advice is to first cut the main vine trunks where they come out of the ground. The ivy on the house walls will eventually die. However, you should pull off the ivy now. In my experience, the vines pull away from surfaces best when they are young and flexible. If you wait until they are brittle, the vine will shatter as you pull, and it will be a tedious job to remove them.

The Brick Institute of America says you can wait for the remaining ivy hold-fasts to dry for a few weeks and then scrub them off the brick with a brush. They caution against letting the tendrils stay on the wall for long, warning that if the rootlets are left alone too long, they will rot and oxidize, becoming nearly impossible to remove.

427 Jack (Sword) Bean

Q: *A friend got some bean seed from his dad, who told him to plant them and they would do great. I think the word* **great** *is an understatement. The beans hanging from the vines are 12 inches long! According to him, they are good eating. Is that true?*

A: Your friend has either a jack bean or a sword bean. The two look about the same, but the "eye" of a sword bean is greater than $1/2$ the length of the seed. They are reported to be edible in the young stage but can cause *great* indigestion when eaten at maturity. The best use of the beans is for telling stories to children!

Q: *Please settle a family argument! I say kudzu has flowers; they say it does not. Who is right? And how do I control it?*

A: How would there be baby kudzu if there were no seed?! Kudzu certainly has flowers: they are small, purple, and appear in late summer. The smell reminds many people of grape Kool-Aid™. The kudzu beans that appear later have been consumed for centuries in the Orient. They are quite tasty stir-fried!

I must confess that my grandfather, Walter Cowart, was a hearty promoter of kudzu in its heyday. But where this noxious vine is concerned, I decline to honor my elders. If kudzu had been around during the Civil War, Atlantans could have planted it on the approach routes to the city and handily tripped up Mr. Sherman and his troops.

Fall is a great time to spray a non-selective herbicide on kudzu. The leaves are much more apt to take the chemical deep into the vine's root system. February is another good time to chop down all kudzu vines on your property so you can gain access to every part of its range in May. Spray the leaves when they are the size of your hand, then respray any remaining sprouts in September.

429 Kudzu – Other Uses

Q: *What's the holdup on using kudzu to power cars? Think how many problems this would solve: no pollution, no foreign oil dependence, no oil slicks, no drilling—the list is endless!*

A: Not to mention the culinary merits of this eminently edible vine! I once made a tasty kudzu leaf tempura for my family. Although it looks like kudzu makes massive amounts of growth, in reality it yields only 2 to 3 tons of dry matter per acre, compared to the 3 to 4 tons per acre bermudagrass hay gives farmers. Also, just a few years of heavy harvests will decimate a kudzu stand, unlike hay crops. Harvesting is also a problem. I imagine the technique of growing the vine on telephone poles, as hop vines are grown in Germany, could be adapted to our needs. Your idea has merit. We just need a George Washington Carver of kudzu!

430 Mandevilla – Winter Care

Q: *I have a five-year-old mandevilla growing on my mailbox. How can I keep it alive during winter?*

A: Mandevilla is not difficult to keep alive from year to year if you have a place to keep it above freezing in winter. Vines can be pruned away from their trellises in late October and cut back to 10 inches tall. Drop the root system into a large pot and put it where it does not freeze. Water it once or twice in winter to keep the soil from drying completely. You can plant it outdoors in May when the ground is warm.

431 Bougainvillea – Winter Hardiness

Q: *My wife and I bought a bougainvillea basket at a flower show. Is it possible to plant bougainvillea in the ground? Will it come back next year?*

A: Bougainvillea definitely won't live outdoors in the winter in Atlanta. You have to keep it indoors until late April, then place it in bright shade outdoors. It will grow huge by fall if you keep it fed and watered regularly. At that time you'll have to chop off most of the stems in order to bring it back inside. Put it in front of a sunny window for winter. Don't feed it, but water when the soil gets dry. Repeat the process each year.

432 Ornamental Sweet Potato – Coverage Area

Q: *How big does an ornamental sweet potato vine grow? I have a 'Blackie' sweet potato planted in a large pot, and it must cover 30 square feet of my deck!*

A: Any gardener who has grown sweet potatoes knows that they are not a shy and timid plant. We are lucky that sweet potatoes are only annuals in Georgia, or we would have another rival for kudzu! An edible sweet potato uses its considerable area of foliage to gather the sunshine that makes for large underground tubers. Ornamental sweet potatoes generate comparatively minuscule tubers as they direct all of their energy into their vines. Other than in neighborhood conversation, there is no national registry for the largest ornamental plants. One Atlanta garden writer owns a 'Margarita' sweet potato that has climbed up a 3-foot picket fence, cascaded down the other side, crawled down a 5-foot bank, and seems headed for the street. Keep your feet moving when you walk past your plant!

433 Ornamental Sweet Potato – Edible?

Q: *Can you eat the potatoes from an ornamental sweet potato vine? They look just like sweet potatoes from the grocery.*

A: Sure you can eat them. And you'll get 200 percent of your daily roughage requirements in the bargain! Ornamental sweet potatoes are the same species as the edible kind, but they have been selected for their interesting foliage, not their tasty roots. You can save the tubers in a cool, dry spot until next March. At that time place them in wet sand to induce sprouts. The sprouts can be planted in warm garden soil when they are 6 inches long.

434 Passion Vine – Identifying

Q: *In summer where I grew up, there were wild vines that bloomed similar to passion vine. They produced a globe-shaped fruit we called maypop. As kids, we'd throw the ripe fruits at each other like bombs. The fruits were edible—they tasted slightly sweet and contained lots of seeds. Is this wild maypop vine the same as passion vine?*

A: Your memories coincide with mine. Maypops made *great* ammunition for war games in abandoned fields! Maypop and passionflower are the same: *Passiflora incarnata*. It produces the edible fruit we pitched so passionately. Like morning glory vine, the seeds of passionflower sprout in abundance. It sometimes becomes an easy-to-control weed. Passionflower foliage is food for Zebra longwing, Julia, and Gulf fritillary butterflies. Observant gardeners have selected improved cultivars of this and other species, including 'Lavender Lady', 'Blue Crown', and 'Ruby Glow'. The frilly flowers, in shades of blue to purple-red, are quite ornamental.

435 Queen Anne's Pocket Melon

Q: *I propagate pomegranates as a hobby. I am quite familiar with the shrub that bears large fruit filled with sticky red seeds each fall. My question concerns a plant everybody in north Georgia calls a pomegranate, but it grows on a vine. The fruit is Ping-Pong-ball-sized, orange in color, and loaded with seed. The most outstanding trait is the very strong incense-like odor. Do you know what it is?*

A: I don't know what it is, but I am fortunate to have a friend who does. Dr. Wayne McLaurin, an organic database of esoteric plants and their common names, says you have a Queen Anne's pocketbook melon. It is a close relative of the grocery store muskmelon. It is called "pocket" melon because in Victorian times the ladies would carry them in their pockets as "perfume," since deodorant had not yet been invented. The scientific name of your vine is *Cucumis melo* var. *Dudaim*. It is also known as pomegranate melon—which explains why your neighbors call it a pomegranate. Its third name is stink melon—because it was used by old timers to mask certain odors in the bathroom.

Q: *We are in the process of building a new house and will have a large, steep bank dividing the yard from the road. What can you recommend for a fast, low-growing, attractive ground cover for this area?*

A: Keep in mind that fast-growing plants can also be invasive. Also remember that *no plant* will thrive unless the soil is enriched around its roots. Make a "pocket" for each plant on the bank using three bricks laid end-to-end, parallel to the contour of the bank. Add two shovelfuls of soil conditioner to the spot and mix it 6 inches deep before planting.

For Sun

- Spreading juniper (*Juniperus chinensis, J. communis, J. conferta, J. horizontalis*); forsythia (*Forsythia intermedia*); Carolina jessamine (*Gelsemium sempervirens*); winter jasmine (*Jasminum nudiflorum*); creeping raspberry (*Rubus pentalobus*); Saint John's-wort (*Hypericum calycinum*)

For Part Shade

- Green 'n' gold (*Chrysoganum virginianum*); ground cover strawberry (*Fragaria* cvs. 'Lipstick', 'Pink Panda'); mondo grass (*Ophiopogon japonicus*); monkey grass (*Liriope muscari*)

Invasive Unless Controlled

- Spreading liriope (*Liriope spicata*); English ivy (*Hedera helix*); periwinkle (*Vinca minor* or *Vinca major*); wintercreeper (*Euonymus fortunei*)

Ground Cover Roses

- *Rosa* 'Carefree Delight'; *Rosa* 'Flower Carpet Appleblossom'; *Rosa* 'Flower Carpet Red'; *Rosa* 'Flower Carpet White'; *Rosa* 'Magic Carpet'; *Rosa* 'Fire Meidiland'; *Rosa* 'Magic Meidiland'; *Rosa* 'White Meidiland'

VINES & GROUND COVERS

437 Ground Cover – Alternatives to Turfgrass

Q: *I am curious about using plants other than grasses for an open area in my backyard. What do you think about growing cover crops such as crimson clover or subterranean clover?*

A: I applaud your curiosity, but I don't think clover will satisfy you. Crimson clover (*Trifolium incarnatum*) is a gorgeous plant when it blooms along the medians of Georgia highways. However, ask yourself, "Have I seen any crimson clover plants along the highway in July?" The answer is "No!" Crimson clover is an annual plant. It germinates in fall, grows through the winter, flowers in spring, sets seed in early summer, then dies. However, its seed does not germinate again readily.

Subterranean clover (*Trifolium subterraneum*) is also an annual, but it buries its seed underground, making it more likely to reseed itself. However, light rains in August often cause the seed to germinate early, and they then die if not given regular moisture.

438 Ground Cover – For Dry Shade

Q: *I would like to put a ground cover in dry shade under an oak, but my husband thinks all ground covers are invasive. Are there any evergreen ground covers that would work?*

A: It is good that your husband is cautious about invasive ground covers. English ivy, dwarf bamboo, and wintercreeper euonymous create virtual green deserts where they are allowed to spread without control. For situations like yours, I am particularly fond of Lenten rose (*Helleborus orientalis*) and mondo grass (*Ophiopogon japonicus*). Both are tough as nails and evergreen but noninvasive. The Lenten rose has attractive flowers from January through April. You'll need to carefully loosen the soil between the roots of the oak and add good quality planting soil to the area before planting.

If you can snake a soaker hose among the plantings, you could include hosta, variegated Solomon's seal, and ferns to the shady spot. Watering in the summer will benefit both your perennials and your oak tree.

439 Poison Ivy vs. Poison Oak

Q: *Does Georgia have poison oak plants?*

A: Poison oak (*Toxicodendron pubescens*) does grow in Georgia, but it is *much* less common than people think. Poison oak leaves tend to have rounded lobes rather than pointed lobes; it always grows as a shrub. Poison ivy (*Toxicodendron radicans*) has leaf lobes that are usually pointed, and it typically grows as a vine. However, when it can't find a tree to climb, poison ivy makes a shrub-like mound. In my experience, most folks who think they've found poison oak are really looking at poison ivy.

440 Poison Ivy – On Dead Tree

Q: *A large dead pine tree at the edge of our property fell recently. All that had been growing on it was a massive poison ivy vine. The base of the vine was at least 12 inches around. We now have about 50 feet of poison ivy tree on the ground with a lot of berries. How can we safely get rid of it?*

A: Whatever you do, always keep in mind that the poison ivy irritant oil is still on the leafless stems, the hairy vine itself, and probably the pine tree trunk as well. The oil is very persistent, so you can't just wait until spring and cut things up then. The best suggestion I have is to wear old clothes, old shoes, and rubber gloves while you carefully prune away the vine and stems. Place them in plastic garbage bags as you work. Once the tree is stripped of vine, use a chain saw to cut it into manageable pieces. The sawyer should wear disposable clothing and preferably a full face shield like a dentist uses. Dispose of all clothing (including shoes) afterward, and take a careful bath using lots of soap.

441 Vinca – Dieback

Q: *The vinca patch in my yard has a fungus that makes the stems turn black. The leaves are first yellow and then turn brown. It appears in patches with no specific pattern. Is there anything I can do to stop it?*

A: Your vinca has *Rhizoctonia dieback*. It's a common disease when vinca foliage is regularly wet from rain or is in the path of rainwater. About all you can attempt is to keep the foliage as dry as possible. Hot weather usually stops the disease's progression. If you *must* do something, spray with fungicide each month and give the whole patch a light feeding with 10-10-10 in April.

442 Wisteria – Make It Bloom

Q: *Let me tell you how my grandfather used to make a wisteria bloom. Each fall he would stand on his shovel blade and slice through the wisteria roots a foot away from the plant. It would bloom the next year every time. How does that work?*

A: Your grandfather was carrying on the tradition of stressing a plant to make it bloom. Hundreds of years ago, monks would beat the trunks of their apple trees with canes to make them produce more fruit.

Whether you chop the roots or wound the bark, a plant responds to damage by producing hormones that affect growth and fruiting. The biggest pecans I ever saw came from a tree that had been struck by lightning early one summer. That tree "knew" that it wasn't long for this world, so it poured all of its reproductive energy into its autumn crop of nuts. It was dead the following spring.

MAINTENANCE
Q&A

443 Almanac – Planting by the Signs

Q: *My grandmother wants to garden again, and she's looking for a garden almanac so she'll know when the signs are right to plant. Can you recommend one?*

A: There are several competitors in the garden almanac genre. The nationally distributed *Old Farmer's Almanac* (**www.almanac.com**) advertises that it has been around for 182 years. But I think you are looking for the locally produced *Grier's Almanac* (770-395-6381), which features an anatomically correct gentleman displaying the zodiac signs and their supposed relation to proper planting. Some gardeners swear by planting root crops, leaf crops, and flower crops according to the relation of the moon, the sun, and the planets. Others would rather plant by the day of the week. I fall into the latter camp, preferring Saturday and Sunday and sometimes Friday afternoon. Everyone has their method. If your grandmother finds success in planting by the signs, more power to her!

444 Artillery Fungus – Identification

Q: *We have a lovely patio with hardwood mulch in nearby flower beds. This past fall we started noticing pinhead-sized tar spots on our patio furniture and privacy fence. We have tried removing these spots with strong cleaning products to no avail. What can we do?*

A: I think the spots are caused by *artillery fungus*, also called *shotgun fungus*. It forms extremely small (0.1 inch) balls on decaying leaves and mulch and ejects spores in tiny globs that tightly adhere to nearby surfaces. Occasionally stirring the mulch adjacent to the fence and patio will keep it dry. Since the fungus discharges toward light-colored surfaces, cover the area near the patio and fence with pine straw.

445 Compost – Controlling Ants

Q: *How do I keep ants out of my compost without harming the good critters?*

A: If you keep the piles damp and if you turn it occasionally, ants won't be able to set up permanent housekeeping. They might build a mound at the edge of the pile, but they don't like living in a moist environment. Further, ants can be a valuable part of a healthy compost pile. They, along with centipedes and beetles, feed on smaller consumers, like springtails, which in turn eat the fungi and bacteria that decompose your leaves and yard debris. Ants help by distributing nutrients throughout the pile. If ants become a nuisance, apply a gel ant bait product nearby.

446 Compost – Tree Roots In

Q: *Tree roots are growing all up into my compost from the ground. Can you tell me how to stop this?*

A: This as an excellent demonstration of how much plants love compost. A nearby tree has discovered your pile and made itself at home. The solution is actually pretty simple. Remove all of the crumbly compost in the pile and spread it around nearby flowers. If some parts of the pile haven't fully decomposed, put them to the side. Now, and in the future, just make a 2-inch-thick layer of small sticks on the ground before you pile on the fall leaves. The sticks will keep the compost supported above the roots until it is completely rotted. I suspect that you haven't been removing compost fast enough (every three months or so). If you do, the tree roots won't get the chance to invade.

447 Compost – Starter Products

Q: *Can you help me find a product that will act as an accelerator for grass clippings in a compost pile?*

A: I don't believe you need such a product. Usually a shovelful of brown dirt from under old trees or some compost or composted cow manure will start and fuel the composting process handily.

448 Compost – Using Shredded Paper

Q: *I work out of my home office and shred considerable amounts of paper, which I would like to use in amending my garden soil. Is office paper usable?*

A: I see no problem at all with composting shredded paper. The ink is carbon- and soybean-based nowadays. You can compost *anything* that is organic in nature: shredded paper, shrimp shells, peanut hulls, etc. All that matters to the bacteria and fungi who perform the composting operation is that they get the moisture and oxygen they need. The problem you'll face in composting the shredded paper is keeping it from matting together and excluding oxygen from the creatures who want it.

If you had unlimited time and muscle power, you could flip the pile every day or two until the microbes did their work. Guessing that this is not what you have in mind, I'd say that a better use of the paper is as mulch under your shrubs and trees. Spread it out, wet it down, and cover it with a bit of pine straw. The resulting paper maché will prevent weeds better than most other mulches but will let water and fertilizer through just fine.

449 Compost – Using Fertilizer

Q: *To make compost, I have no difficulty gathering plenty of brown material like dried leaves and wood chips, but I can't seem to find enough green material to make up a 2:1 green/brown ratio. What can I use?*

A: Anything green will work well, but you could also add a half-cup of 10-10-10 per cubic foot of brown material and get a similar composting effect. In my experience, the ratio between brown and green material is not critical, within reason. It *is* critical that the two materials be mixed with moisture and oxygen in the pile. In addition, the pile needs to be large enough to maintain the heat of composting, approximately 3 feet × 3 feet × 3 feet to 5 feet × 5 feet × 5 feet.

450 Composter – Purchasing

Q: *My wife and I are trying to decide on an economical composter. Do you have any suggestions on the best one to purchase?*

A: It all depends on your sense of aesthetics, your space, and your wallet. If you have a small space in which to put the composter, the upright plastic bins work fine. If you want compost quickly, the tumbler-type units rapidly mix and aerate your landscape debris, but they are a bit unsightly. If you don't want to spend too much and you have a place to hide it, buy a 10-foot length of 4-foot wide fencing and roll it into a wire compost barrel. Composting is simple: "Pile it up and let it rot," then feed your plants with the results.

451 Composting – Fruit Flies

Q: *I am a recent convert to composting. My challenge is my covered kitchen waste receptacle. I put in fruit and vegetable trimmings, coffee grounds, tea bags, egg shells, and even dryer lint. But as the five-liter container fills, I develop fruit flies. What can I do to eliminate this nuisance?*

A: Your enthusiasm is commendable, but your composting receptacle is too big for your waste production. You either need to cook and eat more (or invite more friends to your meals) or get a smaller container. I recommend the later. Plan to empty the container once per week and fruit flies won't be a problem.

452 Composting – Mushrooms

Q: *I know that mushrooms are a fungus. Is it a good idea to take mushrooms that grow in my yard and put them into the compost pile? It seems logical that the mushrooms would be good organic matter.*

A: Your intuition is exactly correct. Mushrooms are nothing but organic tissue produced by underground fungi. They are mostly water and will dry to almost nothing, but grass clippings do the same thing. There is no harm in composting mushrooms; they may help with the composting process as they inoculate the pile with fungal spores.

453 Fertilizer – What to Choose

Q: *How can someone know which combination of fertilizer numbers is right for each shrub, perennial, ground cover, or annual?*

A: Despite the plethora of tomato fertilizers, azalea fertilizers, lawn fertilizers, orchid fertilizers, citrus fertilizers, etc., feeding plants is not so complex. Plant food requirements are pretty basic. They simply need nitrogen, phosphorus, potassium, calcium, and magnesium, plus a few micronutrients that your soil probably already contains.

In general, plants are *grazers*. They absorb what they need from the soil. I apply 10-10-10 to my garden and landscape plants in spring and in summer, turf fertilizer to my lawn three times per year, and water-soluble houseplant fertilizer to my houseplants as needed. Those three products have satisfied my plants for years.

454 Fertilizer - Using Lumpy

Q: *I found a plastic bucket in which some 10-10-10 fertilizer had spent the winter on my patio. When I opened it, I found that the granules were wet and partially dissolved, with a good bit of liquid in the bucket. Can I use this liquid like a compost tea?*

A: Fertilizer does not go bad, but don't use it like compost tea. The dissolved 10-10-10 is too concentrated and will burn your plants. Instead, fill the container with cat litter to absorb the liquid. Put on rubber gloves, and mix the cat litter with the granular fertilizer. Toss the sticky stuff under your shrubs and trees that need a bit of food for spring.

MAINTENANCE

455 Compost – Speeding Up Decomposition

Q: *This is my year to shine in the garden with compost! I have a plastic compost bin, yet everything is slow to decompose. What am I missing?*

A: You need to add some patience to the pile! Compost happens eventually—even for the novice. If you want things to decompose faster, water the pile with a gallon of houseplant fertilizer, mixed according to label directions. This will supply vital nitrogen to the bacteria that disintegrates your landscape trimmings. Keep in mind that piles decompose slower in winter than in summer; cold affects the necessary biological processes. Try stacking hay bales around the bin to insulate it. Eventually the hay will make compost too.

456 Mulching with Straw

Q: *I have removed all pine straw from around my house and plan to replace it. How much of a gap should I leave between the house and the straw?*

A: All mulch should be kept 12 inches away from a home's foundation. This prevents termites from bridging over any injected termite poison at the base of your foundation. Read your termite protection contract closely. It may exclude any termite damage caused by your failure to keep mulch away from the house.

MAINTENANCE

457 Fireplace Ashes – For Roses

Q: *Can I use fireplace ashes as a source of potassium for my roses?*

A: Ashes do provide a slight amount of potassium for plants. They also counteract the natural acidity of soil, so they are a substitute for garden lime. Because ashes are so very alkaline, only a small amount can be applied at a time. Twenty pounds of ashes per 1,000 square feet would be plenty to use at one time on a lawn. If you are preparing a new rose bed, 2 pounds of ashes per 100 square feet would probably be fine. I'm worried that the potential harm from the alkaline ashes would be more than the benefit from their potassium. Sure, you could use a few tablespoonfuls per plant, but you likely have more ashes than that.

458 Fishpond

Q: *I have a large fishpond. I recently built a smaller pond on the other side of the yard. Now it has hundreds of tadpoles. How can I keep from being overrun with frogs?*

A: Frogs are low on the food chain in your landscape. Birds, raccoons, dogs, and snakes eat them regularly, thus limiting their numbers naturally. Enjoy the frogs' croaking each night, but note that their numbers and the volume goes down gradually as the summer wears on.

459 Frost – Forming

Q: *How and why does frost form?*

A: I guess you could say that frost is the same as dew, except colder. When I pour myself a glass of iced tea in summer, humidity from the air condenses on the outside of the glass. If the glass were colder than 32 degrees F, ice crystals would form. That's the simple explanation, but what's curious is when frost forms even though night temperatures *don't* go below freezing. This can happen on clear nights when grass, roofs, and dark-surfaced cars lose heat to the sky faster than the air can warm them. Their surface temperature falls below 32 degrees, and frost forms. This happens to dark surfaces more than light surfaces, because a dark surface usually emits heat faster than a light-colored surface does.

460 Number of Feet – In an Acre

Q: *Could you please tell me how many feet are in 1 acre of land?*

A: It depends on which creatures are standing there. Many more spider feet can fit on an acre than can elephant feet. Now of course, if you're looking for the number of *square* feet in an acre, that's easy: 43,560.

MAINTENANCE

281

461 Full Sun vs. Part Sun

Q: *When a plant tag says "full sun" or "partial shade," how many hours of sun or shade are appropriate?*

A: Sunshine intensity differs across every landscape and garden. Noon sunshine in Valdosta is radically different from noon sunshine in Blairsville. In any area, afternoon sun is stronger than morning sun. This is how I rank sunshine conditions in different parts of the state:

Full Sunshine
- Coast: unfiltered sunshine for six or more hours per day
- Mountains: unfiltered sunshine from morning to night
- Elsewhere: unfiltered sunshine for eight or more hours

Part Sun/Part Shade
- Coast: all-day sunshine filtered through high pine or hardwood (oak, maple, poplar, etc.) trees, or three hours of direct sunshine between sunrise and noon, followed by shade
- Mountains: five hours of direct sunshine between sunrise and noon, followed by shade
- Elsewhere: direct sunshine part of the day, or partial sun (as under high pine trees) all day

Full Shade
- Coast: all-day shade under low evergreen trees (live oak, magnolia)
- Mountains: occasional direct sunshine during the day or dappled shade under low deciduous trees (dogwood, redbud, crabapple, etc.)
- Elsewhere: dappled shade (as under low and high hardwoods) all day

462 Gray Water – Using

Q: *Due to water shortages, I'm considering piping water from my clothes washing machine drain to a 200-gallon cistern outside and using that to water my landscape. Would any of the chemicals in common detergents, fabric softeners, or bleach be harmful to plants or vegetables?*

A: First, be aware that disposing of gray water in any way other than a plumbing-code-approved manner is illegal. That being said, washday products are diluted so much that they should not be a problem for outdoor plants. However, *do not* use gray water on vegetables. A more pressing issue is managing your cistern. If you save wash water for more than twenty-four hours, it will stink to high heaven. Rather than storing it, consider burying a long length of black 4-inch slotted pipe 2 feet away from trees and shrubs. Introduce your gray water directly into the sloped pipe so it can seep into the soil relatively quickly.

463 Weed Barrier Fabric – Using

Q: *I'd like to make the flower beds at the school where I work more low maintenance. I plan to install weed barrier fabric and new pine straw. Is this the proper way to go?*

A: The weed barrier fabric will work fine *if* you remember to remove and replace the straw on it *every* year. Otherwise rain will cause the straw to decompose rapidly, creating a layer of compost on top of the fabric. Weed seeds will germinate in the compost and you'll be back to square one. Make it a yearly parent project to remove the straw, sweep off the fabric, and replace with fresh mulch.

MAINTENANCE

Hardiness Zones – Which One Are We In?

Q: *I have seen several different Hardiness Zone maps for Georgia. Which one should I use to determine which plants will grow here?*

A: You're right—it's confusing. The short answer: Most plant labels include the zones in which the plant will prosper. If the information label on the plant you are considering says it is hardy in Zone 7, it will usually survive our Georgia winters just fine.

Now for the long answer: The zone map story actually begins in Germany, in the early 1800s, where a geographer used lines, called *isotherms*, to delineate regions of equal temperatures in Europe. The United States Department of Agriculture in 1960 mapped and divided the United States into ten zones based on a 10-degree difference in the average annual minimum temperature between each zone. Zone 1 included parts of Alaska, where the two growing seasons are divided into winter and the Fourth of July. Zone 10 encompassed areas in Florida where long pants are considered cold weather dress. Georgia was divided into three parts, placing us in Zone 7 (north Georgia), Zone 8 (middle Georgia), and Zone 9 (south Georgia).

The hardiness map was revised in 1990, dividing each original zone into two subzones, contrasting with each other by only a 5-degree difference in winter low temperatures. Most of the metro Atlanta area falls into Zone 7b, where low winter temperatures are between 5 and 10 degrees F.

MAINTENANCE

465 Irrigation – Pumping from a Stream or Pond

Q: *I have a creek that runs beside my property, roughly 20 inches deep. I would like to pump water to my lawn from the creek. How do you recommend I do this?*

A: Pumping irrigation water from a stream or pond sounds great in theory, but it can be really complicated in practice. A rough estimate is that a lawn needs 600 gallons per 1,000 square feet per week. If you have enough water, you can decide which pump to buy. Others who have done this recommend 220-volt electric pumps because they are cheaper ($200–$350) and easier to maintain. You'll have the cost of installing an electric power line to the creek side. How large should the pump be? Much of the decision depends on how far the water must travel and how high your lawn is above the stream.

The *best* way to buy a pump is to go to a pump/irrigation store and ask a salesman to help you decide. As if all this wasn't complicated enough, you need to find out if removing water from the stream is even legal. The Georgia Department of Natural Resources has regulations about how much of the total flow of a stream can be removed. Their concern is for wildlife living near the stream. You may need a permit.

Including pump (electrical line), suction tube, backflow preventer, supply pipe, valves, sprinkler heads, etc., I don't think you can do it for less than $1,000. You'll need the system for only a couple of months each year, while municipal water costs only a few dollars per 1,000 gallons. Are the savings worth the hassle and equipment expense in your case?

466 Manure – On Top of Bed, Why?

Q: *I was at the Atlanta Botanical Garden the other day, and they were spreading composted manure under shrubs. They were not incorporating it into the soil but leaving it on top. Is this something I should do?*

A: There is good reason for applying a layer of manure on top of the ground. It's to attract and feed earthworms, which carry the material underground. This enriches and loosens the soil. If this were not done, the soil would tend to become harder and harder, and gardeners would have to dig up and amend their beds every few years. I suspect that the secondary reason for applying the manure is a practical one: in winter there is little for the garden interns to do outdoors, so spreading manure keeps them busy.

467 Mowing – Mulching vs. Bagging

Q: *Which is best: mulching or bagging lawn clippings?*

A: I can see value in both mowing techniques. If I were maintaining a candidate for my subdivision's Lawn of the Month, I'd bag my clippings. The mowing and bagging would pick up pine cones, small sticks, and most of the clippings that might mat on the lawn. With that done, I'd put the clippings in my compost pile or use a thin layer as mulch under shrubs. On the other hand, if I wanted to avoid the hard work of collecting the clippings, I'd mulch them. A mulching mower with a well-designed blade chops clippings so fine, you can't usually see them on the lawn surface. The clippings add nutrients to the soil. Contrary to myth, mulching does not increase thatch, as long as you remove only a third of the grass blade at a time, as you ought. Further, mulching does not spread diseases or weed seeds any more than would occur normally.

468 Wood Chips – Composting

Q: *I had some tree stumps ground up and have a lot of mulch. How can I make this into compost at an accelerated rate?*

A: The key is to regularly feed the fungi and bacteria that break down the wood chips. Use your high school math to calculate the volume of the chip pile. Sprinkle 10-10-10 fertilizer over the pile at a rate of 1 cup per 2 cubic feet of chips. Don't be surprised if you see steam wafting from the top of the pile in the next few weeks. Repeat the feeding in two months. You'll have a much reduced pile of brown compost to use as you plant your landscape.

469 Mulch – Pine Straw vs. Nuggets

Q: *I know mulch serves two purposes: appearance and retaining water. Which do you recommend: pine straw mulch or pine mini-nuggets for mulching around plants?*

A: I think it's a matter of appearance more than anything else. Some people like the texture of straw; others like the dark brown of nuggets. My wife uses mini-nuggets almost exclusively because she likes their look. However, we had to buy several brands before we found one that was mostly bark nuggets and not a poor mixture of nuggets, compost, and wood fiber. Do your own research and buy several bags of nuggets at the same time, to avoid differences in batches coming from different companies.

MAINTENANCE

470 Mulching – Correct Procedure

Q: *I'm confused about proper mulching. Could you provide details about how to mulch around trees, shrubs, and perennials?*

A: Mulching is vital for plant health in Georgia, so it is important to know how to do it correctly. In general, wood or pine chip mulch should be no deeper than 2 inches. The same depth applies to shredded leaf mulch. Pine straw mulch can be 2 to 4 inches thick. Mulch should cover the soil wherever roots grow. Tree and shrub roots extend at least out to the drip line but usually further. Do pull the mulch away from the base of your plants: 3 inches away in all directions for annuals and perennials, 6 inches for woody plants. Although some landscapers provide bad examples, *never* pile mulch high around the trunk of a tree.

471 Newspaper – Using to Kill Weeds

Q: *I am thinking of mulching a large weedy area behind my house. Can I use old newspaper instead of black plastic sheeting under the mulch to prevent weed growth?*

A: A great idea! I'd spray with a **non-selective herbicide**,[62] wait until all of the weeds are dead, then mow real low and put down newspaper ten sheets thick. Newspaper is much better than plastic. It allows the soil to breathe and allows moisture to soak through.

62. **non-selective herbicide:** www.gardenword.com/nonselective

472 Pecan Shells – For Mulch

Q: *I have always used pine bark or red oak mulch. I have been seeing pecan shell mulch lately, and it really looks good. What do you think of pecan shell mulch?*

A: Anytime you can beneficially use a material that was formerly considered waste, you'll get my approval. The cracked shells make a fine mulch. You'll have *lots* of bird and squirrel friends in your garden for a few weeks if you use shells that are fresh from the sheller. After that, the animals disappear, and the shells conserve moisture and prevent weeds under shrubs like any other mulch. I wouldn't use them for covering a pathway: they are too sharp on your bare feet!

473 Gutter Cleaning

Q: *This week we had our gutters cleaned out. On the side of the house where the gutters are 20 feet aboveground, the gutter man said he found lots of big, beautiful worms in the accumulated debris. How did the worms get up there?*

A: I consulted two groups of friends on this question. After eliminating any answer that contained the word "magic," there were two schools of thought:

1. A worm crawled up the downspout, passing a very small spider that was on its way down, and deposited eggs in the gutter.
2. A bird eating an earthworm accidentally dropped an earthworm egg sac on your roof. Worms then hatched in your gutter.

Obviously, the question demands further research.

474 Pine Straw – Origins

Q: *Having relocated from the Pacific Northwest, we had never seen pine straw used in landscaping. Where does it come from, and how is it harvested? What are the benefits over beauty bark, which is popular back home?*

A: I don't believe I've ever heard the term *beauty bark*. What a nice phrase! Beauty bark in the Northwest is mainly Douglas fir bark. We recycle pine bark in the same way here . . . we just call it pine bark chips. Pine straw, of course, is composed of the needles that fall from pine trees. South Georgia and north Florida are the centers of pine straw harvesting, in the pine pulpwood plantations. Pine straw is collected and handpressed into bales. Bales are loaded onto trucks and delivered to garden centers all over Georgia. The choice between bark and straw is a matter of personal taste. Both decompose gradually and replenish soil organic matter.

475 Pine Straw Mulch – Replacing Each Year

Q: *A family discussion is left for you to resolve: A pine straw island has tree leaves on it. I say to just cover with new straw. My lovely spouse wants the area raked and new pine straw placed on the cleaned area. Your thoughts?*

A: I spent two hours recently obeying my wife's wishes in the landscape, raking out old straw and replacing it with new. It was strenuous labor, but I did it anyway. One thing I learned from a previous marriage is that a humble attitude toward a spouse's opinion goes far in strengthening a relationship. If my sweetheart wants the old straw removed, I help remove it. I use the stuff to mulch between my garden rows, so nothing goes to waste! And I have to admit the pine island in front of our house is nice looking with fresh straw on it!

476 Plant Trademarks – Explanation

Q: *I have a rose tag that says "The Squire™" and then has the word "Ausire" underneath. What does this mean?*

A: It means that you have a patented rose and propagation is limited by law. Plant breeders, like David Austin, who bred The Squire, go to considerable effort to develop superior plants. They protect their work by patenting their best products. The first-ever plant patent was issued to 'New Dawn' rose in 1931. Plant patents, however, expire after twenty years. To keep continuous control of their products, breeders also trademark plant names. Trademarks can be extended indefinitely. In most cases, the trademark name is not the same as the patented name. Such is the case with your rose. It was patented as Ausire but trademarked as The Squire. You can propagate cuttings of it when the patent runs out, but you'll have to call it something different, perhaps 'Mama's Favorite'.

477 Rainfall – Records and Information

Q: *Is there a Web site I can go to that shows daily rainfall records from a recording station near me?*

A: The University of Georgia has sixty weather monitoring stations scattered across the state. Sensors measure rainfall, soil temperature, wind speed, and solar radiation. All data is open to the public at **www.georgiaweather.net**. Since soil temperature determines when to plant summer bulbs (65 degrees F is best) and when to apply crabgrass pre-emergent (50 degrees F and rising), I frequently use data from the monitoring station nearest my house.

MAINTENANCE

478 Sinkhole in Yard – Correcting

Q: *We have a huge bury pit in our front yard that just caved in! What is the proper way to fix this?*

A: We've all seen the occasional pictures from Florida. Car dealerships, apartment buildings, and homes seem to regularly fall into sinkholes. When you see a big depression in your front yard, is it a signal to call your insurance agent? Fortunately, no. Atlanta perches above a thick layer of granite and clay, not limestone aquifers as in Florida. Our sinkholes are usually nothing to fear. Some occur when a buried mass of construction debris decomposes and allows the earth above to sink. Smaller holes can appear overnight when a buried stump or large root allows soil to subside several inches.

In most cases the simple answer is to fill the hole with soil and replant grass in the spot. If the hole was caused by buried construction debris, tree roots might have grown partially over the hole. They will prevent its true size from being revealed. First use a motorized trencher to encircle the hole, severing any roots. Once you calculate the volume of the hole, you can order a delivery of soil to fill it.

MAINTENANCE

Q: *I recently purchased a house and all of the soil around it seems to be hard, red clay. I want to have flowers this spring, but I know I'll have to make the soil better. What do you personally do to prepare a new bed?*

A: For me, late winter is a great time to prepare the soil in beds. The earth is usually damp and shoveled easily. The sunny afternoons with cool temperatures let me work without sweating too much. Psychologically, the earliest blooms give me that extra push I need to put on my gloves and gather my tools.

I use a long-handled, round-pointed shovel for the initial digging. I heave up big clods of soil and turn them over so any weeds or grass will die in a few days. I don't try to chop the clods apart unless they are semi-dry. Otherwise, the big soggy clumps will just turn into small concrete-like lumps. After a few sunny days, the clumps dry out enough to be broken apart easily. I own a small, two-cycle tiller that does an excellent job pulverizing clods and mixing in organic matter. Usually I use the tiller because it mixes the soil so thoroughly.

After running over the bed with the tiller, I shovel out a wheelbarrow of soil to make room for cow manure or composted pine bark. I add 2 cubic feet of compost per 8 square feet of bed. I also sprinkle a ½ cup of 0-46-0 fertilizer and 4 cups of garden lime into the bed. The tiller is then used to mix everything with the clay. I dump the soil from the wheelbarrow and mix it into the mound too. The result is a flower bed full of soft soil 10 inches deep. Few plants can resist the excellent drainage and easy-to-penetrate conditions.

MAINTENANCE

480 Soil – Components Of

Q: *To better know my soil, I've taken a sample, put it in a jar, added water, then shook it up. In what order does the sand, clay, and silt settle out?*

A: Sand is on the bottom, silt is in the middle, and clay is on top. Some organic particles may float on the surface of the water, and the water itself will remain cloudy forever. If the layer of clay is more than 50 percent of the soil column, more humus and sand is needed for your bed. In a 10-square-foot flower bed area, add a 2-cubic-foot bag of soil conditioner plus two bags of gritty paver leveling sand. Once everything is mixed together thoroughly, the soil stays soft and productive for years.

481 Depth to Which the Ground Freezes

Q: *How deep does the ground freeze in Georgia? This has a great bearing on what I can and can't grow and also on burying my irrigation pipes.*

A: Welcome to the South! The ground doesn't freeze here, at least not for more than a day or two in a severe winter. We don't worry about frost heave like our Northern neighbors do. Irrigation lines are typically buried 12 inches deep, not to protect from cold but to prevent enthusiastic gardeners from slicing them with a shovel. Visit **www.georgiaweather.net** to keep an eye on soil temperatures in your part of the state.

Q: *About three years ago we tilled up our hard clay front yard and added close to a ½ ton of compost and soil amendments. The soil looked really good when we finished. This year, when I dug around some shrubs, the soil was back to mostly clay. Where did my compost go?*

A: Some of your compost cooked away, some eroded away, and some is still there, in the form of humus. Gardeners feel a great thrill when their bad soil has been amended with compost. Imagine, though, what would happen if you put vegetables and water in a slow-cooker and let them simmer, covered, for three years. You would have nothing but thin, indistinguishable gruel. The compost you added to your yard has slowly cooked for the past few years. Particles on top of the soil turned to dust and blew away or washed away. Underground, soil creatures ate and digested large compost fragments. They excreted what they couldn't use in tiny grains, called *humus*.

Humus is great stuff because it holds nutrients for your plants. However, it is so finely divided that is packs tightly with clay. Your once-beautiful soil has reverted back to its former state. You can reverse the process by adding a 1-inch layer of composted cow manure under and around all of your perennials and shrubs. Keep it away from plant stems and cover with a thin layer of pine straw. During the summer, earthworms will find the rich food and will gradually work the manure into the soil. Over the next three years, your soil will improve by itself, without any work on your part!

MAINTENANCE

483 Pond – Leave Pump on in Winter

Q: *I have a pump that circulates the water between my two small fishponds. In cold weather, should I run the pump or leave it off?*

A: During the winter, fish have few needs. They sink to the bottom of the pond, quit eating, and slow down their bodily processes. They do need oxygen, however, and that is where your pump comes in. Leave it on, but be careful that splashing water doesn't freeze outside the pond and eventually drain it dry.

484 Tiller – Choosing

Q: *I have been looking at tillers for several months and have been told that only a rear-tine tiller will cultivate clay. I garden about ¾ of an acre extensively. Can you tell me how to choose a tiller?*

A: It's a matter of matching the tiller to the job, both now and in the future. I have an acre to care for, but I only till beds of 50 to 100 square feet at a time. They are small enough that I can spade up an area, then use my lightweight, two-cycle tiller to mix in my soil amendments. If you commonly till 1,000- to 5,000-square-feet plots, you need a bigger tiller than mine. A friend has a self-propelled heavy-duty tiller that is a dream to use on hard ground. It creeps slowly forward as it churns the earth. Even so, the tines only penetrate 8 inches.

You must also consider your physical strength. Big tillers are *heavy*. Wrestling them around a garden corner or into a shed can be a back-breaking chore. In my opinion, it might be best to rent a big tiller once or twice a year to dig big bed areas. Keep a small tiller handy for day-to-day gardening.

485 Trough Plant Container

Q: *Can you tell me the recipe for making trough containers out of Portland cement and peat moss?*

A: It is a simple recipe: one part Portland cement, one part sand, and two parts peat moss. Once you have mixed the dry ingredients thoroughly, slowly stir in water until the mass is the consistency of oatmeal. After that, the sky is the limit for molding plant containers. For a small trough, cut a 3-gallon plastic pot to 8 inches tall. Line the inside with a layer of plastic film. (A garbage bag works nicely.) Put a 1-inch layer of your mixture on the bottom of the container. Place on it a 1-gallon plastic pot. Fill the space between the two pots with more of your mixture, packing it down with a stick.

When the space is full, cover the whole mold with another plastic bag for two days, to allow the cement to begin hardening. Carefully remove the trough from the mold and set it aside for two weeks to finish hardening. During this time you can use a dull knife or an old fork to roughen the trough sides and make it look more like stone. You can use two cardboard boxes of different sizes to make a larger trough container. Perlite or sphagnum moss can be substituted for the peat moss to cause a different look to the trough.

MAINTENANCE

486 Weed Control – Using Weed Fabric or Newspaper

Q: *I recently removed some bermudagrass in order to plant shrubs. I want to put down a weed block. Which is better: weed block fabric or newspaper?*

A: Both items are somewhat effective weed fighters, but neither one is perfect. More importantly, both require annual maintenance. Any bermudagrass you accidentally leave under the weed fabric will grow up through it eventually, as will also happen with newspaper. Even if no bermudagrass is under the fabric, you'll need to annually remove the mulch you put on top and replace with fresh material. Otherwise the mulch will decompose into a layer of rich soil in which weed seeds can germinate. The newspaper, obviously, will need replacement every year. I recommend a layer ten sheets thick for your project.

487 Wood Chips – Using as Mulch

Q: *What can I do with the chips that are left after a stump is ground up? Can I put them on my flower or vegetable garden?*

A: I think it is best to rake up as many of the chips as you can and use them as mulch under shrubs in your landscape. You don't have to be obsessive about getting them all; just try to get most of the chips. I foresee no harm in using them as mulch under flowers or vegetables either. You could even dig them into the soil of your garden if you occasionally add extra fertilizer to feed the fungi that break down the chips. Without the added nitrogen, your plants will not get all of the nutrients they need. How much extra fertilizer to add? My guess is that increasing your normal fertilizer application by 25 percent should satisfy everyone's needs in your garden.

488 Tree Leaves – Mulching

Q: *Is it beneficial or detrimental to the lawn if I mow over tree leaves and let the shredded pieces lay on the grass?*

A: If the shredded leaves do not mat on top of the lawn grass, it is fine to leave them on the lawn. If great clumps of them remain after you mow, they have to be raked out or mowed again to make the pieces small enough to sift down between existing grass blades. My experience is that dry leaves can easily be shredded and left on a lawn if you mow regularly. Wet leaves, though, make a hopeless mess and have to be raked.

489 Plants – Watering in Summer

Q: *I hear two trains of thought about summer watering: (1) Watering in the morning causes problems because droplets on plant leaves burn them when they are in full sunshine. (2) Watering plants in the evening creates fungus problems if too much moisture sits on the leaves at night. Which is correct?*

A: The first train of thought is headed down the wrong track. Despite tales from supposed garden experts, moisture on the leaves does not cause leaf burning. The second train of thought, though, is exactly correct. Most foliar diseases need twelve to fourteen hours on a wet leaf in order to cause trouble. If you water at 6:00 p.m. after work, leaves stay wet until mid-morning the next day. That's plenty of time for fungi to have a party on your lawn or landscape plants. The best time to water is anytime after midnight until 10:00 a.m. Be sure to follow current local and state watering restrictions.

MAINTENANCE

490 Watering – Before a Freeze

Q: *When you know the temperature is going to be really cold, is it better to water plants or wait?*

A: Water. Many plants protect themselves by drying out their cells as temperatures drop, in order to make them less susceptible to freeze damage. Pansy, aucuba, and daphne plants look horribly wilted during snow and cold, but they perk back up if there is water in the soil the next day.

491 Pinching, Deadheading – Defined

Q: *On your radio show, you've mentioned pinching azaleas to make new buds. For those of us in the slow group, where do you do this?*

A: The reason I advocate pinching azaleas is that the flowers for next year will grow on the tips of branches that grow this summer. It stands to reason that if you help your shrub make more branches, you'll have more flowers next spring.

Sometimes I use garden jargon without properly explaining what the words mean and I apologize for that. *Pinching*, *deadheading*, *nipping*, and *tipping* all mean the same to me: removing the end of a stem in order to encourage new growth. *Deadheading* (removing flowers as they fade) inspires the plant to form new branches, which will grow new flowers. *Pinching* (removing the growing tip of a branch) stimulates new stems to sprout a few inches under where you pinch.

After your azaleas bloom in April, the shrub will naturally send forth new shoots. When the shoots grow to 6 inches in length, use your thumbnail or your pruners to remove the swollen tip on each one. In this way, the plant will resprout even more bud tips by July, and you'll have a plant covered with flowers next spring!

492 Lichens

Q: *I'm having a problem with my azaleas. They seem to have lichens on the trunk. I hate to see them die. What can I do?*

A: I think you should *like* your lichens. Azaleas and older trees of many species often have gray, flaky lichens growing on their limbs. Interestingly, a *lichen* is a "sandwich" made of algae in the center and fungus on the outside. The algae make food from sunlight and air; the fungus protects the algae and supplies moisture. They live together symbiotically. Although lichens are almost always found on weak plants, the fact is, lichens are totally harmless and in no way responsible for the poor health of any tree or shrub. They are simply indicators of the infirm health of the plant.

As a woody plant loses vigor, the number and size of its leaves gradually decreases. This allows more sunlight on the trunks and branches. As soon as enough light is available on the stems, lichens will begin to colonize.

Lichens can be brushed off the plant with a stiff brush, but unless the true cause of decline is corrected, lichens will reappear.

Are your azaleas growing in dense shade? Do they get enough water in the summer? Maybe the best thing to do would be to prune them to 12 inches tall next March and let them grow a better canopy of leaves.

If a plant is helped to become healthier, less sunlight will strike the limbs and trunk. Lichens will then gradually disappear.

MAINTENANCE

493 Mulch – Using Plastic Sheeting

Q: *While cleaning up my backyard, I found black plastic covering the ground under my shrubbery. There is a layer of decomposed leaves two inches thick on top. Should I remove the plastic? Can I add the leaf dirt back under the plants?*

A: Did the plants mulched by the plastic seem healthy? Or, as I imagine, did they appear weak and spindly? While the woven product sold for this purpose is a good weed preventer, plastic sheet is *never* a good mulch for plants. It cuts off the supply of oxygen to plant roots as well as preventing water and fertilizer from penetrating. Rake the rotten leaf mold off the plastic, pull the sheeting up, and throw it away.

Don't be surprised if you see lots of white roots growing on the soil surface. They were trying to find the little bit of air under the plastic. Scatter the decomposed leaves back under your shrubbery. Cover with pine straw or pine bark mulch. Listen carefully as you work—you might hear the plants saying, "Thank you! Thank you! Thank you!"

494 Soaker Hose – Using on a Slope

Q: *Can I use a soaker hose in a sloped shrub and flower bed that is about 100 feet long or should I use another type of irrigation?*

A: You can use soaker hoses on a slope as long as they are laid along the contour of the hill, not up and down the incline. Otherwise, there will be more water pressure in the hose ends at the bottom of the hill and more water will be distributed there.

495 Cistern – For Storing Water

Q: *Are barrels or an underground cistern viable options for storing water?*

A: It all depends on how much water you're trying to store and how much storage you can afford. In a 1-inch rain, 12 square feet of roof surface collects a cubic foot of water. A cubic foot of water equals $7^1/_2$ gallons. A rough estimate is that 1,000 square feet of roof would collect 625 gallons of water, more than 12 fifty-gallon barrels. On the other hand, a buried 4 feet × 6 feet × 6 feet concrete cistern would hold 1,080 gallons. A sump pump could be used to distribute water to your landscape. I'll let you do the math and make the decision.

MAINTENANCE

496 Gardening Memorials

Q: *Can you suggest small gardening charities that accept donations in the memory of people? Some organizations require a minimum amount.*

A: I am positive that any small garden organization would be happy to work with you on a memorial. Before you make a donation, check to see if they are a 501(c)(3) nonprofit so your gift is tax deductible. Books on gardening (or any other topic) can be given to your public library in honor or memory of loved ones. These books for children and adults tend to be expensive, and libraries often cannot afford to purchase them from their own funds. Usually the library can obtain the book at a better price and with library binding, so send your donation to the library with an explanation of its purpose and they will take care of it.

497 Greenhouse – For Homeowners

Q: *I am considering building my own hobby greenhouse. I want to start out with simple flowers and vegetables, but I would like to be able to expand the greenhouse, in case I decide to start a small business with it. Where can I get information?*

A: There are several publications you can study. Your local Extension service office (1-800-ASKUGA-1) has the booklets "Managing a Hobby Greenhouse" and "Heating, Cooling and Ventilation for Greenhouses," Also ask for "Starting a Greenhouse Business." They'll be happy to mail copies to you.

498 Landscape Design – Courses of Study

Q: *What credentials should one have to be a landscape designer or landscape architect? I don't have the time or resources to go back to college full-time.*

A: Landscape architecture is a five-year course of study. It is a very broad-based study of the many aspects of landscape work, including architecture, engineering, design, and horticulture. To be a good landscape designer, one needs an intensive study program in horticulture and training in good design basics. You can take evening courses at Gwinnett Tech, Lanier Tech, or North Metro Tech. The University of Georgia has online horticulture courses as well. Also check out **www.workoutdoors.com**. Georgia landscape companies are begging for more trained employees. You are making a good choice!

499 Master Gardener Program

Q: *Some time ago on your radio show, you mentioned classes for Master Gardener training. Can you tell me where to apply?*

A: The Georgia Master Gardener Program is a wonderful opportunity for you to learn about gardening in Georgia. The classes are taught by professionals and volunteers from the University of Georgia. Once you complete the course, you are expected to share your knowledge with the public. For more details, visit **www.gamastergardener.org**.

500 Swimming Pool - Converting to Garden

Q: *I have a concrete swimming pool that I want to fill it in and create a garden spot. How is this done?*

A: A professional should jackhammer drain holes in the deep end. At the same time, break up the pool apron and the top 36 inches of wall and dump it in. Fill the pool to within 18 inches of the top with #57 stone and compact it with a skid-steer loader or a plate compactor. Fill the last 18 inches of the pool with screened topsoil and plant your flowers!

501 Ultrasonic Watches - Do They Work?

Q: *I recently saw an advertisement for an ultrasonic watch that claims to ward off pregnant female mosquitoes. Supposedly they are the only ones that bite. True or false?*

A: It's true that only female mosquitoes bite, but false that the watch repels them. Mosquitoes hear sound in a narrow range: 200–400 Hertz.

Ultrasound is above 2 million Hertz. Pregnant females of any species are mighty touchy, but even a device designed with advanced harmonics circuitry to emulate and emit the ultrasonic high frequency of an approaching male mosquito isn't likely to bother a female mosquito, pregnant or otherwise. However, if you use the watch to smack the mosquito while she feeds, it will be a 100 percent effective control.

INDEX

308

INDEX

INDEX

INDEX

313

INDEX

INDEX

314

315

INDEX

317

INDEX

INDEX

MEET THE AUTHOR

Walter Reeves is a native Georgian. He grew up on a farm in rural Fayette County, where he gained lots of practical knowledge about plants. His horticulture career began with the University of Georgia Extension, where he served for 29 years. Best known to Atlanta-area listeners as the radio host of *The Lawn and Garden Show with Walter Reeves,* he also reaches gardeners through his weekly columns in the *Atlanta Journal-Constitution.* Walter helps gardeners throughout the state as the host of *Gardening in Georgia,* shown weekly on Georgia Public Broadcasting.

Walter is the coauthor of the *Georgia Gardener's Guide, Month by Month Gardening in Georgia,* and *The Georgia Fruit and Vegetable Book.* His Web site, www.walterreeves.com, contains thousands of hints, tips, and answers for gardeners in the Southeast. He lives with his wife, Sandi, and his son, Grey, on a one-acre "in progress" landscape in DeKalb County.